The
Dictionary
People

The Dictionary People

The Unsung Heroes Who Created the Oxford English Dictionary

SARAH OGILVIE

ALFRED A. KNOPF
New York 2023

THIS IS A BORZOI BOOK
PUBLISHED BY ALFRED A. KNOPF

www.aaknopf.com

Knopf, Borzoi Books, and the colophon are registered
trademarks of Penguin Random House LLC.

Library of Congress Cataloging-in-Publication Data
Name: Ogilvie, Sarah, author.
Title: The dictionary people : the unsung heroes who created
the Oxford English Dictionary / Sarah Ogilvie.
Description: New York : Alfred A. Knopf, 2023. |
Includes bibliographical references and index.
Identifiers: LCCN 2023012911 (print) | LCCN 2023012912 (ebook) |
ISBN 9780593536407 (hardcover) | ISBN 9780593536414 (ebook)
Subjects: LCSH: Oxford English dictionary. |
Encyclopedias and dictionaries—History and criticism. |
English language—Lexicography—History—19th century. |
English language—Etymology. | Lexicographers—Biography.
Classification: LCC PE1617.O94 D53 2023 (print) |
LCC PE1617.O94 (ebook) | DDC 423.0922—dc23/eng/20230718
LC record available at https://lccn.loc.gov/2023012911
LC ebook record available at https://lccn.loc.gov/2023012912

Jacket illustrations by Bill Sanderson / Phosphor Art
Jacket design by Linda Huang

Manufactured in the United States of America
First American Edition

To Jane,
and in memory of Antoinette.

I am sure that lovers of our language will not willingly let die the names of those who, from unselfish devotion and service to that language, have laboured in the cause of the Dictionary.

James Murray, Editor of the OED, 1892

Contents

Contents

Introduction:

Discovering the Dictionary People

It was in a hidden corner of the Oxford University Press basement, where the Dictionary's archive is stored, that I opened a dusty box and came across a small black book tied with cream ribbon. That basement archive is, strangely perhaps, one of my favourite places in the world: silent, cold, musty-smelling; rows of movable steel shelves on rollers; brown acid-free boxes bulging with letters; millions of slips of paper tied in bundles with twine; and Dictionary proofs covered in small, precise handwriting. It is a place full of friendly, word-nerd, ghosts. Perhaps those ghosts were guiding me because the discovery I made that day would lead me on an extraordinary journey and eventually to the book you are now holding.

I was there out of nostalgia more than anything. I used to work upstairs as an editor on the Oxford English Dictionary (OED) and I was filling in time while waiting for my visa to come through for a new job in America. It was Friday, and I had spent the whole week revisiting my favourite spots before leaving the city that had been my home for fourteen years.

Monday had been a walk around the deer park within the walls of Magdalen College. C. S. Lewis had said that the circular path was the perfect length for any problem. It was true. The fritillaria weren't in flower, but the trees were yellow and the leaves on the ground were damp and smelled of the earth. Next, noisy Longwall Street and past the dirty windows of where I used to live at number 13. Through a heavy gate and an arch in the old city wall and into the vast gardens of New College with its immaculate lawn and long border still in colour. The bells rang as I paused at the spot under the oak where the college cat, Montgomery, had been buried by the chaplain. Along the gravel path by the purple echinops, crimson dahlias, and red echinacea with their pom-pom centres. Through the grand gates of the old quad, and into the silence of the cloisters where they had filmed *Harry Potter*. I pushed open the door of the chapel and was immediately hit by the comforting smell of beeswax and the sound of the choirboys rehearsing. I stayed in the antechapel and sat in front of Epstein's *Lazarus* rising out of the tomb and spinning free of his bandages. Tuesday was the Upper Reading Room of the Bodleian Library. Wednesday was the secret bench against the President's wall at Trinity College where I used to worry about my thesis. Thursday was Wolvercote Cemetery and the resting place of my hero James Murray, the longest-serving Editor of the Oxford English Dictionary from 1879 up to his death in 1915.

The Dictionary had started out with three men, Richard Chenevix Trench (1807–86), the Dean of Westminster Abbey, along with Herbert Coleridge (1830–61) and Frederick Furnivall (1825–1910), both lawyers turned literary scholars, who suggested the creation of a new dictionary. This would be the first dictionary that *described* language. Until then, the major English dictionaries such as Dr Samuel Johnson's in the eighteenth century were prescriptive texts – telling their readers what words *should* mean and how they *should* be spelled, pronounced, and used. In 1857, these men proposed to the London Philological Society – one of the scholarly societies that were such a hallmark of their day – the creation of 'an entirely new Dictionary; no patch upon old garments, but a new garment throughout'. Coleridge became the first Editor of the *New English Dictionary* (as the OED was first called), but he died two years into the job. Frederick Furnivall took over for twenty years, until he was replaced in 1879 by a schoolmaster in London called James Augustus Henry Murray (1837–1915).

Before moving to Oxford, Murray tried to combine teaching at Mill Hill School with work on the Dictionary. The Dictionary won out. It was at Mill Hill that Murray had started to compile the Dictionary inside his house, but the vast quantities of books and slips threatened to crowd out his growing family (in time, he and his wife Ada would have eleven children). Ada eventually put her foot down, insisting that he build an iron shed in the garden and use that as his office; it was nicknamed the Scriptorium. When Murray moved to Oxford in 1884 to work solely on the Dictionary, his family and the Scriptorium went with him. It was partially dug into the ground, so Murray and his small team of editors laboured on the Dictionary for the next thirty years in dank and cold conditions, often wrapping their legs in newspaper to stay warm. Over the years, he was helped by paid editorial assistants and joined by three key editors who subsequently became Chief Editors in their own right: Henry Bradley, William Craigie, and Charles Onions.

The new Dictionary would trace the meaning of words across time and describe how people were actually using them. The founders, however, were smart enough to recognize that the mammoth task of finding words in their natural habitat and describing them in such a rigorous way could never be done alone by a small group of men in London or Oxford. The OED was the Wikipedia of the nineteenth century – a huge crowdsourcing project in which, over seventy years between 1858 and 1928, members of the public were invited to read the books that they had to hand, and to mail to the Editor of the Dictionary examples of how particular words were used in those books. The volunteer 'Readers' were instructed to write out the words and sentences on small 4 x 6-inch pieces of paper, known as 'slips'. In addition to being Readers, volunteers could help as Subeditors who received bundles of slips for pre-sorting (chronologically and into senses of meaning); and as Specialists who provided advice on the etymologies, meaning, and usage of certain words. Most people worked for free but a few were paid, and the editorial assistants formed two groups – one under the leadership of Murray in the Scriptorium and the other managed by Henry Bradley at the Old Ashmolean building in the centre of Oxford.

In the first twenty years, this system of crowdsourcing enlisted the help of several hundred helpers. It expanded considerably under James Murray, who sent out a global appeal for people to read their local texts and send in their local words. It was important for Murray that everyone adhere strictly to scientific principles of historical lexicography and find the very first use of a word. Readers received a list of twelve instructions on how to select a word, which included, 'Give the date of your book (if you can), author, title (short). Give an exact reference, such as seems to you to be the best to enable anyone to verify your quotations. Make a quotation for every word that strikes you as rare, obsolete, old-fashioned, new, peculiar, or used in a peculiar way.' He distributed the appeal to newspapers and journals, schools, universities, and hundreds of clubs and societies throughout Britain, America, and the rest of the world.

The response was massive. In order to cope with the volume of post arriving in Oxford, the Royal Mail installed a red pillar box outside Dr Murray's house at 78 Banbury Road to receive post (it is still there today). This is now one of the most gentrified areas of Oxford, full of large three-storey, redbrick, Victorian houses, but the houses were brand

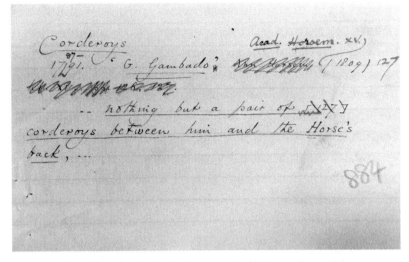

A 4 x 6-inch 'slip' sent in by one of the most prolific female contributors, Edith Thompson of Bath, who sent in 13,259 slips. The underlinings and markings were made by Dr Murray.

new when Murray lived there and considered quite far out of town. He devised a system of storage for all the slips in shelves of pigeonholes that lined the walls of the Scriptorium.

We know some of the contributors' names from brief mentions in the prefaces to the Dictionary that accompanied each portion (called a 'fascicle') as it was gradually published between 1884 and 1928. Other historical documents, such as Murray's presidential addresses to the London Philological Society, also mention groups of contributors: some are famous, some ordinary, and some unpredictable – perhaps most notoriously the murderer and prisoner William Chester Minor, so brilliantly depicted by Simon Winchester in *The Surgeon of Crowthorne* (1998). Through these sources, historians have thought that there were hundreds of contributors, but have not known who they all were.

Today, crowdsourcing happens at extraordinary speed, scale, and scope thanks to the internet. In the mid-nineteenth century, the launch of 'uniform penny post' and the birth of steam power (driving printing presses, and leading to railway transport and faster ocean crossings) enabled this system of reading for the Dictionary to be so successful. The growth of the British Empire, the proliferation of clubs and societies, and the professionalization of scholarship throughout the century all conspired to create the conditions for a global, shared, intellectual project that continues to this day.

The OED is now on its third edition, and still makes appeals and invites contributions from the public (via its website), but is chiefly revised by a team of specialized lexicographers. As one of those lexicographers, my job was to edit the words that had originally come from languages outside Europe – words from Arabic (*sugar, sofa, magazine*) or Hindi (*shampoo, chutney, bungalow*) or Nahuatl (*chocolate, avocado, chilli*) – in the third edition. Apart from the use of computers, the editing process I followed was exactly the same as that masterminded by Murray: each lexicographer was given a box of slips corresponding to our respective portion of the alphabet and, aided by large digital datasets, we worked through slip by slip, word by word, striving to piece together fragments of an incomplete historical record, until we had crafted an entry and presented a logical chain of semantic development in much the same way that Murray and his editors had. We also worked in a silent zone, just as it was in the nineteenth century. It has relaxed a bit now and editors work in small groups, but when I first started there if you wanted to speak to a colleague you were encouraged to whisper or to go into a meeting room to do so.

It was only natural that on my final day in Oxford I should want to bid farewell to the Dictionary Archives, where I had spent so many happy hours in the past. On that cool autumn Friday in 2014, when I casually popped by to pass some time, I could not have imagined what I was about to discover.

I collected my visitor's badge from the reception and made my way along multiple corridors, down some stairs, along a tunnel. I had walked this way many times because I had also written my doctorate on the OED using historical materials stored down there. As a previous employee, I have always been granted exceptional access to the stacks. One last swipe and a loud click, and I was inside the inner sanctum of the archives. Bev and Martin greeted me; I passed through another door into the OED section of boxes and paraphernalia. It was the material relating to the first edition of the OED which drew me. It was a treasure trove. You could pick any box and it held something of interest.

I don't even remember what was written on the one that I pulled off the shelf, but I noticed that it was lighter than the others. I placed it on the floor and lifted the lid. There, right on top, was a black book I had never seen before, bound with cream ribbon.

I carefully picked it up and removed the ribbon that held the stiff black covers together, and looked more closely. It was the size of an average exercise book; the spine had disintegrated to reveal fine cotton binding; the pages were discoloured at the edges, slightly foxed. When I opened it, the first thing that struck me was the immaculate cursive handwriting. I recognized it as the familiar hand of James Murray.

He had written the names and addresses of not just hundreds but thousands of people who had volunteered to contribute to the Dictionary.

Finding Dr Murray's address book was one of those moments when everything goes into slow motion. I immediately appreciated the significance of the find. I realized I held a key to understanding how the greatest English dictionary in the world was made: not only who the volunteers were, where they lived, what they read, but so many other personal details that Murray often included on their deaths, marriages, and friendships.

I was stunned by the sheer numbers of people who had contributed. Murray had not only listed the names and addresses of his contributors but had meticulously recorded every book title they had read, with the number of slips they sent in, and the dates received. Every page was filled with black ink: names, addresses, and titles of books with numbers beside them, small symbols and notes, ticks and checks, stars and scribbles.

I wondered whether I was the first person to open the address book since Murray had last used it. Had it remained closed for almost a century? Not quite: there was an archival classification number written in pencil at the top of one of the pages, and I knew that the dictionary archive had been re-organized and categorized by the Dictionary's wonderful archivist, Bev. However, I was familiar with the books and articles written about the OED over recent decades, and I knew that it was likely that no one else had seen Murray's address book or, if they had, they had not deemed it valuable. I was the first person to take this opportunity to track down who the contributors really were, and to build as comprehensive a picture as possible. I had found the Dictionary People.

The box in the archives held two further address books belonging to Murray, and the following summer, in a box in the Bodleian Library, I found another three address books belonging to the Editor who had preceded him, Frederick Furnivall. As I worked my way through them, it became clear that there were thousands of contributors. Some three thousand, to be exact.

The address books provided me with the kind of research project that scholars can only dream of. My excitement was followed by long, hard detective work. My visa came through and with the help of a team of tech-savvy student research assistants at Stanford (where I was by then teaching) I used the information from six address books (Murray's and Furnivall's) to create two large datasets of the thousands of Dictionary People and the tens of thousands of books that they read. In tracking contributors across the world, I visited libraries, archives, and personal collections in Oxford, Cambridge, London, New York, California, Scotland, and Australia. I also gathered portraits and digital photographs of the contributors, scanned hundreds of letters and slips showing the handwriting of the contributors, as well as great lists of the words and quotations they collected.

Murray's address books were clearly the work of an obsessive. Piecing together the stories of the Dictionary People from his brief and often cryptic notes required a similar focus. Some pages held original letters from the addressees, and almost every page contained signs that needed decoding. What did Murray mean by D4, D6, a tilde accent, or a U with a cross through it? It took me a while to work those out, while others I immediately grasped – '11/2/85' clearly meant 11 February 1885. Some people in the address books had cryptic marks and ideographs above their names. Others had not-so-subtle descriptors: 'dead', 'died', 'gone away', 'gave up', 'nothing done', 'threw up', 'no good'. I sat with the books and studied their pages, and other patterns emerged. Some names were underlined in bright red pencil, and gradually I realized this meant they were Americans, while others were crossed out in blue pencil with the letters 'I-M-P-O-S-T-O-R' written over them.

For the past eight years I have pored over these address books, researching the people listed inside them – where they lived, what they did with their lives, who they loved, the books they read, and the words they contributed to the

Dictionary. Some people have remained mysteries, despite my trawling through censuses, marriage registers, birth certificates, and official records, but many more have come to life with such force it is as though they have been calling out for attention for years.

The Dictionary was a project that appealed to autodidacts and amateurs rather than professionals – and many of them were women, far more than we previously thought. It attracted people from all around the world as well as Britain: from Australia, Canada, South Africa, and New Zealand, to America, Europe, the Congo, and Japan. Remarkably, they were not generally the educated or upper classes that you might expect.

Over the years that I have been researching them, I have fallen in love with the Dictionary People. Most of them never met each other or the editors to whom they sent their contributions, and most were never paid for their work. But what

Some pages of Dr Murray's address books contain
letters from contributors.

united them was their startling enthusiasm for the emerging Dictionary, their ardent desire to document their language, and, especially for the hundreds of autodidacts, the chance to be associated with a prestigious project attached to a famous university which symbolized the world of learning from which they were otherwise excluded. The Dictionary People could also be cranky, difficult, and eccentric – as James Murray often found out – but that, paradoxically, also makes them lovable, or at least fascinating.

Tracking the lives of these three thousand people has been a long task and, yes, a labour of love. I have wanted to tell the story of the OED from the 'bottom up' through the eyes of the volunteers rather than from the perspective of the editors or the scholars. Murray's incredible record-keeping in his address books made much of this possible, though some of those three thousand were easier to track through the many archives I consulted than others: the biases within record-keeping meant that there were sometimes frustrating gaps in the evidence and a skew towards certain classes, genders, and ethnicities. And yet the stories of so many were findable – and I often found them on the margins. Even James Murray was unusual in not being part of the Oxford Establishment – he was Nonconformist and Scottish, and had left school at fourteen. He was an expert in the English language but he was also somewhat on the fringes. The OED was a project that attracted those on the edges of academia, those who aspired to be a part of an intellectual world from which they were excluded. While I always wanted to find out more about Miss Janet Coutts Pittrie of Chester who is marked in the address book as 'Friend of Miss Jackson'; Mr John Donald Campbell, who was possibly a factory inspector in Glasgow; and Miss Mary A. Pearson, who was possibly a cook and servant in Eaton Square, London, the details of their lives eluded me. But there were so many more whose life stories popped out in technicolour as I was doing my research. I was thrilled to discover not one but three murderers, a pornography collector, Karl Marx's daughter, a President of Yale, the inventor of the tennis-net adjuster, a pair of lesbian writers who wrote under a male pen name, and a cocaine addict found dead in a railway station lavatory. In the process of searching for these people, I have come across many hundreds of fascinating and often unexpected stories – dramatic and quotidian. I became obsessed with shining a light on these unsung heroes who helped compile one of the most extraordinary and uplifting examples of collaborative endeavour in literary history.

The time that the Dictionary was being written was an age of discoveries and science, an explosion of modern knowledge, and we see in so many of the rain collectors, explorers, inventors, and suffragists how much our current world was shaped by this relatively short period. There is a paradox about the very project of the Dictionary, the words collected for it and included in it. The Dictionary enterprise can easily be seen as a mastery of the world for the sake of the English language and the intellectual passions of white people. Murray's commitment to including all the words that had come into the English language may be seen as colonizing – or it may be seen as inclusive. Murray went out of his way to include all words, often being criticized for it by reviewers of the Dictionary and his superiors at Oxford University Press. This means that the pages of the Dictionary incorporated words from the languages of Black and indigenous populations, and of people of colour. The Dictionary People who sent in those words were, for the most part, white, because of their privileged access to literacy in the period. The published sources of those words drew originally on the language of members of Black and indigenous communities whose names never made it into the pages of Murray's address book, and it is

Dr Murray and his editorial team working on the OED
in the Scriptorium, a shed in his back garden.

important to acknowledge those often unseen and unre-
corded interlocutors.

A myth of Murray has persisted as the Editor who
devotedly and single-handedly created the world's largest
English dictionary with its half-million entries – only to die
during the compiling of the letter T in 1915, not knowing
whether his life's work would ever be finished. While Murray
was clearly a master-manager of the whole Dictionary project
and had a small number of paid staff in the Scriptorium, this
oft-told story ignores all the many people who corresponded
with him and sent him words and quotations which made
the Dictionary happen. The photograph in the Scriptorium
might show only five men, but a careful observer will see the
volunteer contributors clearly present, there in the thousands of word slips they sent, poking out of the pigeonholes.

It is their lives that I unearthed and relate in this book.

The story here is one of amateurs collaborating alongside the academic elite during a period when scholarship was being increasingly professionalized; of women contributing to an intellectual enterprise at a time when they were denied access to universities; of hundreds of Americans contributing to a Dictionary that everyone thinks of as quintessentially 'British'; of an above-average number of 'lunatics' contributing detailed and rigorous work from mental hospitals; and of families reading together by gaslight and sending in quotations. This extraordinary crowdsourced project was powered by faithful and loyal volunteers who took up the invitation to read their favourite books and describe their local words not just so that the bounds of the English language could be recorded for future generations but so they could be part of a project that was much bigger than them.

They are the Dictionary People, largely forgotten and unacknowledged – until now.

A

for ARCHAEOLOGIST

Which of the Dictionary People should start this book, I wondered, and be given the honour of representing the letter A? There are many 'Americans' I could, and will, tell you about, some autodidacts, and quite a number of activists. However, for me, archaeologist Margaret Alice Murray deserves to be at the beginning, not least because recognition for her came late in life. Despite being one of the most famous archaeologists of her day, she had to wait until the age of sixty-one to be made, in 1924, an Assistant Professor at University College London. Margaret was indefatigable: she embarked on a lecture tour to Norway, Sweden and Finland aged seventy-two, and on reaching her century she optimistically titled her memoir *My First Hundred Years*. The story of her involvement with the Dictionary begins when she was just eighteen years old, shortly after Dr James Murray (no relation) made his general appeal to English speakers around the world in 1879, asking them to read their local books and send him words and quotations on small slips of 4 x 6-inch paper. National and international newspapers picked up Murray's appeal and advertised the project in their pages. It is likely that this is how Margaret heard about the OED and its call for contributors: her family, then living in Calcutta (now Kolkata), regularly read the weekly edition of *The Times* newspaper, distributed throughout the Anglo-Indian community, which carried Murray's advertisements.

Margaret's mother was an English missionary. Her wealthy father – of British descent born in India – was managing partner of a firm of Manchester paper merchants. The family lived in a grand white stone-and-stucco house at 8 Elysium Row, in the Anglo-Indian quarter of Calcutta not far from the Anglican Cathedral. The houses here were neoclassical in design, with floors of polished chunam, high ceilings, ornate cornices, and marble pillars. In fact, none of the large homes on Elysium Row would have looked out of place on London's Pall Mall, were it not for the Anglo-Indian addition of jill-mills (wooden louvres) and plaited-grass screens that hung between the columns of the verandahs to provide a cool flow of air. But even these grand spaces could not escape the heat, sounds, and smells of the city, situated as it was on the Tropic of Cancer along swampland and salt marshes. There were (and still are) few places on Earth hotter and more humid.

Margaret had a routine of getting up at sunrise and taking a book to the balustraded, flat roof to read alone in the cool early-morning air. As she read, the smells of the dawning day would drift up to her: incense from the Hindu house servants performing their first devotions, and the pungent odour of spicy jhalmuri (Bengali street food). She underlined words in her books to the background noise of the kitchen staff preparing breakfast, the slap of laundry on stone, and the far-off clatter of the street traders, astrologers, and chaiwalas (tea sellers) setting up their stalls. And then, as the day got hotter and stickier, she made her way downstairs to write out her selected words and quotations on slips of paper at a desk on the shaded verandah. At night, she would continue the work in her bedroom, in the company of her cat, Dapple, working by the soft, smokeless light of a small pottery lamp half-filled with water and castor oil.

Margaret was so dedicated to reading for the Dictionary that she persisted even during insect plagues. One evening at the end of the rains, while she was reading by oil light with all the windows open, Calcutta was hit by a swarm of emerald-green insects with black spots. They got into Margaret's hair, down her back, up her sleeves. Under every light in the house the harmless beetles started to accumulate until reading was impossible and the rooms on the windward side were uninhabitable. Another time she had to stop because a plague of fleas had formed a solid wainscot on the walls and had to be removed by spreading fresh-cut grass on the floor for an hour, which attracted the fleas and was swept up and taken to the garden for burning, and then every wall and floor washed in strong tobacco water.

Margaret's situation as an Englishwoman in India directed her choice of reading. She drew on the religious books in her English mother's library but also on the Indian world in which she was living. She started with William Lisle's edition of Aelfric's *Saxon Treatise Concerning the Old and New Testaments* and, 300 slips later, moved on to Thomas Fuller's *Abel Redevivus*, a set of seventeenth-century biographical sketches of key figures in the English Reformation. Her reading of a 1665 translation of the Italian Pietro della Valle's *Travels in East India*, and the 600 slips which she sent of words from that text, opened the Dictionary to language from the part of the world where she was living. Pietro della Valle was a young Roman from a noble family who, depressed after a failed love affair, was advised by his doctor to travel. His letters from seventeenth-century India, translated from Italian into English, provide an insight into the new customs and people that he encountered.

Margaret sent in words that only made it into the

Dictionary because of her reading, such as the rare word *spicerer*, someone skilled in the nature of spices or drugs, which has a singular citation sent in by Margaret. She also sent in *chinch*, a bedbug; and an obsolete sense of *breeze* meaning the specific cool wind that blows from the sea by day on tropical coasts. But it was a sixteenth-century translation of the Bible that took up four years of the young woman's life, resulting in 3,800 slips from the *Bible Douay* (a translation of the Bible undertaken by Roman Catholics in response to the Protestant Reformation), and many new and obscure words were, as a result, added to the Dictionary such as *ethecke*, a porch or gallery; and *superexalt*, to praise excessively.

Margaret was also familiar with local words and terms from the team of Indian servants who ran the house for her Anglo family: all dressed in long white coats, the Muslim table servants were distinguished by their colourful cummerbunds and the Hindu house servants by their puggaree turbans. It was from Margaret's beloved personal servant, 'Baba Ayah', a tall and graceful woman who cared for her from her birth in Calcutta on 13 July 1863 until the time she left India at the age of twenty-five, that she would have first learned local words and phrases. But there was also a durzee tailor, who made clothes for the family; a mehtar sweeper; a khansamah and several khidmutgar table servants; a mussalchee washer-up; and a Malay cook called Teeloo who made special children's curries for Margaret and her older sister Mary.

These Indian-English words, along with many others, made it into the Dictionary with published quotations written out on slips. The Dictionary project was a concerted effort, and Margaret was one of many Readers who sent in words from books relating to India. Others included William Francis Grahame, a civil servant living in Madras; John Wesley Caldwell, a school superintendent in America; John Thompson Platts, a school inspector from Benares (now Varanasi) who retired to Oxford; and Charles Sutton, a librarian in Manchester.

If all of this paints a picture of a young Anglo-Indian woman idly passing her time in a marble mansion, then you would be mistaken. As a child and teenager Margaret accompanied her mother on visits to provide medical treatment to orphanages and zenanas (the secluded sections of Muslim or Hindu households for women) around Calcutta. From the age of twenty, working during the day and often through the night on twelve-hour shifts, Margaret was a nurse, as the first 'lady-probationer' in India, in one of the world's busiest hospitals, Calcutta General Hospital. Her forthright, competent and calm demeanour helped to save hundreds of lives during a cholera epidemic and, when the sister-in-charge collapsed from overwork, Margaret was promoted to this role at the age of twenty-one. Her medical knowledge would come in handy later, once she became an archaeologist and was working at excavation sites.

Margaret sent slips to Murray from 1881 until 1888, first from Calcutta, and then from England. During this time, she had no idea that her future mentor, the archaeologist William Matthew Flinders Petrie, was doing exactly the same thing from his home in Bromley, Kent. His reading was quite different from Margaret's. The contributors to the Dictionary had the freedom to read whatever they wished, and while Margaret Murray had chosen religious books and travellers' tales, Flinders Petrie chose poetry, the works of John Ruskin, and William Dampier's *Voyages*. The contributors' paths did not cross until the next decade, in 1894.

In her mid-twenties, Margaret moved from India to England with her mother and sister Mary, settling first in Rugby where her uncle was Rector, and then in the village of Welwyn, Hertfordshire. There were height requirements for nurses in England in those days, and Margaret, who was only 4 foot 10 inches, was not deemed tall enough so she tried her hand as a social worker and district visitor instead. She later referred to these years as 'failed attempts to find a career'. Nothing suited her, and in 1893, she returned to India to visit Mary who had gone back and was now living in Madras with her husband and new baby. It was the height of the hot weather, and the sisters were sitting in the coolest room in the house reading the weekly edition of *The Times*. 'It says here that Flinders Petrie is going to hold classes for Egyptian hieroglyphs in London at University College,' said Mary. 'Who is Flinders Petrie?' asked Margaret.

Back in London, at the age of thirty-one, Margaret attended Petrie's lectures and her life changed. She had found her passion, and, in January 1894, became a student of Egyptology at University College London which was (radically) co-educational. Petrie's bold lectures captivated his audiences. As Margaret explained in her memoir, 'On the occasion when he expounded his system of sequence-dating, Sir Herbert Thompson, who was sitting next to me, whispered in my ear, "But this is Epoch making." And more than once at the close of a lecture the audience has clapped vigorously, a rare thing for a college audience to do after listening to a routine lecture.' Margaret excelled at her studies, and soon became Petrie's research assistant, helping him write papers and filling in for his teaching when he was away on archaeological digs. She eventually attended those digs alongside him, working in Abydos, Saqqara, Malta, Minorca, and Palestine.

Margaret managed to forge her way against the odds in the male world of professional Egyptologists, and was known for her support and mentorship of female colleagues. She published more than one hundred books and articles, and became famous not only for her work in Egyptology but also for her groundbreaking books on witches. It was reported by her friends that, later in her life, she herself practised witchcraft. If she did not approve of an academic appointment, she would try to reverse it by casting a spell in a saucepan. Known for her wit and humour, she was interviewed by the BBC at the age of ninety-six and commented, 'I've been an archaeologist most of my life and now I'm a piece of archaeology myself.'

Margaret Murray's work eventually came full circle back to the OED when some of her own writings were quoted in the Dictionary. Entries such as *talayot*, a Bronze Age tower;

Margaret Alice Murray (1863–1963) who sent
in slips from Calcutta.

torba, a kind of cement made with broken pottery in Malta; and the term *witch dance,* a ritual dance performed by witches, were taken from her controversial book *The Witch-cult in Western Europe* (1921). The citations from her writings were added to the OED in the 1970s, after her death, and some ninety years after she had contributed words and quotations to the Dictionary from her own reading, but we can imagine that she would have been pleased. The whole world of scholarship delighted her. She wrote of the exhilaration that she felt when her first article was published, 'I often wonder whether great writers have that same feeling of sheer unadulterated pleasure when their first writings appear in print. But I think that researchers have a keener pleasure, for besides the glory and splendour of becoming a real author there is the additional splendour of having added to the knowledge of your subject, of having filled a small and possibly not a very important gap, but still a gap. This is one of the purest joys that life can give.'

B

for BEST CONTRIBUTOR

Over the seven years that archaeologist-to-be Margaret Murray sent in words to the Dictionary, she managed to contribute 5,000 slips. This was impressive, but there were many others who sent in far more, testifying to extraordinary industriousness and commitment, often over long periods of time, on the part of the people who were inspired to help with the project. If we define best contributor or OED Reader in terms of number of slips, then the outright winner was a mysterious character called Thomas Austin Jnr who sent Dr Murray an incredible total of 165,061 over the span of a decade. Second place goes to William Douglas of Primrose Hill who sent in 151,982 slips over twenty-two years; third place to Dr Thomas Nadauld Brushfield of Devon, with 70,277 over twenty-eight years; with Dr William Chester Minor of Broadmoor Criminal Lunatic Asylum coming in fourth place with 62,720 slips. Dr Minor was not the only one in a mental asylum – all four were, for some period or another, suggesting a connection between word obsession and madness. More about that later.

Mr Austin caused Dr Murray a lot of trouble. He started out a loyal and faithful friend of the Dictionary, frequently visiting the Editor for tea and dinner during his time in Mill Hill. However, Austin became increasingly enraged that he

wasn't being recognized or paid for his work on the Dictionary. After Murray moved to Oxford, Austin also moved there
and would wait outside the Oxford Scriptorium, pestering
the Dictionary staff. Dr Murray called him 'a painful case'. He
was a painful case for me in a different way. Of the hundreds
of people whom I researched for this book, Austin was one of
the most difficult to identify. He has several addresses crossed
out beside his name in the address books which shows that he
moved between Hitchin, Oxford, and London. At one stage,
I thought he might be a servant of the same name at Exeter
College, Oxford, who started work at the age of fourteen,
never married, lived on the seedy side of town in a squalid
boarding house behind St Ebbe's and racked up a huge tab
on his battels (college food and drink account), was eventually fired from Exeter College, and spent the rest of his life in
and out of mental asylums, and even had a stint at an abattoir
for pigs. I loved the idea of an uneducated servant contributing the most slips to one of the most prestigious scholarly
projects in the world, and even pictured this Mr Austin sitting in the college porters' lodge during the night, as drunk
students came back, busy sorting out quotations from the
books listed beside his name in Dr Murray's address book:
Thackeray, Byron, Defoe, not to mention Dryden, Milton,
and innumerable volumes of the *Philosophical Transactions of
the Royal Society.*

Alas, there was a piece of the puzzle which did not fit
the servant theory – the OED's Mr Austin read some very
rare manuscripts only found in the Bodleian Library and
the British Museum (which at that time incorporated the
British Library). How could a servant in Oxford in the 1870s
get access to these rare materials when such a person would
not usually be granted membership to these libraries? I so
wanted to believe that the Exeter servant was our Mr Austin
that I even imagined he might have got a job as a porter at

From Dr. MURRAY,
(Sunnyside, Banbury Road,)

OXFORD, 7 Nov. 1887

Dr Murray writes to Frederick Furnivall in 1887,
'Austin's <u>is</u> a painful case.'

the Bodleian so as to gain entry, but a search of the employment records came up empty.

I kept searching for answers: had he been one of Murray's students at Mill Hill School (where Murray worked before becoming full-time Editor of the OED)? The school's historical records said there was no Millhillian with that name. Was he the same Thomas Austin Jnr, a civil engineer, who wrote a scholarly paper about a Crinoidea sea animal fossil with his distinguished father, Fort Major Thomas Austin

FGS? No, that man moved to Canada in 1860. Was he the Thomas Austin Jnr of Hitchin who submitted two comments to the *Notes and Queries* journal in April 1871 about the etymology of a French word and about the date of a sixteenth-century hymn? Very likely, as Murray's address books record him as living at one point in the town of Hitchin. Was he therefore the only son of Mrs Annie Austin who, with Emily Davies, was one of the founders of Girton College, and lived in Hitchin at the same time? No, her son was called Gerald. Was he the same Thomas Austin who edited *Two Fifteenth-Century Cookery Books* in 1888 for the Early English Text Society? Here is what I found out.

The OED's Thomas Austin Jnr was born in London in 1835 to Eliza and Thomas Austin (Snr), a prosperous brewer. The only boy amongst six sisters, Thomas Jnr grew up in a large house with three servants at 29 Liquorpond Street, Middlesex. After school, he followed his father into the brewery, moving to Hitchin and boarding with various families and their lodgers. He never married. He started contributing to the OED when he was forty-three years old, but how his path initially crossed with Murray's we do not know.

Five years into his devoted service for the OED, the strain on Thomas Austin's mental health began to show. By that time, he had successfully sent in 121,190 slips but the rest of his life was falling apart. He lost his job at the brewery. He was trying to survive on a small allowance from his father, but then his father died and grief was compounded by disappointment and frustration when he was left nothing in the will. He fell out with his sisters and could not return home to Middlesex so, with scant savings, he moved from one house to another, lodging with strangers until finally settling with a family of six in Hornsey.

These conditions were far from ideal for Dictionary work and so, when Murray moved to Oxford in 1884 to work full-time on the Dictionary, Austin decided to move there too, in the hope of getting tuition, or a job at Oxford University Press, or, better still, a place in the Scriptorium on Murray's editorial team. His hopes came to naught.

Austin should have seen the writing on the wall. When the first part of the Dictionary was published that same year, he received very little credit or recognition in the book. The only mention of his name appeared in a footnote in the preface: 'T. Austin, Esq., jun., Hornsey, stands first with a total of 100,000 quotations.' Four years later, in 1888, when the first volume (A and B) was published, there was more disappointment. Murray used his preface to give credit to the scholars and Specialists who had worked on the Dictionary, most of whom were well-known, but the majority of volunteer Readers who had sent in slips, such as Austin, were relegated to the appendix, listed after the Subeditors.

Nothing was further from Murray's mind than employing Austin, and he was shocked when, soon after moving to Oxford, he received 'a violently abusive letter' from Austin which, as he would later write to Furnivall, 'fell on me like a bomb-shell, and for which I could not account, as we had never even had one word of unpleasantness during all the time I had known him'. While Austin industriously read books and sent in thousands of slips with the hope of employment, from Murray's point of view, Austin 'had no qualifications for constructive work'. To pay him for his reading 'was quite out of the question', wrote Murray, who 'had never even for a moment thought of such a thing'. Receiving a torrent of abuse from Austin, Murray vowed to leave him alone and hoped he would go away.

Murray's side of the story shows a discrepancy between how he saw the role of Readers and how Readers, such as Austin, understood their work. Austin called his reading 'work for the dictionary', but Murray's view was that it was support for Dictionary work. This made me wonder how many other Readers misunderstood the importance of their contribution? In fact, we might have some sympathy for Austin who did the equivalent work of hundreds of people, and the Dictionary would not be the esteemed volume that it is today without his extraordinary contribution.

As far as Murray was concerned, most Readers and volunteers did not turn up on his doorstep pleading for recompense. Despite Murray's attempts to ignore Austin, the two remained in contact as Austin continued to try to find work in Oxford: a sad affair of failed job applications and hustling OED editors for money (and not paying them back). Austin spent his days in the Bodleian Library, still gathering quotations for the Dictionary. He asked Murray to recommend him for a job with Clarendon Press, which Murray willingly did, but it came to nothing. They even met, when Austin came to the Scriptorium and, as Murray wrote, 'behaved just as if he had never written the letter, & had been on the best of terms with me all his life'. Things continued to be difficult and Murray had to tell him clearly that he 'had not a penny to spend on reading for the Dictionary however valuable, the Delegates would only pay for work which was devoted directly to expediting the appearance of the book, not a farthing for work such as his which only tended to reinforce its quality or to give earlier or later quotations'. Austin made a final attempt at getting a job, this time with the Bodleian Library. Murray gave him half a sovereign to keep him going and begged the Librarian, Edward Nicholson, to employ him – but Nicholson 'could not or would not do anything'. Murray encouraged Austin once again to leave Oxford, offering to pay his expenses to return home to his sisters in Middlesex, but as Murray explained to Furnivall, 'He would not go: he still "entertained hopes" that something "would turn up" here, and meanwhile would "work for the dictionary". As I found that this merely meant fastening him[self] upon my assistants, borrowing of them, plaguing them at their lodgings etc, I had to write more firmly, telling him that he was under a mad delusion which I could not countenance; that I could not sanction his working any further for the dictionary, till he was in a position to afford to do it. I have not seen him since.'

After his failure to get paid work in Oxford, Austin stopped speaking to Murray but amazingly he did not stop helping the Dictionary. He moved to London and boarded at 45 Gower Place, St Pancras, with a family of five and three other lodgers, an upholsterer, a cabinetmaker, and a commercial traveller. The conditions were cramped but all that mattered to Austin was that the house was a mere three-minute walk from the library at the British Museum, where he spent each day collecting quotations for the Dictionary and sending the slips to Murray via the editorial assistants with whom he surprisingly remained friends.

It was Frederick Furnivall, Murray's predecessor as Editor of the Dictionary, who came to the rescue with a paid editing job for Austin with the Early English Text Society. His volume, *Two Fifteenth-Century Cookery Books*, was published in 1888 and Austin's name rightfully appears on the title page. Thomas Austin stopped contributing to the OED the following year, aged fifty-four years old. His death date is unknown.

C

for CANNIBAL

As I pieced together the list of contributors, it became clear that the Dictionary People came from varied backgrounds and had very different reasons for giving their time to the OED. Margaret Murray used it as a way to connect with her English roots while living in tropical India, and to use her academic gifts at a time when she did not yet enjoy other opportunities. For Thomas Austin it was perhaps to connect with a scholarly world from which he was otherwise excluded. But for other volunteers, such as the surgeon and Arctic explorer Sir John Richardson, it may have been for more personal reasons, not immediately obvious.

The final years of Sir John Richardson's life were spent in quietude in the Lake District surrounded by birdsong, butterflies, and the beautiful gardens of Lancrigg, his large seventeenth-century house by the River Rothay, just outside Grasmere (today a boutique hotel in Alastair Sawday's guide). It was the late 1850s and Richardson, a retired surgeon and explorer, spent a portion of each day reading Scottish ballads and poetry alongside his daughter Beatrice, each of them sitting side by side at a large wooden table in front of French windows overlooking gardens designed by William

Wordsworth, and the hills beyond. Together they would write out slips and send them to the Dictionary.

This genteel picture of retirement belies Richardson's early years of dangerous adventure in the Arctic. He had been the surgeon and naturalist on John Franklin's infamous and doomed first voyage in search of the Northwest Passage from 1819 to 1822. Eleven men perished of starvation; three were killed by fellow crew, including one murdered by Richardson himself; and the expedition was plagued by scandalous tales.

I first discovered Sir John Richardson's role in the OED while looking through Frederick Furnivall's photo album, which is now housed in the Bodleian Library. In the early days of the OED, when Furnivall was Editor (1861 to 1879), he collected autographs and photos of the contributors. This wonderful visual catalogue of the early volunteers contains many pictures of grey-haired and balding men, but one of them, wearing a bow tie and black velvet jacket with silk trim, stands out as particularly cantankerous- and impatient-looking, under which Furnivall wrote, 'Sir John Richardson, the Arctic Voyager, Florence 1863 died June 1865.'

Sir John and his daughter Beatrice were asked to help the fledgling Dictionary by Frederick Furnivall, long before Dr Murray became Editor. They were two of an initial 147 helpers who found themselves swept along by Furnivall's enthusiasm, willingly reading books and sending in words.

Reading for the Dictionary was an opportunity for Sir John to reminisce and reconnect with his Dumfries childhood through the ballads and poems of his old family friend Robert Burns. He also enjoyed reading once again the bawdy fun and romance of fifteenth-century Scottish village life in the anonymously authored 'Christis Kirk on the Green' (influential upon his friend's writings), and the supernatural tale 'Kilmeny' from James Hogg's *The Queen's Wake*. Beatrice,

Photograph and signature of Sir John Richardson as
recorded in Frederick Furnivall's photo album.

meanwhile, wrote out quotations from Jane Austen's novels,
Thomas Arnold's *History of Rome,* and Sir Walter Scott's novel
Old Morality.

It is easy to imagine that these idyllic days at Lancrigg,
re-engaging with the literature of his Scottish homeland, were
soothing for Sir John Richardson. His life had been long,
active, and sometimes controversial. Like Thomas Austin, his
father was a prosperous brewer, but that is where the similarities end. Richardson was born the eldest of twelve children
in Dumfries in 1787. He studied medicine at Edinburgh University, publishing a thesis on yellow fever, and went to North
America as a surgeon with the Royal Marines.

When Richardson was thirty-two years old, he was offered the chance to be surgeon and naturalist on John Franklin's Coppermine expedition to explore the Northwest Passage, a putative route through Arctic Canada which would give Europeans a trade route to Asia. He would become one of Franklin's loyalist supporters and closest friends. Fourteen years later he would marry Franklin's niece (this was his second wife, Mary, the mother of Beatrice).

The voyage was a failure. The crew of twenty-one men never found the elusive Northwest Passage, and the journey came at great cost: icy and treacherous rivers, wild animals, starvation, and the death of more than half the expedition. They had planned and managed their provisions poorly. They did, however, manage to chart 500 miles of previously unmapped Arctic coastline, and Richardson described many new species of plants and animals.

The deadliest part of the expedition came two years into the three-year journey when they were trying to reach Fort Enterprise. Bad weather and shortened rations, combined with a treacherous trip in canoes down the Coppermine River in which Richardson nearly died swimming in the icy waters without a lifeline, left the group weak and exhausted.

One of the men, a cartographer named Robert Hood, was too ill to continue towards Fort Enterprise, so Richardson and another of the party, John Hepburn, offered to stay back with him. Franklin pushed on with the others, leaving Hood, Richardson, and Hepburn alone.

Writing in his journal, Richardson recorded that they soon ran out of provisions and had to survive by searching for small amounts of tripe de roche (lichen), even resorting to eating their moccasin boots: 'Every little scrap of shoe leather is now highly prized, and after boiling is greedily devoured.' They scavenged for old bedding made of deer skins that the indigenous peoples of the region had discarded the previous winter, ravenously eating whatever was possible. 'There were about 26 [skins] collected', reported Richardson, 'but many of them are rotten and most of them very thin. Those that contain the larvae of the oestrus [warble fly] are most prized by us, and eagerly sought after.'

One morning, when the snow had stopped and the sky was clear, Richardson went out to look for tripe de roche, leaving Hood ill in bed, and Hepburn to cut willows for a fire. He returned to camp empty-handed, feeling weak and dispirited – only to discover that a new person had arrived. Michel Terohaute, an indigenous Iroquois voyageur – one of the men employed to help carry goods – and one of Franklin's forward party, had walked back to deliver a message. Franklin wanted to let the three men know there was a better location amongst pine trees a mile ahead and encouraged them to move camp.

Terohaute received a hero's welcome among the men: he brought them pigeon and hare meat, killed that morning, which they cooked immediately and devoured. 'This unexpected supply of provision was received by us with a deep sense of gratitude to the Almighty for his goodness,' wrote Richardson, 'we looked upon Michel [Terohaute] as the instrument He had chosen to preserve all our lives.' Terohaute told them that he had originally been walking back to them in the company of two other members of Franklin's team, voyageurs called Perrault and Belanger, but they had been separated in the snowy forest.

That evening, the four men read the evening prayer service together under a clear, but cold, sky. With full stomachs for the first time in months, they bedded down to sleep. Terohaute complained of cold, so Hood offered to share his buffalo robe with him and Richardson gave him two of his warmest shirts. Hepburn, who was suspicious of voyageurs, whispered to Richardson, 'How I shall love this man if I find that he does not tell lies like the others.'

The next day they moved camp a mile on, into the pine trees, as planned. There was still no sign of Belanger and Perrault, and the men lamented that they must have got lost, or have perished. Terohaute went out hunting with a hatchet and came back at dusk with part of a 'wolf' which, he said, he had found abandoned after it had been killed by a deer. Again, the hungry men cooked and ate the meat, praising Terohaute for his great hunting skill.

'We implicitly believed this story,' explained Richardson, 'but afterwards became convinced from circumstances, the detail of which may be spared, that it must have been a portion of the body of Belanger or Perrault.'

Richardson became suspicious when he noticed that whenever Terohaute went out hunting, he took a large hatchet. Not only was a hatchet very heavy to carry for someone in an emaciated state, it was a poor choice to kill a warm-blooded, live animal: a sharp knife was a better weapon for hunting animals. A hatchet was better suited to hacking off pieces of meat from a frozen animal – or, as it turned out, the bodies of men which Terohaute knew to be frozen. Richardson now suspected that Terohaute had killed Belanger and Perrault, hidden their bodies close by, and that his 'hunting trips' with his hatchet were in fact walks to the place where he had sequestered them, feasting on the meat himself and bringing chunks of so-called wolf back to the camp.

Tension between the men mounted. Terohaute became increasingly belligerent and uncooperative, going out by himself with the hatchet each day, presumably to eat portions of Belanger and Perrault. The denouement came with the murder of Hood. The morning of his murder, the men said Morning Prayer together and, at noon, Richardson went out to gather tripe de roche. Hepburn was cutting firewood close by. Hood sat by the fire in front of the tent, arguing with Terohaute whom he reproached for leaving the group so often.

Richardson heard a gunshot and rushed back. 'When I arrived, I found poor Hood lying lifeless at the fire-side.' Edward Bickersteth's *Scripture Help* lay beside the lifeless body as if it had fallen from his hand; 'it is probable that he was reading it at the instant of his death', wrote Richardson. They removed the body into a clump of willows behind the tent, and returned to the fire for a short funeral service. That evening, the hungry men took the dead man's buffalo robe, singed off the hair, and boiled and ate it. Richardson salvaged the watercolours which Hood had painted on the expedition, which visually captured the journey for future generations.

According to Richardson, Hood had been shot by Tero-haute who in turn claimed that Hood had shot himself as an act of suicide. Richardson calculated that this would have been impossible because the long gun was shot from behind Hood's head, the bullet exiting his forehead, and 'the muzzle of the gun had been applied so close as to set fire to the night-cap behind'. Richardson wrote in his journal, 'We passed the night in the tent together without rest, every one being on his guard.'

It is important to remember that we do not have Tero-haute's side of the story, and are relying entirely on the word of Richardson, a white man who, within that context, had power over Terohaute, an indigenous man. At this point in the events, Richardson reported, Terohaute began to act erratically and the two men felt threatened: 'He gave vent to several expres-sions of hatred towards white people . . . whom he said had killed and eaten his uncle and two of his relations.'

After two days of thick snowy weather, which forced all three of them to be incessantly together, Richardson secretly conferred with Hepburn and decided 'there was no safety for us except in his death'.

Richardson killed Terohaute with a single shot to the head. 'I was thoroughly convinced of the necessity of such a dreadful act, to take the whole responsibility upon myself; and immediately upon Michel's coming up, I put an end to his life by shooting him through the head with a pistol.'

Two days of snowfall followed the death of Terohaute. They found lichen, which they moistened and toasted over the fire, and ate the remaining singed hide of Hood's cloak, before packing up camp and moving on in the hope of re-uniting with Captain Franklin and the rest of the party at Fort Enterprise. Trudging through blizzards, and with nothing to eat, they frequently sank into snowy pits and were too weak to get up without the help of the other. Although they saw a large herd of reindeer their hands were too unsteady to shoot accurately. Crossing a frozen lake, they followed the tracks of a wolf and came across the carcass of a deer. 'It was clear picked and at least one season old; but we extracted the spinal marrow from it, which even in its frozen state was so acrid as to excoriate the lips.' Richardson fell ill, but the two men pressed on. 'During the last few hundred yards of our march, our track lay over some large stones, amongst which I fell down upwards of twenty times, and became at length so exhausted that I was unable to stand. If Hepburn had not exerted himself far beyond his strength, and speedily made the encampment and kindled a fire, I must have perished on the spot.'

The two exhausted explorers eventually reached Franklin, who had lost many of his men to starvation and was argu-ably in an even worse state than they were. They exchanged news of the deaths of their companions. Richardson, as the surgeon on the expedition, gave medical aid to Franklin's men, only three of whom were still alive. He recorded in his journal the next day that two of them were too weak and dis-pirited to cut wood, and were unable to eat from the soreness of their throats. They died later that night. The third man was 'much distressed with oedematous swellings, I made several scarifications in his scrotum, abdomen, and legs and a large quantity of water flowing out he obtained some ease'. That evening they ate singed skins and the soup of a few pounded bones.

The next day, Richardson and Hepburn left the others in bed, while they ventured out to cut wood. They heard a musket and a great shout, and looking out saw a group of indigenous people on the river. 'The Indians treated us with the utmost tenderness', remembered Richardson, 'they gave us their snow shoes and walked without themselves, keeping by our sides that they might lift us when we fell . . . The Indians cooked for us and fed us as if we had been children.'

The indigenous people walked the white men to safety, and the survivors spent the next six months recovering first at Fort Providence and then at Fort Resolution in the house of Robert McVicar, chief trader of the Hudson's Bay Company. On 27 May 1822, they returned to England where Franklin received a hero's welcome, an honorary doctorate from Oxford University, and a knighthood. Richardson was not so well-received: the execution of Terohaute, and the rumours of cannibalism, caused great controversy, with some critics calling for him to be punished as a murderer. This did not happen. On his return to England he managed to resume his medical career and eventually became Chief Medical Officer of Royal Haslar Hospital in Hampshire, which at the time was the largest hospital in the world. It contained an asylum for sailors with psychiatric disorders, and Richardson pioneered humane treatments for the mentally ill. He was good friends with Florence Nightingale and advocated for radical nursing techniques: cleanliness, fresh air in wards, and general anaesthesia.

Despite the disastrous maiden expedition, Franklin was determined to find the Northwest Passage and made two more attempts (without Richardson). On his third journey in 1845 he perished, along with all 128 members of his crew. It became known as 'Franklin's Lost Expedition'.

Despite – or perhaps because of – everything he had gone through on previous expeditions, Richardson believed that he had a 'sacred duty' to find his friend, and in 1848, he returned to the region with fellow Scottish surgeon John Rae, to search for Franklin's team. They failed to find the ships, HMS *Erebus* and HMS *Terror*, but they did recover some human remains. 'From the mutilated state of many of the corpses and the contents of the kettles', Rae reported, 'it is evident that our wretched countrymen had been driven to the last resource – cannibalism – as a means of prolonging existence.' This news was not well-received by the British public, especially the widow of Franklin and her friend Charles Dickens who ensured that Rae was ostracized and never acknowledged or awarded for his efforts to retrieve Franklin and his men. Richardson, on the other hand, had clearly learned his lesson from the controversy that followed his own experience of cannibalism thirty years earlier, and made absolutely no mention of the taboo topic. He was duly knighted in 1846, while Rae received no recognition whatsoever. Franklin's ships, HMS *Erebus* and HMS *Terror*, remained lost until local Inuit communities and historians located them near King William Island in 2014 and 2016 respectively.

Richardson published the story of searching for Franklin in *Arctic Searching Expedition* (1852), which was later read for the OED. Richardson's book is therefore quoted in the Dictionary, just as Margaret Murray's work is. His writings provided words relating to the animals, plants, and geological forms of Arctic Canada – *laughing goose*, a North American goose; *beaver*, the rodent; *beech*, the tree; *butte*, an isolated hill with steep sides; and *rock butter*, soft crystalline deposits on rock – as well as words related to indigenous cultures: *parka*, a hooded jacket; *Dogrib*, an Athabaskan language;

Mingo, a member of the Susquehannock people; and *Slave,* an Athabaskan language. He was the first person to use the geological terms *prairie plateau* and *non-conformably* (meaning 'in a manner that is not conformable'), and therefore his book provides the first quotations for these words in the Dictionary.

Richardson was close friends with Charles Darwin; he advised him on how to get government funding for scientific projects and frequently answered his queries about fish, Arctic plants, and ice formations. Darwin nominated Richardson for the Royal Medal, which he received in 1856, two years before he started contributing to the OED.

Richardson contributed to the Dictionary right up until his peaceful death at Lancrigg on 5 June 1865, having sent in a total of 23,568 slips. Upon his death, Frederick Furnivall wrote, 'we have suffered a great loss in the death of Sir John Richardson, one of the most careful and accurate of our contributors. His last work was for the Dictionary; his pen had just finished a verse from the Wycliffite version of Isaiah, when his gentle, able, and manly spirit was called to its rest.' Furnivall recorded the death of 'the Arctic Voyager' in his photo album, alongside Richardson's signature which he had cut and pasted from a letter. Richardson is buried in Grasmere churchyard with the inscription 'Heroic Sailor-soul' on his tombstone.

D

for DICTIONARY WORD NERDS

One summer morning in 1883, Alexander John Ellis sat at his desk in front of three large bay windows, opened wide to catch any breeze that London's Kensington had to give. From his chair, he could hear the birds in the plane trees and see right down Argyll Road, its five-storey white stucco Georgian houses resembling layers of an expensive wedding cake. By the time everyone else was rising, Ellis had generally already been up for several hours. Early morning was his favourite time of day. Ellis loved the notion of getting ahead while others were sleeping, and getting work done before his neighbour, a master singer, started his scales and taught his students by the open window. 'The nuisance is awful at times', he wrote to Murray. Ellis always ate the same light breakfast of a French roll with butter, and drank his signature beverage: a cup of warm water with a little milk.

This day, as every day, his first act on waking was to weigh himself naked, before dressing for the day. Always the same boots and coat, affectionately named Barges and Dreadnought, before heading straight to his desk on the second floor. He needed to weigh himself *before* putting on his clothes for one main reason: Dreadnought was heavy. Dreadnought had twenty-eight pockets, each one stuffed full with eccentric items. Ellis made a noise like a kitchen drawer as he walked. When he sat down, eyewitnesses said that his pockets 'stood upright like sentinels'. They were variously full of letters, nail clippers, string, a knife sharpener, a book and philological papers in case of emergency, and two things that a teetotaller and someone who watched his weight rarely needed: a corkscrew and a scone, just in case friends were in want of either. These last two items sum up Ellis; he was kind-hearted and always thought of his friends before himself.

On his desk, there were signs of everything that he held dear: a draft of the fifth and final volume of his monumental book, *On Early English Pronunciation*, daguerreotypes of Venice and his three children, a tuning fork, and a favourite quotation from Auguste Comte, the founder of altruism, 'Man's only right is to do his duty. The intellect should always be the servant of the heart, and should never be its slave.'

This morning held a special excitement: also spread out in front of him were Murray's proof sheets for the first section of the Dictionary (words A to Ant) – all 362 pages of them. Murray had sent them to Ellis for his comment. As Ellis's eyes skimmed the proofs, he could not help looking for his own name in the Introduction. He felt a sense of profound satisfaction to see 'A. J. Ellis, Esq, FRS (Phonology)' listed between Prof. Frederick Pollock (Legal terms) and Dr P. H. Pye-Smith (Medical and Biological words).

Ellis's passions were pronunciation, music, and mathematics, and his expertise in all of these areas had been sought by Murray who had had difficulty finding British academics to help him (by contrast, American scholars were eager to be involved). He had helped Murray with the very first entry in the Dictionary – A: not only the sound A, '*the low-back-wide vowel formed with the widest opening of the jaws, pharynx, and lips*', but also the musical sense of A, '*the 6th note of the diatonic scale of C major*', and finally the algebraic sense of A, '*as in a, b, c, early letters of the alphabet used to express known quantities, as x, y, z are to express the unknown*'. Ellis was happy to see these and other results of his work on the printed page, including the words *air, alert, algebra.*

Many people, not only in Britain but around the world, were eagerly awaiting the appearance of the first part of the Dictionary, and Murray particularly wanted Ellis's opinion on the draft Introduction, which he knew he had to get just right. It all read perfectly to Ellis except for one section. 'The Dictionary aims at being exhaustive', Murray had written. 'Not everyone who consults it will require all the information supplied; everyone, it is hoped, will find what he actually wants.'

Is it really exhaustive? Ellis wondered. What about slang and coarse words? He scribbled to Murray in the margin (and the page with the scribble still survives today in the archives), 'You omit slang & perhaps obscenities, thus are by no means exhaustive. Though disagreeable, obscene words are part of the life of a language.' Feeling satisfied with his contribution to Murray's landmark first part of the Dictionary, and admiring of the project as a whole, Ellis placed the corrected draft into an envelope and placed it by his front door, ready for the morning post.

Ellis had raised an important question about inclusion, but he was not quite right about the boundaries of the Dictionary. Murray *had* included slang but it was true that, so far, he had left out obscenities. We can only imagine the uproar in Victorian society had he not. Murray would agonize over his decision to leave them out, but also had to be mindful of the Obscene Publications Act of 1857 which made it illegal to expose the public to any content judged to be grossly indecent.

Murray's caution proved wise when, a few years later, a fellow lexicographer and one of the Dictionary People, John

Stephen Farmer, had his own legal drama. Farmer was writing a slang dictionary with William Henley, and was struggling to publish the second volume (containing the letters C and F) of his work on grounds of obscenity. Farmer took his publisher to court for breach of contract in 1891, and tried to convince a jury that writing about obscene words in a dictionary did not make him personally guilty of obscenity, but he lost the case and was ordered to pay costs. Eventually, he found fresh printers and avoided the Obscene Publications Act by arguing that his dictionary was published privately for subscribers only, not the public, and the remarkable *Slang and Its Analogues* by Farmer and Henley was published in seven volumes (from 1890 to 1904), with *cunt* and *fuck* and many other words regarded as lewd on its pages. Farmer's legal case and the public outcry that ensued was a clear deterrent for Murray.

By the time that section of the letter C was published for the Oxford English Dictionary the only cunt that was listed by Murray was *cunt-*, a cross-reference to the prefixes *cont-, count-* with no mention whatsoever of the female body part. *Fuck* was also left out. Although these old words had been in use since the thirteenth and sixteenth centuries respectively, they would have to wait until the 1970s to be included in the OED. Murray did, however, include *pudendum,* a word derived from Latin for 'that of which one ought to be ashamed', which he defined as 'the privy parts, the external genital organs' with no reference to a woman or – God forbid – her vulva.

Each of Murray's advisers had different notions of what was offensively salacious. His adviser on medical terms, James Dixon, who was a retired surgeon living in Dorking, Surrey, had been all right with including *cunt,* but absolutely drew the line with a word which he considered so obscene it had to be sent to Murray in a small envelope marked PRIVATE, sealed within a larger envelope. Inside the intriguing packaging was a message advising him not to include the word *condom*. 'I am writing on a very obscene subject. There is an article called Cundum . . . a contrivance used by fornicators, to save themselves from a well-deserved clap; also by others who wish to enjoy copulation without the possibility of impregnation', he wrote to Murray. 'Everything obscene comes from France, and I had supposed this affair was named after the city of Condom, which gives title to a Bishop.' But he had found a quotation from 1705 referring to a 'Quondam' which made him rethink his assumption that it was named after the town in France. 'I suppose Cundom or Quondam will be too utterly obscene for the Dictionary', he concluded. Murray left it out.

Dixon was the man who unwisely advised Murray to delete the entry for *appendicitis* because it was, according to Dixon, just another itis-word. 'Surely you will not attempt to enter all the crack-jaw medical and surgical words. What do you think of "Dacryocystosyringoketokleitis"? You know doctors think the way to indicate any inflammation is to tack on "itis" to a word.' The word's deletion turned out to be an embarrassment to Murray and Oxford University Press when, in 1902, the coronation of Edward VII was postponed because of the King's attack of appendicitis. Suddenly everyone was using the word, but no one could find it in the Dictionary, and since the letter A was already published it could not be added until the Supplement volume in 1933.

But back to the summer of 1883. Murray received the corrected proofs from Ellis. He not only appreciated Ellis's feedback but also trusted his judgement: he promptly deleted all claims to exhaustiveness and wrote, 'The aim of this Dictionary is to furnish an adequate account of the meaning, origin, and history of English words now in general use, or known to be in use.'

*

I had been wondering how Ellis got to be such a word nerd? I was fascinated by what I discovered. To begin with, something very unusual happened when he was eleven years old. His mother's cousin, a schoolmaster called William Ellis, offered to give the young boy a substantial inheritance if he would change his surname from Sharpe to Ellis. Mr and Mrs Sharpe agreed, and from then on 'Alexander John Sharpe' became 'Alexander John Ellis'. The young boy was enrolled at Shrewsbury School and Eton, educated at Trinity College, Cambridge, and never had to earn money for the rest of his life.

Ellis's wealth enabled him to be the quintessential 'gentleman scholar', an expert in almost everything he did, be it music, mathematics, languages, phonetics, travel, or daguerreotype photography. He was a polymath for whom life was more a science than an art. He published over 300 articles and books, and his works are quoted in the OED 200 times.

His interest in accent and pronunciation was inspired by the fact that he was born to a middle-class family in Hoxton, east London, where he was exposed to working-class cockney speakers, followed by schooling at Shrewsbury with its Welsh and English accents, and then exposed to the Received Pro-nunciation of the upper and upper-middle classes at Eton and Cambridge.

Words were like children to Ellis. He loved them equally, regardless of whether they were common, technical, scien-tific, slang, or foreign. He read the Dictionary as though it were a novel. Some words gave him pure delight in both their sound and meaning such as *absquatulate*, to abscond or decamp, with a quotation from Haliburton's *Clockmaker*. 'Absquotilate [*sic*] it in style, you old skunk . . . and show the gentlemen what you can do.' But it was their sounds that captured his imagination most. The quality of a whisper or a creak; the stress of a syllable; high pitch or low pitch.

Most people *hear* sounds, but Ellis *saw* them. He saw the air move in the mouth, the way the tip of the tongue touched the ridge of the teeth for a t; the vibration of vocal cords to change it to a d; and how the base of the tongue moved back in the mouth to block the flow of air for a g. Every sound was a picture for Ellis. He devoted his life to painting these pictures, describing their systematic order so the world might better understand the fundamentals of language.

His book *On Early English Pronunciation*, published in five volumes between 1869 and 1889, traced the pronunciation of English from the Middle Ages to the late nineteenth century and established him as a world authority on English phonology, a pioneer in the field of speech-sound studies. For the nineteenth-century section of the book, Ellis enlisted the help of hundreds of informants across Britain and a small group of experts, including Murray and others within the OED network. The result was the first major study of British dialects.

No language yet existed for the patterns Ellis was identifying, so he often had to invent the words, which subsequently made it into the Dictionary: *palatalized*, to make a palatal sound (by moving the point of contact between tongue and palate further forward in the mouth); *labialization*, the action of making a speech sound labial (articulated with both lips); and *labiopalatalized*, a sound made into a labiopalatal (articulated with the front of the tongue against the hard palate and the lips). He also invented the words *septendecimal*, relating to a seventeenth (in music); and *phonetician*, which originally referred to an advocate of phonetic spelling, rather than its current meaning of 'an expert of phonetics'. Quite a few of his inventions have since fallen out of use and appear in the Dictionary with a dagger sign (which indicates obsolescence) beside them, such as *vocalistic*, of or relating to vowels, and *phonotyper*, an advocate of phonotypy (another term which Ellis invented, meaning 'a system of phonetic printing').

Ellis was one of the phoneticians on whom George Bernard Shaw modelled the character of Henry Higgins, that master of pronunciation, in his play *Pygmalion*, later turned into the musical *My Fair Lady*. Higgins (as a bet with his gentlemen friends) teaches Eliza Doolittle to speak 'proper' English; but Ellis had none of Henry Higgins's snobbery or arrogance. He was a generous, down-to-earth man, a frequent correspondent with friends, happy to offer advice when asked, and always working to bring people together and support them.

Ellis spent every Sunday carrying out experiments in musical pitch at the house of musicologist Alfred Hipkins. He arrived at the Hipkinses' by horse cab, the pockets of Dreadnought full of tuning forks, measuring rods, notes, and resonators. So as not to cause any trouble to the Hipkinses' servants, the thoughtful Ellis even filled his experiment jars with water for refreshment before leaving home. Ellis's work with Hipkins is preserved in the Dictionary in certain words which they alone invented and used – but as no one else did they are now obsolete, for example *mesotonic*, relating to the mean tone.

After a full afternoon of experiments with Alfred, Ellis would join the Hipkins family for lively conversation around the tea table, although he refrained from eating lest it interfere with his supper of warm-water-and-milk. Hipkins's daughter Edith remembered these Sundays and commented that for someone who became famous for sound, Ellis actually had a bad ear: 'Dr Ellis was tone deaf and could not distinguish between "God Save the Queen" or "Rule Britannia"! Happily my father had an unusually sensitive ear and as Dr Ellis arrived at conclusions entirely by calculations he would call upon his "other self" in time of trouble with "Lend me your ears!"'

Edith Hipkins described Ellis as genial and happy, but we know from his letters in the archives that he suffered from bouts of depression and burnout. His way of dealing with his depression was what he called 'mental hygiene', a type of fasting from one's passions. This included days, or even weeks, of reducing his diet, and taking long walks of an hour and a half each day.

It seems very likely from the language that Ellis used when talking about his mental health that he had read the book *Mental Hygiene* (1843) by the American doctor William Sweetser. A Harvard graduate, Sweetser encouraged people suffering from depression to examine their intellects and passions, and to abstain from them in order to regain their equilibrium, health, and happiness. Ellis would resist reading, intellectual work, and attending talks at his favourite clubs and societies. His letters to Murray are intimate and honest about his state of mind. 'I feel as if I were going to be quite well again soon', he wrote in 1871, 'but I am going to keep on my scheme of abstention for sometime to come. It was just because I knew I should be interested by Nichol's paper that I did not go. After Easter I hope to attend again [the Philological Society meetings]. I won't read Nichol's paper yet (perhaps not this year) as I have Payne's – out of a respect for mental hygiene.'

He wrote to Murray during another bout of depression, 'I was not at home when you left your note about ten days ago, but it was as well that I did not see you, for I find it best for me to abstain as much as possible from having any conversation which interests me, philological or other. By preserving a strict regime I am certainly improving, and therefore always feeling a desire to kick over the traces, as it's weary work doing nothing when one is longing to be doing something.'

I was struck when reading Ellis's letters that the Victorians were much more open to discussing their well-being than later generations, except perhaps Generation Z today. Ellis wrote to Murray in February 1882, 'A cough, not bad in itself but provoking in keeping me awake most of the night & hence rendering me stupid and unfit for work during the day, will prevent my being at the Philological Society on Friday so I must ask you to take the chair from me.' In November 1883 he wrote, 'This morning I am much washed out. I nearly broke down altogether on Wednesday & only with great care came up to the scratch.' And ten days later, 'I got sadly overworked by my preparation for my paper & had to take half holidays in the mornings of the preceding Wednesday and Thursday to get it done at all. Afterwards I was unable to do writing for want of head power till the following Wednesday, when I wrote the enclosed slips but could not finish them for I had to write a lecture to be read tonight which has destroyed my greatly needed rest & from which I shall probably be the rest of the week recovering. I am sorry your influenza still continues. You are always sadly overworked. My overwork is as nothing to yours – except in my additional years, 69 in June. Don't think of coming out at night in this cold weather.'

When he was well, much of Ellis's correspondence related to queries about pronunciation. In 1884, one of Murray's assistants, Alfred Erlebach, who kept a kind of secret diary on humorous happenings in the Scriptorium, recorded that Ellis had written to the biologist Thomas Henry Huxley to ask how he pronounced *abiological*. Huxley replied that he had no idea how to pronounce the word because he had never seen it before. It occurred on the first page of his book *Manual of the Anatomy of Invertebrated Animals*.

Ellis and Murray first got to know each other in the 1860s (before Murray worked on the OED) while Murray was still living in the Scottish village of Hawick where he worked as a schoolteacher. Alexander Melville Bell, father of the inventor of the telephone, had introduced them: Bell thought

An image of Alexander John Ellis in Furnivall's
photo album: 'Alexr J. Ellis b. 14 June 1814
photo'd 10 June 1890'.

that Murray could help Ellis with his book on pronunciation, which he was then researching and writing. Murray did help Ellis with Scottish and northern dialect, and they travelled together with the express purpose of observing and noting pronunciations around Britain. Murray continued to help Ellis through all five volumes of his book, and the two men exchanged letters on the subject up until Ellis's death in 1890.

Without Bell's introduction of Murray to Ellis, Murray would never have become Editor of the Dictionary. Ellis, twenty years older, became a mentor and father figure, introducing Murray to all the right people, bringing him into membership of the London Philological Society, and frequently inviting Murray to his house for meals. Ellis's letters are full of invitations to dine at 25 Argyll Road. 'We lunch at 1.30 & dine at 7.0. Come when you like & stay for one or both meals as you like. But I must get a walk, & so I shall be out from 11.30 to 1.15 if it does not rain.' Ellis twice served as President of the Philological Society and was therefore a key figure in the creation of the OED. Alongside colleagues Henry Sweet and Frederick Furnivall, Ellis was instrumental in negotiating Oxford University Press as the publisher for the Dictionary, and paved the way for Murray to become Furnivall's successor in the role of Editor.

I wanted to know how news about the Dictionary project spread and who among the Dictionary People were key connectors for that communication. We knew that Murray advertised for volunteers in journals, newspapers, and pamphlets and leaflets, but what about news spreading by word of mouth? In his *History of London in the Nineteenth Century* (1909), the historian Walter Besant wrote that 'without doubt the greatest social force of modern time has been the club'. If this was true, and clubs were indeed conduits and breeding grounds for connection and communication among the Dictionary People, which club was the most helpful for spreading the word about the OED? And which Dictionary contributor was the strongest connector amongst the club network? I had my suspicions that Murray and Furnivall were probably the key connectors, and that the Philological Society was the key club, but it turned out I was wrong.

I worked with a colleague at Cambridge and students at Stanford to apply graph theory and network analysis to the database of Dictionary People belonging to clubs and societies. First, we trawled through the membership lists, memos, and minutes of meetings of 1,000 clubs and societies in Britain, America, Europe, and elsewhere to see who were members. We found that 671 contributors to the Dictionary belonged to 918 clubs and societies. Most of this could be done electronically but some of it had to be done manually and involved a trip to London and the kindness of archivists in 'Clubland', the Athenæum, and the Oxford and Cambridge Club on Pall Mall, who let me sit in their basement offices and scour their huge leather-bound membership books.

When we applied network analysis to these people, we discovered there was no one in the network who was more powerful or influential in connecting other people to each other (technically called 'betweenness centrality') and being connected themselves to influential people ('eigenvector centrality') than Alexander John Ellis. He was a 'superconnector' among the Dictionary People. He brought other people to the project and those people were influential. Just as Murray would never have become Editor without Ellis, many people would not have become Dictionary volunteers without Ellis's encouragement. Today social media is a meeting place and platform for gossip, news, and discussion. The equivalent in the nineteenth century was the club. The volume of one's letter-writing and correspondence was a barometer of popularity and influence just as our number of followers and likes is today. Ellis belonged to many clubs and societies and he was a prolific correspondent, as glimpsed in his letters to Murray: 'I have no time for more now. This is my 10th letter. Thanks for the proofs. Truly yours.'

Clubs and societies proliferated in the nineteenth century and played an important role in the social, cultural, and intellectual life of Ellis, as they did for hundreds of other Dictionary People. Sometimes within the same day, he would rush from the London Library to the British Museum, from the Royal Society to the New Shakspere Society, the Palaeographical

Society, and Philological Society. He used these social networks to spread the word about the Dictionary project and to recruit volunteers for it.

The most influential society among the Dictionary People was the Early English Text Society. This surprised me. After all, the OED had been founded by the Philological Society and for decades had been called 'the Society's Dictionary'. The Early English Text Society was one of the eight societies founded by Frederick Furnivall, all of which were vital to the work of the Dictionary. Some have criticized Furnivall for not doing enough in his role as Editor in its first twenty years, because he was too busy starting new amateur organizations, but they fail to understand that these initiatives were vital to the work of the Dictionary. They produced reprints and edited copies of publications which provided quotations without which the Dictionary could never have been written; they also gave a steady supply of contributors – Readers, Specialists, and Subeditors.

The particular mission of the Early English Text Society was to bring unprinted works of early literature, written in Old English and Middle English, to a wider audience by printing them. Today, the handsome brown volumes embossed with the symbol of King Alfred's jewel are known and beloved by medievalists. Furnivall commissioned colleagues and friends to edit the texts – Old English epic poems such as *Beowulf*, or Middle English *Morte Arthure, Piers Plowman*, and *Cursor Mundi* – and to write introductions to them, thereby contextualizing them and aiding in their reception. Some of the titles might seem obscure to those untrained in Old and Middle English – Murray, for example, edited *The Romance and Prophesies of Thomas of Erceldoune* – but they were invaluable to the fledgling OED because they allowed Murray to show evidence of a word right back to the tenth century. Works attributed to King Alfred, for example, are quoted over 2,000 times in the Dictionary and take words such as *darling, dwell, laughter, lust, merry, mirth,* or *bliss* (which was originally a verb meaning 'to rejoice') or common words such as *each, her, his, off, on, only, that,* or *rather* back to 900 CE. Murray was grateful to Furnivall for having the ingenuity to start such a society; without it, the Dictionary would have been limited in its ability to give full biographies of words and to trace their origins fully.

The members of Early English Text Society who helped the Dictionary usually did so in the role of Specialists who provided advice on the meaning of certain words or their etymologies. If we look at the number of Specialists versus those who were Readers in the UK, we see that there were fewer Specialists than Readers. But there was one part of the world that had a higher proportion of Specialists than Readers, and that was Europe, to where we now turn.

E

for EUROPEANS

A few years ago, I was standing in front of a glass case in a small museum in southern Germany. I was on holiday with friends but, of course, was still thinking about the Dictionary. Looking at a display of small pieces of paper nailed to a wall, I suddenly had an aha moment.

The museum was the Grimmwelt Museum in Kassel, former home of the famous Brothers Grimm, who in the nineteenth century had written the children's fairy tales 'Snow White', 'Sleeping Beauty', 'Little Red Riding Hood', and 'Cinderella'. More importantly, for those of us who love dictionaries, Jacob Grimm and his brother Wilhelm were also lexicographers who created and edited the *Deutsches Wörterbuch*, the German equivalent of the OED. Or rather I should say, the OED is the English equivalent of the *Deutsches Wörterbuch*, because the German dictionary was started first (even if it ended up being finished later because the Brothers Grimm died before the letter G, and it took another hundred years to complete).

The museum got unfairly low scores on Tripadvisor. One American tourist said, 'Not enough about the fairy tales and too much about the boring dictionary.' Another wrote, 'Just leave your children at home and bring your reading glasses.' Which, of course, is why I loved it. It is one of my favourite museums. If you haven't visited it, you are missing out on something very special, so plan a trip and pack your spectacles.

As soon as I walked into this beautifully designed museum, which tells the story of the lives and work of the Brothers Grimm, I realized the similarities between the two dictionaries. There was a dramatic wall of vast numbers of slips, or 'zettel', hanging from long nails. They looked exactly like the slips sent into the OED by the Dictionary People. There was a world map showing the hundreds of volunteers who corresponded with the brothers; the editors' lists of words and statistical counts of entries; the tracing of etymology using the new scientific philological methods of the day; the gathering of citations from historical, published sources. I had worked in the OED archives for years and the contents of the Grimmwelt Museum looked identical.

Walking through the museum, I was struck by the myriad ways in which the OED editors, who began work on their Dictionary twenty years after the Brothers Grimm, had 'borrowed' their working methods. Could, I wondered, the OED have existed without the Grimms' dictionary? The OED editors were able to learn from the lexicographic successes and mistakes of their European counterparts, not least the Germans who had already pioneered crowdsourcing and experienced the difficulties of coordinating volunteers of unreliable ability and indifferent adherence to deadlines.

By the time the OED project commenced, Europe already had major dictionaries under way or completed in German, French, Italian, Russian, and Dutch, all of which were taking advantage of the new methodologies of Continental philology. In Germany, the Brothers Grimm had begun the *Deutsches Wörterbuch* in 1838. In France, Émile Littré had begun the *Dictionnaire de la langue française* in 1841

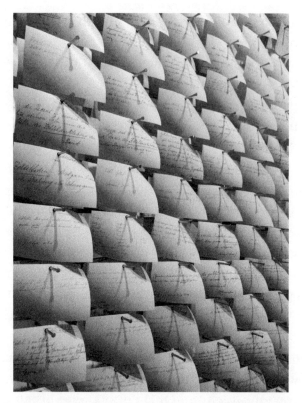

A section of a wall of slips in the Grimmwelt Museum
showing how the Brothers Grimm pioneered the
methods used by the OED twenty years later.

(a dictionary of post-1600 French). In the Netherlands, Matthias de Vries had begun *Woordenboek der Nederlandsche Taal* in 1852 (a dictionary of post-medieval Dutch).

We think of the OED as a radical dictionary because of its size, its scholarship, and its methods, and it was radical *for English*. But if you compare it with other languages, there was nothing about its creation in the mid-nineteenth century that had not been done before in Europe. English was relatively late to the table. The English editors were able to pick and choose the best methods from different European dictionaries. The OED implemented European lexicographic practices, and advanced upon them, to create something truly revolutionary, something that would in fact end up being the envy of Europe.

If we're being generous we would say Britain was 'inspired' by Europe to write its own massive dictionary. If we were being real, we might say Britain was playing catch-up. There was no way Samuel Johnson's dictionary, already a century old, or any others published in the meantime, neither Charles Richardson's *New Dictionary of the English Language* (1836–7) nor John Ogilvie's *Imperial Dictionary of the English Language,* not to mention what had been going on in America with the dictionary wars between Noah Webster and Joseph Worcester, could match what was happening in Europe.

It was not only the size and scale of European dictionaries that were superior, it was also the scholarship which underpinned them. The study of words and language, otherwise known as 'philology', was all the rage in Europe at the turn of the nineteenth century. European scholars had developed their own methodologies to compare languages and to trace the source of a word, which became known as 'Continental philology'. It was half a century until Britain took up these methods, which are still practised today and form the basis of comparative linguistics. As Murray put it, 'The scientific and historical spirit of the nineteenth century has at once called for and rendered possible the Oxford English Dictionary.' It was time for Britain to equal Europe in terms of the study of philology, etymology, and, most specifically, the creation of dictionaries based on scientific principles.

It was left to a handful of keen British scholars, by no means part of the mainstream, to encourage others to take up Continental philology. Murray and his colleagues at the London Philological Society, especially its founders Edwin Guest, Henry Malden, and Thomas Hewitt Key, were main players in enlivening the British linguistic scene and adopting the methods of Continental philology. Now

known as 'the oldest learned society in Great Britain dedicated to the study of language', the Philological Society
was founded in 1842 as a forum for discussion, debate, and
work on developments in philology. But all this innovation
came comparatively late, and the Grimms, who were made
honorary members of the London Philological Society in
1843, were at the heart of the European innovations. They
influenced Continental philology; they practised the application of historical principles; they pioneered the descriptive method of defining and tracing a word's meaning
across time; and they forged the crowdsourcing techniques
and lexicographic policies and practices adopted by the
OED editors.

Given how advanced Europe was in the philological world, it probably comes as no surprise that contributions from Europeans are prominent among the Dictionary
People. There were fifty-six people living in Europe who contributed to the Dictionary. This is not a huge number but if
we compare these volunteers with the thousands of others
in Britain and around the world, we detect a pattern. The
numbers were relatively low, but the quality was high; they
were learned and scholarly. Most of them lived in Germany
(fourteen) and France (eleven), followed by the Netherlands
(nine) and Austria (six), Denmark (five), Sweden (four),
Italy (two), Belgium (one), Norway (one), Poland (one),
Madeira (one), and Switzerland (one).

European contributors filled all the volunteer roles –
Reader, Specialist, and Subeditor. Not only were there proportionally more Specialists than Readers in Europe, which
was unusual when compared with the UK and the rest of
the world, but there were also half as many female contributors in Europe as elsewhere. This is because Europe had a
higher proportion of contributors who were specialist consultants, and in the nineteenth century more of those would

have been male because of inequalities in access to higher education.

Only a fraction of all Subeditors were located in Europe, but they covered the proofs of nearly half the Dictionary. And, amazingly, the lion's share was done by one man, Mr A. Caland, a Dutch schoolmaster and lecturer in English who lived in Leeuwarden, followed by Wageningen, and subedited twelve letters of the alphabet. Caland and Murray became good friends, writing to each other most weeks for twenty-five years, only stopping shortly before Caland's death in 1910. They shared an interest in stamp collecting. Strangely, we do not know Caland's first name. He only ever signed himself 'A. Caland' and Murray called him 'Mr Caland', and my efforts to discover what the A. stands for drew a blank. When Caland died, Murray wrote in the preface to the letters Q and R: 'The whole of the proofs of Q and R were read by Mr. A. Caland of Wageningen, whose death on Feb 18 of this year has deprived the Dictionary of one of its most devoted and helpful voluntary workers.' Not long before his death, Caland had told Murray that 'this interest was the one thing that kept me alive'. His enthusiasm was not shared by his wife who called the OED 'that wretched dictionary'. I suspect quite a few spouses of the Dictionary People felt the same.

It is perhaps strange to think that someone in the Netherlands was regularly reading *The Times* but Mr Caland sent in over 1,000 slips from the newspaper along with thousands of others from Thomas Hardy's *Tess of the D'Urbervilles* and *Far From the Madding Crowd*, Elizabeth Gaskell's *Mary Barton*, Henry Sweet on *Phonetics*, Thackeray's *History of Pendennis*, and Dickens's *Little Dorrit*. Sometimes Murray lacked quotations for specific entries that he was editing, and he would ask his most trusted Readers to find them. Caland was one of Murray's most reliable collectors of these 'desiderata' (marked in the address book with a capital D followed by numbers according to the list of desired words). As a Specialist, he answered Murray's queries about the words *bosch,* *bowery, parole, pensionary, pingle, pistol,* and *pouch.*

The most prolific Reader in Europe – we might call him a 'super-contributor' – was Hartwig Helwich, a professor at the University of Vienna who wrote out the entire *Cursor Mundi* onto 46,599 slips. His efforts made the medieval poem the second-most-frequently cited work in the Dictionary after the Bible (though in the current OED, it has dropped to eleventh in the top sources).

Of all the Dictionary People around the world, Helwich was the fifth-highest contributor. Born in Austria, he had lived in London for a period teaching German and studying artefacts in the British Museum, and copiously adding notes to his own copy of Stratmann's *A Dictionary of the Old English Language* which he gave to the OED editors, before returning to the University of Vienna and giving so generously of his time to more Dictionary work. His copy of Stratmann still exists in the small library in the OED offices in Oxford, and is consulted regularly by editors in the etymology group.

Murray took advantage of the standard of scholarship and expertise among the European Dictionary People. He had thirty-eight Specialists in Europe, one of whom was the notable Danish linguist Otto Jespersen. As a student in 1887, Jespersen had travelled to Oxford to meet with the phonetician and philologist Henry Sweet. Perhaps Sweet introduced him to Murray because Murray began seeking Jespersen's expertise soon after his return to Denmark. Jespersen contributed to the OED for seven years while working on his doctoral dissertation on the English case system. It is surprising that Jespersen's contribution appears to have stopped once he was promoted to Professor of English at the University of Copenhagen in 1893, because this university was a hub for contributors to the OED with consultants such as the Icelandic scholar Professor Jón Stefánsson and the expat archaeologist and philologist Professor George Stephens. They were later joined (in 1899) by the Nordic languages specialist Professor Verner Dahlerup who also consulted for the OED. The University of Vienna was likewise a hub with Murray getting help from several professors including the founder of the Vienna School of English Historical Linguistics, Karl Luick.

Murray got help on etymologies for thirty years from Friedrich Kluge, a Swiss-German professor at the University of Freiburg – famous for 'Kluge's Law', a proto-Germanic sound change, and his *German Etymological Dictionary*. Another key source of etymological advice came from Paris where Marie-Paul-Hyacinthe (Paul) Meyer was Keeper of National Archives at the Bibliothèque Nationale. Considered one of the leaders of twentieth-century medieval studies, Meyer's skills as a palaeographer were consulted in connection with the Dreyfus affair in 1898. (Of a key document, Meyer concluded, 'I swear that this cannot be the writing of Dreyfus.') There is a postcard in the archives from Meyer to Furnivall, which shows his respect for Murray: 'Murray's Dictionary is a beautiful thing. The man is not to be deceived. When in despair of finding any good explanation, I send him bad stuff, he at once detects it.'

In the early days of the English Dictionary, the editor of the famous French Dictionary, Émile Littré, was himself a contributor, as was Rufino José Cuervo, the Colombian linguist who lived in Paris, specialized in varieties of Spanish, and wrote the *Diccionario de construcción y régimen de la lengua castellana* (Dictionary of the Construction and Regime of the Spanish Language).

In the late 1880s, Murray began corresponding with a Welsh woman in her mid-fifties, Miss Caroline Pemberton, who was living in the Austrian spa town of Meran for two years. While in Austria, she sent in 3,060 slips from *The Rule of St Benedict* and William Paley's *Evidences of Christianity*. Miss Pemberton knew about the Dictionary project because she was one of the few female members of the London Philological Society, and on her return to England devoted many years to preparing Queen Elizabeth I's translation of Boethius's *The Consolation of Philosophy* (1899) for the Early English Text Society.

There were many regular, non-specialist, volunteers too, including a number of expatriates. Living in Florence was an American Reader called E. E. Goodrich who sent in slips for five years from 1879 to 1884 and later moved to California to set up an olive grove. A local newspaper reported in 1897 that the venture failed because the delicate species of Italian olive trees, which he and his wife had brought from Florence, were not suited to California. (A century later, the retired proprietor of the *San Francisco Chronicle*, Nan McEvoy, did successfully grow Italian olive trees on her farm outside San Francisco, despite the naysayers, and McEvoy Ranch Virgin Olive Oil is now rated amongst the finest in the world. But she wasn't a Dictionary person.)

One of the earliest contributors from Europe was a friend of Frederick Furnivall living in Hamburg. Maria Bathoe was a British expat who sent in slips for twenty-five years, initially from Hamburg and then from London. Her reading included Dickens's novels, Darwin's *On the Origin of Species,* and John Ramsay McCulloch's *Political Economy*, resulting in a total of 4,750 slips. Born Maria Hume in 1817, she was the daughter of Joseph Hume, the Scottish surgeon and radical politician. She had lived in India in the 1840s and 1850s, where she had married Charles Gubbins of the Bengal Civil Service. These years provided fodder for stories she would later share with Charles Darwin. The Darwin archive at Cambridge preserves a letter from Mrs Bathoe in which she writes to him about her unusual pets. Responding to his publication *The Descent of Man,* she shared with him her own story about the pet antelope, hog deer, and mongoose she had kept while living in India. After reading her letter, Darwin scrawled on the envelope, 'nothing of actual use'.

One of the more glamorous contributors lived in spa hotels throughout Europe. The Hon. Beatrix Lucia Catherine Egerton Tollemache was a polyglot who had been born in Cheshire, England, on an estate neighbouring that of William Gladstone (her father was Baron Egerton of Tatton). She became a noted translator of Russian, a language which, remarkably, she taught herself in her seventies. Although a poet and writer herself, often published in the *Spectator,* her reading for the OED focused on scientific texts such as Darwin's *The Power of Movement in Plants.* This is the book that gave the world many botanical words that had never been written before: *apheliotropic,* bending or turning away from the sun; *apogeotropic,* bending or turning away from the ground; and *circumnutating,* bending or leaning in a direction which is continually revolving or rotating in a horizontal path. Letters to Murray from her and her husband, the Hon. Lionel Arthur Tollemache (son of the first Lord Tollemache), who was also a writer and a contributor to the Dictionary, show that they stayed for long periods at luxury hotels. Hôtel Sonnenberg in Engelberg, Switzerland, and Hôtel d'Angleterre in Biarritz were frequently named on their letterhead. They were probably in search of spa cures because Lionel suffered from ill health, was disabled from childhood, and became increasingly blind over his lifetime: most of the letters are in Beatrix's hand.

The European contributors differ quite radically from the other Dictionary People from around the world. The learned expertise of many of them helped the OED maintain an important rigour and standard, ensuring its reputation as the definitive record of the English language from the twelfth century to the current day. Because of their scholarly expertise, the European contributors had a cachet with which Murray wished to be associated. It is no surprise therefore that 70 per cent of the Europeans who helped him were given credit in the OED prefaces. This is over three times more frequent than the mention of non-Europeans in the prefaces. Why? The quality of their work was high and deserved credit, but also they were powerful and well-respected leaders in the field of philology. Murray was shrewd enough to know that mentioning them helped boost the standing of his Dictionary. He may have been a word nerd, but he was also savvy and knew that the success of his Dictionary depended on creating a prestigious brand and building a loyal audience – we might think of it as the 'content marketing' of the nineteenth century.

F

for FAMILIES

'Ha, I smell the northern air!' exclaimed James Murray, his head out the carriage window. His children always relished the train journey to the Lake District because it announced the start of their annual three-week holiday. Although their father always took dictionary proofs with him, the holiday gave the children respite from the intensity of living in a household of thirteen plus a very big dictionary. From the moment in March 1879 when Murray signed the contract with Oxford University Press to be the next Editor of the Dictionary, and he took possession of 2 tons of slips at his house, his family was immediately part of the project (whether they liked it or not) sorting out the slips. Their house was a workplace and the family a workforce.

A surprising discovery in the address books was that the Murray clan was not the only family group engaged in Dictionary work. Listed together in Murray's impeccable handwriting were fathers and daughters, sisters, couples, cousins, and parents and children. Across the country, indeed the world, families were engaged in communal reading and the writing out of slips. We can imagine them reading aloud in front of the fire or sitting around the gas lamp together, choosing words and quotations. If only it were possible to go

The Murray family on an annual hiking holiday in the Lake District.

back and enter the homes of the Dictionary Families – the
Cooper sisters of Bristol, the Thompson sisters of Reigate,
the Jacksons of the Isle of Wight, the Canns of Plymouth, the
Creak siblings of Stockport, the Curgenvens of Hyde Park,
the Curteis family of Rye, the Custs of Eccleston Square, the
Dobsons of South Shields, the Lees of Reigate, the Dowdens
of Dublin, the Matthews brothers of Boston, the Pope family
of Clifton, the Porter sisters of North Finchley, the Richardson sisters of Newcastle-upon-Tyne, the Druitt sisters of Kensington, the Foster family of New Hampshire, USA, the Fry
family of Exeter, the Leonard family of Clifton, the Goodier

sisters of Manchester, the La Touche family of Dublin, the Green sisters of Leicester, the Ward sisters of Bridgwater, the Shadwells of Marylebone, the Shakespeares of Regent's Park, the Gregg brothers of Ledbury, the Rivington sisters of London, the Ruthven family of New Zealand (Ada Murray's relatives), the Bousfield family of Maida Vale, the Saunders sisters of Surrey, the Scott sisters of Leamington, the Skegg family of Jersey, the Tanners of Somerset, the Tarbolton family of Yorkshire, the Taunton sisters in Wiltshire, or the Yonges of Winchester.

The Dictionary People and their families volunteered their labours from domestic settings, just as the world of lexicography had done for centuries. Homes were the principal location of dictionary creation and consumption. Samuel Johnson wrote his dictionary in the attic of a house in Gough Square, London. The regular meeting place for the founders of the OED – Trench, Coleridge, and Furnivall – was Richard Trench's house, the Dean's residence at Westminster Abbey. Herbert Coleridge began the Dictionary at his home at 10 Chester Place, Regent's Park, London. Frederick Furnivall collected the dictionary materials and stored them at his home at 3 St George's Square (now called Chalcot Square), Primrose Hill, London. And James Murray worked from his house at Mill Hill and subsequently his house at 78 Banbury Road, north Oxford. Homes meant families. Wives and children, and sometimes servants, all got in on the act.

Murray's wife, Ada, was his private secretary and all his eleven children were co-opted to help and in the case of his daughters, Rosfrith and Elsie, work as editorial assistants in the Scriptorium. Henry Bradley's daughter Eleanor worked alongside her father as an editorial assistant for most of her life. All three women were working on the Dictionary until the end, well beyond the deaths of their fathers. William Craigie had no children but his wife, Jessie, worked on the

Dictionary as a Subeditor – she took on particular responsibility for the letter U during the First World War when most
Dictionary staff were serving the war effort in some way.

Charles Onions was the only exception. He had nine
children, two of whom – Giles and Elizabeth, by then in their
eighties – were still alive in my own graduate student days in
Oxford. I visited them at the old family home at 7 Staverton
Road. The house was unchanged since their father had done
his lexicographical work in the front study (his papers and
books still lining the shelves), and the house was so crammed
with 'stuff' that it was difficult to get through the front door.
Giles suffered from a hoarding disorder, and the pair were
forced to sleep in the kitchen because it was the only room
not full of newspapers, junk mail, warplane magazines, boxes
of stuffed birds (nothing sinister, just a taxidermy collection),
and suitcases filled with clothes which once belonged to siblings now dead. A tree was growing through the dining-room
wall and into an upstairs bedroom. I asked them about their
father, and they described a strict and distant figure whose
primary relationship was with the Dictionary rather than
them. Unlike the other editors, Charles Onions did not bring
any of his children into Dictionary work, but after his death
in 1965, Giles, who had idolized his father, did some reading
for the OED under the direction of the later OED Editor
Robert Burchfield. He proudly showed me a volume of the
OED Supplement, published in the 1970s, which listed his
name as a contributor. Getting his name in the learned tome
meant a great deal to Giles who told me that, as he was the
youngest child, his father had refused to pay for his education beyond thirteen (secondary education was not free in
Britain until 1944).

Of all the families helping the OED, the model dictionary family was, of course, the Murrays. When the slips
started to stream in from around the world, and Murray was

overwhelmed by the sheer volume, he called on everyone to help put them in alphabetical and chronological order. Harold, Ethelbert, Wilfrid, Oswyn, Hilda, Ethelwyn, Aelfric, Elsie, Rosfrith, Jowett, and Gwyneth – were paid between one penny and sixpence an hour depending on the child's age. A couple of them even made it into the Dictionary. We know from the diary notes of one of Murray's assistants that the work-obsessed Murray took Dictionary work with him to the hospital when Ada was giving birth. If you look at page 2, column 1 of the first volume of the printed Dictionary, twenty-third line from the bottom, you will see a sentence Murray wrote on the proof sheets while sitting by Ada's bedside just after the birth of their daughter Elsie. 'As fine a child as you will see' appears as an example of when *a* follows an adjective ('as fine a . . .'). Likewise, under the word *arrival* he added the sentence, 'The new arrival is a little daughter', referring especially to the birth of his next daughter, Rosfrith, after a quotation from Tennyson. Both family example sentences were published in the quotation paragraph as 'Mod.' (Modern), an unusual case of words not having written sources.

The life of a lexicographer was better suited to a monk than a doting father of eleven. Murray, instinctively a family man, found the Dictionary work all-consuming, which created a tension that he could never resolve. Not long before his death, he looked back on his career and wrote to his son, 'The greatest sacrifice the Dictionary entailed upon me, by far, was the sacrifice of the constant companionship of my own children; and I doubt it was worth the sacrifice. I have tried, as a husband and father, to do what should have been the work of a celibate and ascetic, a Dunstan or a Cuthbert: no wonder it has been a struggle. But has it been worth it?'

The Dictionary was ever-present in family life. Murray was always up by 5 a.m., often at his desk in the Scriptorium long before the sun rose. With so many children, rules were needed to maintain order. Home life was strict and ran on bells: a wake-up bell at 7.30 a.m., followed by a prayer bell at 8 a.m., followed by breakfast. At meals, the children were served in order of age, the youngest last. Idle chit-chat and fidgeting at the table were prohibited. Murray joined the family for lunch at 1.30 p.m. As his granddaughter explained in her wonderful biography, *Caught in the Web of Words*, 'Usually James arrived a few minutes late, carrying a handful of Dictionary slips, about which he would talk during the meal. If by chance he arrived early and found no one else there, he would bang on the table with a knife handle till everyone flung down what he was doing and came running. Mischievous members of the family sometimes made this signal for the fun of seeing the pandemonium it caused.' Each Sunday the family walked into town for the morning service at the Congregationalist Church on George Street. Murray, upright and spry, marched in front with the children following. Locals referred to them as 'The Dic and the little Dics'.

Although Murray was austere and abstemious (he never smoked or drank alcohol, and made his wife and children sign the teetotal pledge and join the Blue Ribbon Temperance Army), he had a great sense of humour and fun. He valued time playing with his children, loved a practical joke and engaging in banter. His children remembered his dramatic recitations of parts of *The Queen's Wake*, a legendary poem by the Scottish poet James Hogg. Murray was poorly paid by Oxford University Press and was always struggling for money, but the family never let it dampen the Christmas spirit. They would exchange 'haves', joke presents of lumps of sugar or an old fork or toothbrush, wrapped in many layers. As his granddaughter explained, 'James joined in the fun and Gwyneth remembered her anguish as a little girl at finding nothing in her parcel but a Garibaldi ("squashed fly") biscuit, and then, as she began to cry, catching the twinkle in her father's eye and discovering the coin he had embedded in it.'

Their father put their favourite games in the Dictionary – *nievie-nievie-nick-nack, leap-frog, Puss in the Corner, Tom Tiddler's Ground, Mumble-the-Peg,* and *pat-a-cake.* He furnished the latter with a quotation from Lord Tennyson, and a delightful definitional note with the full rhyme: 'Pat a cake, pat a cake, baker's man! Bake me a cake as fast as you can, Shape it and prick it, and mark it with [B], And put it in the oven for baby and me!' The family owned several bicycles and two tricycles, including the first Humber tandem tricycle. Murray rode the tandem for fun with his children and sometimes Ada, and not always successfully – on one occasion the brakes failed going down a steep hill. He and Ada ended up in a ditch, still in one piece but covered in mud.

The Dictionary was a huge part of Ada's life. The family employed a nanny called Emma to help with the children, which allowed Ada to manage Murray's finances and travel arrangements. She often wrote letters on his behalf and took visitors on tours of the Scriptorium when Murray was too busy. After his death in 1915, when the Scriptorium in her back garden was dismantled and its contents moved to the Old Ashmolean building in the centre of town for the other editors to take over, she wrote, 'I cannot tell you what a blank [loss] this removal means to me and my children – it has been an intimate part of my life and they scarcely remember the first building being put up. From the very start I have worked with my husband . . . being in and out of the Scriptorium constantly – if a book or pamphlet or letter was wanted Sir James always came to me for it – so the Dictionary has been a part of our lives.'

It seems that a Dictionary childhood did not do much harm to the young Murrays. The eldest, Harold, graduated with a First from Balliol College, Oxford, authored an

A photograph from a family photo album of James
Murray and Ada (on his left) linking arms with their
eleven children (plus a friend's son).

erudite history of chess, and went on to become Her Maj-
esty's Inspector of Schools; Ethelbert was an electrical engineer in London; Wilfrid was Registrar at the University of
Cape Town in South Africa; Oswyn, who became Sir Oswyn
in 1917, obtained a triple First at Exeter College, Oxford,
and was Permanent Secretary to the Admiralty. Although
women were not granted degrees from Oxford until 1920,
they could study at the university, take the university examinations and their results were classified. This is what Hilda
did, and in 1899 she achieved First Class honours (special
subject Old Norse). Her father had enlisted her to maintain
the Scriptorium and to help him with statistical analysis of the
number of quotations and entries for current, obsolete, alien
or naturalized words in each 'fascicle' (section of the Dictionary as it was gradually published). But Hilda had other

ideas. Having done so well at Oxford, she followed a career in academia, ultimately becoming Vice Mistress at Girton College, Cambridge. A photo of her in the *Girton Review* shows her as the classic spinster don holding a book while sitting by a fireplace in a book-lined room. She is wearing a tweed skirt and jacket and is in active discussion with a student. Her younger sister Ethelwyn married the civil servant Clarence Cousins and lived in South Africa. Aelfric was ordained an Anglican priest and also went to work in South Africa. Elsie and Rosfrith were the only two children who kept working on the Dictionary into adulthood. They devoted their lives to it as their father had, seeing it through to completion. Their younger brother Jowett achieved a triple First at Magdalen College, Oxford, and became a missionary and professor in northern China; and Gwyneth, the baby of the family, was a suffragist who achieved a First at Girton College, Cambridge, and married a young Canadian Rhodes scholar called Harry Logan – their (erotic) love letters can be consulted in the National Library of Canada.

*

The Murrays provided inspiration for the Elworthys, a family living at Foxdown, a sheep farm in rural Somerset. Frederick Elworthy, his wife, Maria, and two daughters, Florence and Mary, are listed in the address books as having sent in 18,000 slips. The two families had a close friendship and the Murrays made visits to Foxdown every year.

The more I researched the Elworthys, the more I could picture them in the drawing room at Foxdown, reading and writing out slips together. Mrs Maria Elworthy read *The New-comes*, a family saga that was Thackeray's most popular work with Victorian readers. Her slip for *crumpling irons*, 'In Miss Ethel's black hair there was a slight natural ripple which others endeavoured to imitate by art, paper, and I believe crumpling irons', was one of 700 which she sent in from the book including the word *bouderie*, pouting, which had never occurred in a printed source before.

Their elder daughter, Mary, read the poetry of William Cowper, and Florence, who had a preference for female authors, scoured Anna Jameson's *Sacred and Legendary Art*. She wrote out slips for words that were sophisticated for a teenager: *myrrhophore*, each of the women who carried spices to the sepulchre of Christ, and *motif*, the dominant idea of a composition. These words had never appeared in print before Anna Jameson wrote them and would not have entered the OED had it not been for the reading of the young Florence Elworthy.

Frederick Elworthy and James Murray had become firm friends after Alexander John Ellis had introduced them at a London Philological Society meeting in the early 1870s. Although Elworthy was the wealthy owner of a sheep farm, he and Murray had several interests in common: regional dialects, folklore, gardening, and painting watercolours. It was regional accents that first brought the two men together. Elworthy was writing a dictionary and a grammar of the west Somerset dialect and he sought Murray's expertise. Murray had been warned by Ellis that Elworthy's word lists of the Somerset dialect were excellent but his phonetic transcriptions of the words were, as Ellis put it, 'in an alarming state'. Elworthy had attempted to spell the Somerset words using Glossotype (of which more soon) but Ellis was not satisfied with his application and asked Murray to help sort it out.

When Elworthy's grammar was published in 1877, Murray described it as 'the first grammar of an English dialect of any scientific value'. The key word in this sentence is 'English' – Murray, never one to underestimate his own scholarship, had, of course, already published his own grammar of a Scottish dialect four years before Elworthy's, in which he had admirably applied the scientific methods of Continental philology, the same methods which he brought to his work on the OED.

The friendship had its benefits for Murray. A man of Elworthy's stature and wealth would prove helpful, especially when it came to negotiating the conditions of his employment at Oxford University Press. Besides, Murray enjoyed his company, and could think of nothing better than joining Frederick in outdoor painting on hidden parts of the farm, going for long hikes and discussing discoveries in folklore and regional dialect.

Elworthy's interest in folklore was more extreme than Murray's. It extended to witchcraft, superstition, and the occult. He had one of the world's largest private collections of folklore charms and amulets. He spent much of his wealth travelling through Europe and the Middle East collecting artefacts, 700 of which are now housed in the Pitt Rivers Museum in Oxford, but back then they were displayed throughout Elworthy's house as though it were a living museum. The family lived with curious charms and counter-charms hanging from doorways, nailed to chimneys, and displayed in glass cabinets. There were winged figures and hearts stuck with thorns, engraved gems, horse amulets, ancient crosses, and a Fattura della Morte, or 'the death-maker', which he had collected in southern Italy. It was a shrivelled green lemon that had been pierced with thirty nails, a single piece of string twisted around each one. It may have been a little spooky to visit the Elworthys and stay amongst such paraphernalia, but for the Murray family visiting Foxdown was an annual highlight.

Coming from a prominent woollen manufacturing family, Frederick Elworthy was well placed to advise the Dictionary on sheep-farming terms. Letters in the archives show him patiently explaining to Murray the details of words such as *broke*, short locks of wool found on the edge of a fleece, and *noil*, knots of wool combed out of a long staple. He also subedited the letters A, B, C, and D. His reading for the Dictionary included Daniel Rogers's *Naaman the Syrian His Disease and Cure*, a seventeenth-century commentary on the Book of Kings. It contained many words that occurred nowhere else (hapax legomena) and would otherwise be lost to history: *loggish* meaning 'heavy, sluggish'; *to howster* meaning 'to oust'; *to encredit*, to gain credit (for a person); *to ejure*, to renounce; *bunch*, a punch; and *basking*, beating, flagellation.

But it was Elworthy's specialism in folklore that made the greatest contribution to the Dictionary. He invented the term *ophiolaters* for people who worship snakes, especially those in Egypt and West Africa. He delighted in telling tales of those who possess magical powers and are able to foresee the future by observing certain natural phenomena such as the pattern of stones, *lithomancy*; the movement of air, *aeromancy*; the shape of figs and fig leaves, *sycomancy* (in which the diviners wrote names and questions on leaves, which were exposed to the winds, and those remaining gave the answers sought); or the movement of molten lead, *molybdomancy* – all words which made it into the Dictionary. He told stories of *onychonomancy*, practised by the Ancient Greeks who 'took the fingernails of unpolluted boys, covered them with soot and oil, and when turned to the sun they reflected the desired image'. More than 100 -*mancy* words made it into the Dictionary including *cephaleonomancy*, divination by placing a donkey's head on coals, and watching the jaws move at the name of a guilty person.

F might also be for Fairies. Elworthy was the man who put magic spells in the Dictionary with hundreds of words relating to witches, fairies, ghosts, pixies, and devils. His own books on dialect and folklore are cited over 700 times in the Dictionary for words as varied as *pharmacy*, the use of potions in divination or witchcraft; and a folklore sense of the word *phallus*, an image of the (usually erect) penis, especially as a symbol of the generative power in nature, venerated in various religions: 'In compounded amulets the commonest of all objects was the phallus or some other suggesting the ideas conveyed by it.' The entry for *horns*, as those attributed to deities or demons in images and pictures, appears with a most unusual quotation paragraph: two quotations from the same book, in this case Elworthy's *Evil Eye* which was published in 1895, with examples of horns in images from the Middle Ages and in carved wood worn on the heads of idols in Tahiti.

It seems that when it came to Elworthy, Murray was open to breaking the rules a little. It was rare to use a private letter as a quotation in the Dictionary but Murray did so twice with letters from Elworthy which described farming terms. The first was for the expression *all to a beat* which was evidenced by '1885 F. T. Elworthy (in letter) A field is described as "all to a beat" when it has become matted with weeds, especially couch-grass or twitch.' The other was for the verb *to dag*, to cut off the dags or locks of dirty wool from a sheep: '1890 F. T. Elworthy (in letter) In Kent these clots of dung which are apt to stick to the wool around the tails of sheep, with the wool attached, are called "daggings".'

Elworthy's writings revealed that many superstitions stemmed from farming communities, and that his interests were not that disparate after all. This is evident in entries such as *overlook*, to bewitch, which is supported by a quotation from Elworthy, 'In England, of all animals, the pig is oftenest overlooked'; and *needfire*, a fire credited with magical properties, especially in protecting cattle from disease.

Elworthy's favourite topic was the 'evil eye', the power to cast a malicious look which is believed to do harm, and his book was read for the Dictionary and quoted many times for a host of bizarre words relating to superstition and magic, including for the word *mumbo-jumbo*, defined by Henry

Bradley as 'an object of unintelligent veneration', which may have been Bradley's way of signalling what he thought of it all.

Elworthy's book came out a year too late for it to be quoted for the most obvious entry, *evil eye* (this part of E had been published in 1894). Instead, Henry Bradley who edited the letter E included a fabulous quotation from the book of another contributor, Miss Georgina Jackson, whose *Shropshire Wordbook* included this: 'E's a nasty downlookin' fellow – looks as if 'e could cast a nev'l-eye upon yo'.' Miss Jackson ran a school for young ladies in Chester and devoted many hours each day to dictionary work not only for Murray's Dictionary and Joseph Wright's *English Dialect Dictionary*, but also for her own three-volume dictionary of the Shropshire dialect. She was probably the person who Murray meant when he wrote 'Friend of Miss Jackson' beside the entry for Miss Janet Coutts Pittrie. She corresponded with Murray, and in the archives I found a letter which gives us an insight into her dedication to lexicography. In 1880 she was finishing the third volume of her *Shropshire Wordbook* and pushed on in great physical pain: 'I have a great deal of pain to bear, and the book work is a severe strain upon my power of endurance. Pt III nevertheless is steadily advancing, and I hope to see the end of it before very long. I feel very thankful that I have been able to do some useful work in the cause of the Mother Tongue for "useful" I am assured it is on all hands.' Miss Jackson's book certainly proved useful to the OED which ended up citing her 555 times for words such as *afterclap*, an unwelcome surprise; *bowk*, a milk pail; and *cakey*, silly or foolish. Most unusually, Murray even referred to Miss Jackson in a definition for the verb *to delve*, to dig, in which he wrote, 'In Shropshire, according to Miss Jackson, *to delve* is spec. to dig two spades deep.'

As Murray's children grew up, they kept in touch with

the Elworthys – Wilfrid, the third-eldest, often went by himself to stay at Foxdown. The vast correspondence between Elworthy and Murray shows the depth of their relationship; they shared intimate details of their lives with each other, from concerns about their children to details about Elworthy's state of anxiety and depression, and his failing eyesight. Elworthy mentored Murray with career advice right up until his death just before Christmas in 1907. It had been a particularly brutal year for Murray because he had also lost his loyal Subeditor and financial backer Henry Hucks Gibbs, the indefatigable Subeditor Jemima Brown, the American journalist Wendell Phillips Garrison, the schoolmaster William Moore, the zoologist Alfred Newton, and the exceptional volunteer and expert in Indian languages Edward Lyall Brandreth. The Dictionary Family was dwindling, and Murray acknowledged the loss to the Philological Society: 'Thus one by one, they pass away, and one has ever the anxious question Who is to be the next? . . . If good wishes and good counsel can prolong my days, they are not wanting.'

Although the Dictionary advertised for contributors in newspapers and journals, and through global appeals, a recurring pattern amongst contributors was for them to recommend directly the project to their friends and local communities. Then, as now, word of mouth was a stronger recommendation than any official advertisement. The Elworthys spread the word about the Dictionary project amongst their own local community, enlisting the local vicar, Revd P. N. Bisson, who sent in over 200 slips from his reading of Scott's *The Monastery* and *The Abbot*. They also inspired the women in another family, the Walters, who lived at Ford House, Wellington, to give time and attention to the Dictionary; Murray sometimes called on them when he stayed at Foxdown. When one of the girls became ill and died, he wrote to express his condolences and her mother wrote to Murray, 'I want you to know how great value my darling set upon her acquaintance with you, and that some of the most en-joyed half-hours of her life were those brightened by your very kind visits to her.' Her other daughter continued to read for the Dictionary for another decade, sending in 5,000 slips from texts such as *The Elizabethan Homilies* (1623) and Ephraim Pag-itt's *Christianographie, or The description of the multitude and sundry sorts of Christians in the world not subject to the Pope* (1636) to the recently published Mrs Oliphant's *Makers of Florence* (1877). She also contributed to the creation of Joseph Wright's *English Dialect Dictionary*, as did other contributors to the OED.

In the address books, I spotted recurring themes in families who helped the Dictionary. There were cousins (the novelist Charlotte Yonge and her cousin Henry Hucks Gibbs subedited part of the letter N together). There were also many father-and-daughter unions, perhaps none more strik-ing than James Blomfield and his four daughters from Upper Norwood in south-east London.

James Blomfield was a wool merchant who as a boy had been taught by Murray at Mill Hill School. He and his four daughters – Alice, Jane, Mary, and Emily – read for the Dic-tionary over five years and sent in a total of 7,000 slips. The youngest daughter, Emily, provides an excellent test case for understanding the particularity of reading for the Dictionary.

When someone read for the Dictionary their choice of words was a personal decision. Unless a contributor sent in a word, there was a risk that word would be missed. If it weren't for Frederick Elworthy, the Dictionary would lack many words pertaining to folklore and magic; without Margaret Murray it would not have as many words from India; without Alexan-der John Ellis it would lack words related to phonetics and phonology. This is how important the contributors were to the creation of this text.

Emily Blomfield's reading of a book by the explorer David Livingstone demonstrates the subjectivity of the word-gathering process. It is fascinating to compare the words she chose with the words chosen by another contributor, Mr John Griffiths from Kingsland in Hereford, who read a similar book by Livingstone.

Miss Blomfield chose a balance of African words borrowed into English such as *gnu*, wildebeest; *banian*, a Hindu trader; *baobab*, a tree found in Africa and India; as well as common English words such as *fold, bundle, convert*, and *everyday*. Mr Griffiths, on the other hand, only chose common words or words with long histories in English such as *barter, bawling, blatter, boil, brattle*, and *brookle*. You would have no idea that the book from which these words came was Livingstone's *Expedition to the Zambesi*. In fact, I read this second book myself and discovered hundreds of loanwords that Griffiths had ignored: *borassus*, a palm tree with large edible nuts 'of a sweet and fruity taste'; *head man*, chief of a village; *hornbill*, the bird Buceros cristatus; *Makololo*, a tribe living near Lake Nyasa; *sura*, a type of palm wine of which Livingstone wrote 'when fresh, it is a pleasant drink, somewhat like champagne'.

The OED word-gathering process was certainly unpredictable but it also had a safety net: the sheer numbers of contributors ensured that if one of them missed a word, it would often be picked up by someone else who read another book, which is what happened with all these words that were missed by Griffiths. A project of this ambition could only succeed at scale and with a diversity of perspectives from a family living on a sheep farm, to a young woman reading on her rooftop in India, and a group of men who, as I discovered from letters in Murray's papers, wrote in what looked like a secret language.

G

for GLOSSOTYPISTS

I went through a stage in my research when I seemed to spend every holiday in Britain and every day of my holiday in the Bodleian Library. I delighted in sitting for hours in the Rare Books and Manuscripts Reading Room, working my way through the archive of correspondence between James Murray and the Dictionary People. I missed it so much when I got back to Stanford that I found a website playing Sounds of the Bodleian – silence, snuffles, shuffles, page turns, footsteps, and whispers. One day when I was physically there, I sat at a desk by one of the large windows overlooking the King's Arms. Sunlight streamed through as I delicately opened letters between James Murray and Alexander John Ellis: 'Wee must not ekspekt ordineri ruyterz too ruyt widh dhe preesizhun ov paliohtuyp; in fakt dhai kahnt doo it, and it iz verri diffikult too maik up wunz mund abuwt unaksented silublz.'

I realized it wasn't a secret code or even a new language, but Ellis's invention of a new spelling system for English, which – I gathered from other letters in the Murray Papers – had been enthusiastically embraced by quite a few philologists (including Murray) in both Britain and America, who were advocates for what was known as 'Spelling Reform' or 'Simplified Spelling'. They were striving to make English spelling more consistent and easier to read and write. For Ellis, this was a justice issue: he wanted the poor and working classes to be educated, and he believed that a major obstacle to literacy was the tricky spelling system of English.

English is a notoriously difficult language to read and write because there are so many inconsistencies in its spelling system. There are words which require context before we know how to pronounce them (think *minute, read, bow*). Some words contain silent letters (*psalm, knife, debt*) or letters that sound different in different word environments (the final /f/ sound in rou*gh*, and the initial /g/ sound in *gh*ost) or ones that sound different in the same word environments (the final sounds in *rough* and *though*). In all, there are hundreds of ways of spelling the forty-four different sounds in English. With all these possible permutations, linguists today joke that the word *fish* could be spelled 'ghoti' (using the 'gh' spelling for /f/ in *rough*, the 'o' spelling for /i/ in *women*, and the 'ti' spelling for the /sh/ sound in the middle of *nation)*. Ellis himself joked in 1845 that the word *favourite* might be spelled 'phaighpheawraibt' using *ph*ysic, str*aigh*t, ne*ph*ew, *ea*rth, *wr*ite, capt*ai*n, de*bt*.

The craze for spelling reform really took off in the 1870s and 1880s. Ellis and other Dictionary People were central to the movement. Ellis had been working on spelling reform since the 1840s when he and Isaac Pitman, the inventor of shorthand, began efforts to influence schools, government, and institutions by arguing that if spelling was simplified it would improve reading skills and help forge the way for English to be used as an international language. He invented several new spelling systems, but his two most successful were named Glossotype and Palaeotype. Murray had used Ellis's systems in his book on Scottish dialect, and I had spotted it scattered throughout his personal lecture notes and memos. But it was among a core, and influential, group of

Dictionary People who specialized in philology and pronunciation that the strongest advocacy took place. Walter Skeat, Henry Sweet, Archibald Sayce, Daniel Jones, Richard Morris, Max Müller, Frederick Furnivall, Alexander Melville Bell, and Prince Louis Lucien Bonaparte (Napoleon's nephew who was exiled in England and specialized in British regional accents) were all Glossotypists or advocates of Glossotype. They met regularly in each other's houses, most usually Bonaparte's, and wrote articles, pamphlets, and books on spelling reform.

Other Dictionary volunteers who also joined the movement included Samuel Seville, Frederick Fleay, and the extravagantly named Dictionary contributor, Tito Telemaco Temistocle Terenzio Pagliardini, who taught French at St Paul's School in London and in 1864 wrote *The International Alphabet: Or, a Plea for Phonetic Spelling* (ironic, given his name). Pagliardini was described by George Bernard Shaw as 'impossible to dislike'. Shaw himself, although not a contributor to the Dictionary, was a strong supporter of spelling reform. He wanted to do away with the Roman alphabet and left £8,300 in his will especially for the development of a new English alphabet called 'Shavian' in which an edition of his play *Androcles and the Lion* was published in 1962.

The movement was popular among some of the Dictionary People in America too. Francis March, the OED's American coordinator, founded the American Spelling Reform Association and served as its president. Other advocates included the educationalist Robert Koch Buehrle of Pennsylvania, the philologist Hermann Brandt of Hamilton College, and the lexicographer William Dwight Whitney of Yale who edited the *Century Dictionary*. Their campaign gained influential and powerful followers, most famously President Theodore Roosevelt and the Scottish-American industrialist and philanthropist Andrew Carnegie who helped found the American Simplified Spelling Board in 1906 with a huge donation of $300,000. Murray was immediately elected a member. At one stage it looked as though the Board was going to succeed in getting simplified spelling rolled out in all official American government publications. The Board suggested 300 new spellings for English words (e.g. *altho, tho, kist* instead of kissed, *wisht* instead of wished), which Roosevelt ordered the Government Printing Office to use in all government documents, but soon afterwards the mandate was quashed by Congress and never came to fruition.

Murray and Ellis used reformed spelling in their letters as early as 1869, a decade before Murray took up the reins of the Dictionary. Murray's support of Ellis's spelling systems would have played a large part in cementing their friendship. Sometimes entire letters were written in the new spelling, other times only a paragraph or a sentence. Later, they switched to Glossotype when discussing issues related to pronunciation or events involving other Dictionary People who were Glossotypists. Ellis used it to tell Murray about a visit to Bonaparte: 'I kauld on Prins Looee Luisian yesterday & had a long tauk widh him about foanetiks faur ei woz dizeir'rus ov getting sum infaurmai'shen out ov him.' Ellis was planning his next paper (on Glossotype) for the Philological Society: 'Mei paiper for dhi Filoalojikel iz "Glosik, a neu system ov Ingglish speling, proapoazed faur konkurent eus, in aurder too remidi dhi difekts widhout ditrakting from dhi value ov dhi present aurthografi". Ei am thinking ov reiting it, after dhi ferst paij, in Glosik soa dhat it wil serv az its oan specimen!'

In one letter he invited Murray to join him for a spelling reform meeting at the house of Bonaparte: 'Kan eu kum? If soa let me noa az ei promist too reit and infaurm dhi prins this week. Ei think wee shuod bee about 3 ourz dhair faur dhi Prins iz an interminabl tauker. On leeving him, will eu wauk hoam & dein widh mee? Wee dein at 6.30.' On other occasions, they used reformed spelling to discuss the very mechanics of devising the new spelling systems: 'On goaing too mei glosoateip ei feind dhat oaing too dhi eus of aa, oa, uo, eu in glosik, ei must modifei meni ov dhi ekstra leterz', explained Ellis, signing off 'Yoorz trooli, Allegzahnder Jon Ellis'.

Enthusiasm among the Dictionary People for new ways of spelling came out of a deep knowledge of the complicated history of the language. They knew that English words had not always been spelled the way they are today, that spelling varied widely in past centuries, and that the English language is a composite of words from many different sources. Some are based in Old English; others come from Scandinavian and Viking traditions, from Norman French with their own spelling conventions, or are borrowed from other European languages or indigenous languages from around the world. All of this was complicated by the Great Vowel Shift that took place between the fifteenth and eighteenth centuries in which pronunciations changed in spoken English but not necessarily in written English. Superimpose this complexity on a context in which writing went from handwritten manuscripts to the mechanization of the printing press, alongside the evolution of dictionaries as tools of linguistic standardization, and English spelling gradually narrowed in its variation. When monolingual dictionaries of English first appeared in the early seventeenth century, there was no concept of 'correct' spelling, and there was no belief that the ability to spell was a sign of general intelligence or a good education. The idea that someone is 'good at spelling' is a relatively recent phenomenon – because, previously, there was no spelling standard against which the 'good' or 'bad' speller could be measured.

English spelling varied widely in the sixteenth and seventeenth centuries, and it took hundreds of years for English spelling to settle on what it is today. Dictionaries helped with this standardization, and it is therefore no surprise that the push for spelling reform in the nineteenth century came from those within the world of dictionaries. But despite their being advocates for a new spelling system, it was tough to institute any real change. They underestimated what it would take to modify the spelling rules amongst the public. The nineteenth-century world was different from previous centuries – far more people could read and write, printing now happened on a massive scale, and a small group of men had less power to control the future of spelling.

The number of letters in the English alphabet was only settled in the seventeenth century. Before then, i and j were different forms of the same letter, as were u and v (the form used depended on the position of the letter in the word), s was used for the voiced sound /z/, and f, aka the 'long S', represented the voiceless /s/ we know it today.

By the beginning of the nineteenth century, American spelling was being revolutionized by Noah Webster who created an American variety of spelling in his *American Dictionary of the English Language* (1828) and changed -our to -or (*humor*), -re to -er (*center*), -ce to -se (*defense*), and -ll- to -l- (*canceled*). If it weren't for Webster, Americans would still be spelling English like Brits. Dictionaries were that important back then – they could change spelling and standardize language. Well, *most* of the time. There were some spelling changes that Webster tried to institute which did not catch on. He spelled *group* with 'oo' (groop), and dropped the 'a' in *bread* (bred) and *leather* (lether).

Ellis's Palaeotype alphabet was based on Visible Speech, a reformed spelling invented by Alexander Melville Bell (the man who had taken Murray under his wing as a young man and introduced him to Ellis). Ellis's system in turn was built on by Henry Sweet to produce Narrow Romic, which itself evolved into the International Phonetic Alphabet (IPA) – the

pronunciation system still used today by many linguists, lexicographers, journalists, and actors who want to transcribe
an accent or capture how a word is pronounced. The OED
needed its own pronunciation system (each entry has a pronunciation after the headword) so Murray devised one, in
collaboration with Ellis, Thomas Hallam and Alfred Hipkins,
which proved so robust that, when the OED was revised in
the 1970s, the system only needed slight alteration.

In 1900, Henry Bradley gave the words *Glossotype* and
Glossic their very own entries in the Dictionary, for ever me-
morializing the spelling system invented by Ellis. He defined
Glossotype as 'one of the systems of phonetic symbols invented
by A. J. Ellis (afterwards improved into Glossic)' and Glossic as
'applied by A. J. Ellis to a phonetic system of spelling invented
by him in which each letter or digraph represents the sound
which it most commonly expresses in English'. Not long afterwards, in 1904, Murray put the word *Palaeotype* in the Dictionary. It was listed between the words *Palaeotropical*, 'belonging
to the tropical parts of the Old World or eastern hemisphere,
considered as a zoogeographical region', and *Palaeotypography*,
'ancient typography, early printing'. His friend Ellis featured
heavily in the definition, 'a system of writing devised by A. J.
Ellis in which the "old types" (i.e. existing Roman letters and
other characters) in their various forms and combinations,
are used to form a universal phonetic alphabet'.

Murray's enthusiasm for spelling reform, and the use
of Glossotype and Palaeotype, waned over time. He kept his
advocacy for the movement largely separate from his Dictionary work, except for a few re-spellings which had crept
into the first volume. He warned the reader in the preface
that he had chosen a preferred spelling for *ax, connexion*, and
rime, which 'is not that at present favoured by the prepon-
derance of usage but is intrinsically the best, and therefore
is recommended'.

These early spelling quirks meant that, in order to maintain consistency, all the editors were forced to continue those
re-spellings throughout the entire Dictionary whenever that
word appeared in a definition or etymology. Because Murray
had spelt 'axe' as *ax* in the letter A, the editors had to continue spelling it as such whenever they wanted to use the word
'axe' throughout the whole Dictionary, e.g. in the definitions
of *tomahawk* and *twibill*, and the verbs *chop, cut*, and *hew*. Similarly, Murray had used *rime* instead of *rhyme* in the etymology
of *amound* and the definition of *assonate*, and thus it remained
in the rest of the Dictionary. Charles Onions mentioned this
in an obituary of Murray; it was clearly something that he and
the other editors found irksome. You will not find them there
any more; all traces of Murray's spelling-reform fad have been
deleted in the current version of the OED.

Murray's decision not to include more reformed spell-
ings in the Dictionary cost the project money. Murray wrote
to the philanthropist Andrew Carnegie, hoping that he might
help fund the publication of Volume VII of the Dictionary
in exchange for a dedication on the title page but Carnegie
refused for two reasons. He preferred the American *Century
Dictionary* and he was disappointed that Murray's Dictionary
was not including simplified spelling. 'I consider every letter
dropped from a word as a gain', he wrote to Murray. No more
letters were dropped, and the dollars were not given. But
money was always an issue for Murray, as was revealed when
he was dealing with one of his most hopeless contributors.

H

for HOPELESS CONTRIBUTORS

The year 1881 was not easy for Eleanor Marx. Her mother, Jenny, whom she had nursed through illness, died, and her father, Karl, needed her care and attention. Her long engagement to a radical French refugee, twice her age, Hyppolite-Prosper-Olivier Lissagaray, was dragging on. She was feeling confined by him; her parents had always disapproved of the engagement, and she knew she should break it off but couldn't bring herself to do so. She even had to sort out a strange situation in which a cousin had hallucinated that she had written *Little Women.* It fell to Eleanor to correspond with Louisa May Alcott and then to explain the confusion to her misguided cousin and her mother. Eleanor felt the strain. Her health was weak, she stopped eating and barely slept, and by winter the twenty-six-year-old was close to a breakdown. Her father's solution that she needed to lose her virginity was hardly helpful. And yet, in the last months of that awful year, she managed to get herself to the British Museum for at least a few hours a day to do some work for James Murray on the Dictionary. This was not out of love for the project – as it was for so many of the Dictionary People – but rather out of necessity. As she wrote to her sister Jenny (all four children in the Marx family, including Eleanor, were nicknamed 'Jenny' but only the eldest had it as her given name), 'You don't know how many people – most far better qualified to do the work than I am – try to get what I've been doing – and if I once give it up I may whistle for something else.'

Eleanor Marx needed to earn a living. The recipient of an inadequate education as a girl, she had to find a way to become financially independent, especially if she didn't marry Lissagaray. Her first wish was to be an actress. That very year, she had started to take acting lessons from a Mrs Vezin who had moved near to where she lived on Maitland Park Road. She confided her ambition to Jenny in early January 1882: 'Much and hard as I have tried I could not crush out my desire to *try something*. The chance of independence is very sweet . . . You see I'm not clever enough to live a purely intellectual life nor am I dull enough to be content . . . to do nothing.' Eleanor wanted to act but, so far, she had had to earn her living by editing and translating.

On 22 October 1877, Eleanor had stepped for the first time into the imposing circular Reading Room at the British Museum where, under its vast dome and huge windows, her father had written *Das Kapital*. She had been employed by Furnivall to help with his work for the Philological Society and the Chaucer and New Shakspere Societies. Despite her love of Shakespeare, she was easily distracted. Her reading at the end of 1877 included the naturalist Alfred Russel Wallace on spiritualism, and John Nevil Maskelyne's exposure of spiritualist frauds. She also embarked on her translation of Lissagaray's *History of the Paris Commune of 1871* – an account based on his participation in the event.

Four years later, in 1881, she was still working in the British Museum Reading Room, surrounded now not by volumes of Shakespeare or books on spiritualism, but *Cassell's Dictionary* and a variety of glossaries, as she searched for words for

Murray's Dictionary. Eleanor's connection was to Furnivall, not Murray. She often had tea with the Furnivalls or went on picnics and walks to the river with them. So when she completed her work and turned it in, she expected to be paid, as Furnivall had promised and arranged. This was, of course, unusual: most of the Dictionary People were volunteers, and Murray didn't like to pay anyone unless he had to. Oblivious to all of this, Eleanor sent in her words – 144 of them – and claimed 110 hours of labour in finding them.

Murray was not impressed by Eleanor Marx's work. On 25 January 1882, he wrote to Furnivall to say that he would pay Miss Marx if that was what she expected, but he could have done in twelve hours what she had done in a hundred and one. He wrote that it would have been cheaper for him to send one of his assistants from the Scriptorium *and* pay their rail fare. Moreover, the work was close to useless: there was little point in taking words from such works as *Cassell's* and glossaries, words which he had already included in the Dictionary. He was cross at himself for not giving clearer instructions and yet, he wrote rather testily to Furnivall, he had had no idea that in hiring Miss Marx 'that was what you meant'. He didn't hold back his irritation as he finished the letter: 'It is a deal to pay for the satisfaction of knowing that my own idea that we have all words (I don't say quotations for them – but these are not quotations, only a register of words to guide us in our list) was well-founded.'

Nearly five months later, Murray still had not paid Miss Marx. On 5 June 1882, Eleanor wrote to Furnivall, 'Do you think that you could induce Dr Murray to pay me (whatever he thinks fit) for that dictionary work?' She had written to Murray two weeks earlier, chasing the matter up as Furnivall had suggested she do, and had received no money, nor any reply. She remained indignant: 'That I did not find any words that Dr Murray did not know isn't my fault' and 'the work, such as it was, was consistently done'. She had even used the books she had been instructed to use for an earlier task she had done for Murray's assistant, Mr Herrtage, for which she had been paid £4. She needed to pay for her acting lessons 'and so should be very glad if I could get what Murray owes me'.

We do not know if Murray ever paid Eleanor Marx. We do know that Eleanor never became an actress, despite her lessons with Mrs Vezin. Soon after the unfortunate Dictionary episode, she came to the reluctant conclusion that she would not make it on the stage. Another hard year was 1883, in which both her father and her eldest sister died. But there was liberation in that too, and in 1884 she began to live with the fickle, feckless, and married Edward Aveling, a zoologist who shared Eleanor's love of the theatre and her politics. She took his name and became known as Eleanor Marx-Aveling. Despite the unhappiness he caused her through his many infidelities, her attachment to him seemed to bring a new sense of purpose to her life. She flourished as a writer and translator (rendering into English many of her father's works). In 1886 she published a tract entitled *The Woman Question* and translated Flaubert's *Madame Bovary* into English. She even learned Norwegian so to be able to translate Ibsen. From 1887, she became increasingly involved in radical politics, defending Jewish workers in the East End of London, and supporting the gas workers' and dockers' strikes in 1889. She frequently lectured and spoke at labour meetings and congresses and, when those meetings were in Europe, she was a tireless translator. She became known as 'the foremother of socialist feminism' and is credited for unionizing working-class women and campaigning for an eight-hour working day. The 1890s brought sadness, as she realized that her father's ideas would have less influence on British Socialism than she had hoped. And she was devastated when Aveling, by now freed from his former wife, took the alias Alec Nelson and secretly married a twenty-two-year-old woman named Eva Frye. Eleanor's end was tragic; she took her own life, with chloroform and prussic acid, on 31 March 1898 at her home in Sydenham, Kent.

By the end of her life, her Dictionary debacle was long forgotten, and yet there is satisfaction in knowing that, after all, her own work appears in the Dictionary, added in the twenty-first century. Under the entry for *ruffle*, to rumple, to destroy the smoothness or evenness of something, an illustrative quotation is taken from Eleanor's 1886 translation of *Madame Bovary*: 'a gust of wind that blew in at the window ruffled the cloth on the table'.

*

When Eleanor Marx had been trying to get money out of Murray in 1881, Murray himself had been trying to get money out of Oxford University Press. He was deeply concerned about the survival of the Dictionary project as a whole, and suffering from anxiety. All the expenses of the Dictionary had to come out of his own meagre salary from OUP, and now, in his third year as Editor, the Dictionary was going much more slowly and costing much more than he had expected.

He found himself caught: should he confess to OUP that progress was slow and that he was struggling financially, and risk them discontinuing the project? Or should he persevere in silence for the sake of the Dictionary's survival but risk personal financial ruin? He confided to Henry Hucks Gibbs, a Subeditor and wealthy friend to whom he often went for loans, 'I have feared that if they [the OUP Delegates] realized that the work was really to take so long a time, the majority (who care nothing especially for English, & do not realize a priori the grandeur of the work) might put up their backs & say "We won't stand for this, we will rather stop it" . . . The thing worries me and interferes with my mental peace.'

At the same time that Furnivall was pestering Murray to pay Miss Marx her dues, Murray was sharing his personal troubles with Gibbs. 'I have not felt since Christmas that I could spare a moment for anything but work, work, work! . . . It is I on whom the consequences fall, and whom they threaten to crush. It does trouble me when I see my prospects.' He had spent too much of his wages on paying Scriptorium staff and general Dictionary expenses of books, paper, printing of slips, and postage, and was struggling to cover living and education expenses for his children – Ada was pregnant with their eighth child, and at this point they were still living in Mill Hill. 'I have really, in my anxiety to press on & complete the preliminary work, spent far more than I ought upon it', he told Gibbs. Furnivall's employment of Miss Marx without seeking Murray's permission, but expecting him to pay, only added to Murray's stress. Murray admitted that he had been 'partly goaded to it by Mr Furnivall who has continually said "You must get this, & you must do that, & you must pay somebody to do the other thing" and whose possessing idea seemed to be the fear that I should make money out of the work!'

Perhaps it was Miss Marx and her father's philosophy that was on Murray's mind when he wrote to Gibbs, 'I am not a capitalist but a poor man . . . I have bought all the books needed, paid for all the paper, printing, special reading in the British Museum, and of the Philological Transcriptions of the Royal Society – everything . . . while the expenses of assistants, carriage of boxes to & fro to sorters and Subeditors, postage etc. go on week by week.'

The problem was the financial agreement which he had signed with OUP. Estimating that the Dictionary would only take ten years to complete, Murray had agreed to be paid a fixed sum of £9,000 over ten years (£900 per year) out of which he had to pay himself, his staff, and the Dictionary expenses. A much wiser way of structuring it would have been to accept a personal salary from OUP and to make OUP or the Philological Society pay for the expenses.

To make matters worse, in reassessing in February 1882 that the Dictionary would take sixteen years to finish, rather than ten, Murray had failed to renegotiate the fixed sum with OUP. Instead, he agreed to take less money over the longer period, to eke out the £9,000 over sixteen years. It would be impossible for him to live on £500 per annum, given that so much had to come out of it: 'When it comes to facing the future upon less than £500 a year', he told Gibbs, 'I am filled with perplexity, and at times my heart quite fails me. It has done so a good deal of late; and the state is not favourable to work . . . The outlook is gloomy and tends at times to unnerve me.'

*

Eleanor Marx is not in Murray's address book because her connection was not to him but to his predecessor, Furnivall. But if she had been, he might have written 'hopeless' or 'no good' by her name, as he did by the entries of all those who failed to send in words, caused him trouble, or left tasks incomplete. At the same time that Murray was sharing his money problems with Gibbs, he was busy chasing another hopeless Reader in Yeovil, Somerset, to whom he had sent Mansel's *Metaphysics* and 500 blank slips. Receiving nothing, an exasperated Murray put a cross beside the entry of Mr J. Johnson Hoyle, 'to return book at once 10/2/82', 'nothing done', and finally 'lost his slips!'.

Across the entry for T. W. Tonkin of Barnes, who had sent in nothing for a sixteenth-century polemical work against female monarchs, *The First Blast of the Trumpet Against the Monstrous Regiment of Women* by the Scottish Protestant Reformer John Knox, he wrote in blue pencil, 'Impostor – Stole the Book'.

Miss Clowes of Ipswich and Miss Wheaton of Bloomsbury Square 'threw up' (gave up); W. Doig of Sheffield was 'gone, no address'; Mr Spaulding from New Jersey and Mr Bigmore of 4 Trafalgar Square were 'no good'. Mr Ferguson of Indianapolis had 'nothing done'. Mr Chisholm of Charleston, South Carolina, had 'thrown up, slips lost'. Mr R. A. Clarke of Edgbaston had also lost his slips. It was noted beside Dr J. Raymond Brackett of New Haven, Connecticut, 'promised by "end of year" ', and then 'nothing done'. Miss Edith Lucas of High Wycombe had 'gone to Melbourne' (and was never heard of again); L. W. Gatward from Hitchin had 'slips returned undone', and W. Stockley of Dublin 'threw up' and

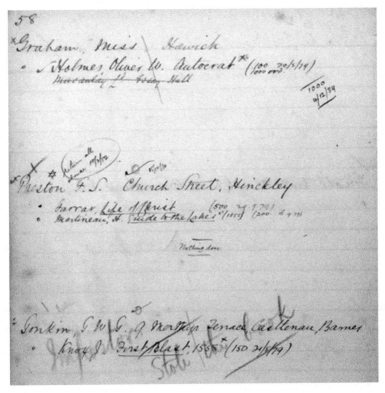

Hopeless contributors in one of the address books
('nothing done'), including the entry for Tonkin,
'Impostor – Stole the book'.

'ill' in 1881. Frank Preston, an Old Millhillian of Hinckley in Leicestershire who was clerk of the Hinckley Local Council Board, and famously caught a man attempting to break into the Board safe and chased him off with a stick, was meant to read F. W. Farrar's *Life of Christ* and Harriet Martineau's *Guide to the Lakes.* After three years Murray wrote to him to 'return all at once', but never received anything. Farrar's *Life of Christ* was taken up instead by an accountant in Bath, but many other books were left untouched by Readers.

The physician Dr Brinsley Nicholson of Shepherd's Bush, who is thanked in the prefaces for 'various help', has 'no good' scrawled across his entry in the address book in 1879 (he had suffered a stroke in 1875 and was paralysed for the rest of his life). One might have expected that the architect responsible for the Liverpool Public Library, and after whom its main reading room is named, Sir James Allanson Picton, would have been an ideal Reader for the OED but Murray wrote 'no good' and put a red squiggle through his entry.

Some Readers misunderstood the coverage of an English language dictionary. Mr Rainbot from Peckham who read Edward William Lane's *Manners and Customs of Modern Egyptians* has a big squiggly line through his entry and the note 'took Arabic words out only'.

Volunteers died on the job – Mrs Campbell of Peckham 'died 11/11/81', Revd Penny of Berkshire 'died Mar 30, '98', Edward S. Wilson of Yorkshire 'died Xmas 1904'. The archive contains letters from loved ones who thoughtfully returned the partially finished work or books the Readers were reading when they died. Murray received a poignant letter in 1906 from the wife of William Sykes of South Devon who had been a one-time assistant, and faithful Reader and Specialist for twenty-two years, sending in a total of 16,048 slips: 'My dear husband died last Friday, the day he received your letter, he was able to read it, and wrote your name in one of the books

I am going to send you eight hours before he died. It took him an hour to write it, but he made up his mind to do it, and did. The last words he ever wrote were to you.' A poignant last line from the impoverished widow reads, 'I shall send the books when the probate duty has been paid.'

At any one time there was always a procrastinator who needed chasing. The address books are littered with notes of exasperation. Mr Eastwood of Birkenhead had 'Does he mean to read or no?', 'written again 18/11/79' and then 'dead', struck through with blue pencil. Mr Edwards of Grosvenor School in Bath had 'nothing done' and 'send all at once 10/2/82' of Olinthus Gregory's *A Treatise of Mechanics*. A music teacher on Long Island, Miss Alberta Selleck, failed to read Horace Greeley's *The American Conflict* and returned 250 blank slips a year later.

When a Subeditor, William Crane in north Brixton, refused to return the first part of letter O materials, Murray resorted to visiting the man at his house. Still, he did not hand over the slips but reassured Murray that the materials would soon be back in the Scriptorium. A month and no slips later, Murray wrote to Crane on 25 October 1881:

> *Excuse me for remonstrating with you as to your inattention to my letter of a month ago. I certainly expected that after coming over to see you expressly about the portion of the Dictionary materials which you have in hand, you would have paid a little more attention to my desires on the subject . . . On not receiving them, I then wrote to you pointing out how seriously your delay was incommoding me, and wasting the time of my sorters. For a whole month you have disregarded that letter. I beg you to send off the slips at once, and not further waste my time every moment of which is required to complete the task which I have undertaken. Yours obediently, James A. H. Murray.*

When the recalcitrant volunteer still refused to send the slips, Murray sent an assistant, Herbert Ruthven (Ada's brother), around to his house to try to collect them. Crane was out and his daughter refused to hand them over. The next day, Mr Crane wrote a letter to Murray dated 10 November, 'I am sorry that Mr Ruthven stayed about so long last evening but it should have been obvious to him that my daughter could not deliver the dictionary material to him in my absence and without my permission, especially as she had no means of packing it. I shall in the course of time forward the parcel to Skipper [Miss Skipper, one of Murray's assistants]. With compliments, I remain Dear Sir, Yours truly, W. J. E. Crane.' Murray did finally receive the materials. Suffice to say, Crane never volunteered again.

Murray and his team had a postcard system for chasing people. They sent out postcards to remind Readers to send in their slips, and devised a code for recording these in the address books. A blue or red cross beside someone's name denoted whether a first or second form of postcard had been sent and answered. A number 2 with a check or tick mark beside it denoted a second postcard sent. A triangle with a line through it signalled that a third postcard had been sent.

Some volunteers started out hopeless but ended up helpful. Sir Howard Warburton Elphinstone of Lincoln's Inn 'threw up' reading Sir Edward Coke's first part of *The Institutes of the Lawes of England*, but eight years later sent in 200 slips from Sir Henry Spelman's *Of Law Terms*, and was twice thanked in the prefaces for help with legal terminology in 1899 and 1903.

It is a hazard of all crowdsourced projects, including the OED, that a small proportion of contributors will do the bulk of the work, and a large proportion will comprise a 'long tail' of people who each contribute a very small amount. Of the

A page of one of the address books showing
the various symbols and codes used to
track a volunteer's work.

latter, there are bound to be those who do nothing or, worse, something that is of bad quality, and end up causing more trouble than they are worth.

Murray was not the only OED Editor who had this problem. In 1860, the first Editor of the Dictionary, Herbert Coleridge, had written of his despair with a portion of his 147 volunteers:

Fifteen more I set down as 'hopeless'; most of these consist of contributors who volunteered to aid us under our first scheme, and have since either forgotten their promises, or found the task more irksome than they anticipated, and so thrown it aside, remaining deaf to all applications made to them on the subject. The loss is not very important, as in most cases the works undertaken by this faithless band are of secondary value; and in some instances I have succeeded in substituting fresh contributors in their places.

Coleridge said that he had fifty reliably efficient contributors of the one hundred and forty-seven, and remarked that this was favourable in comparison with the Brothers Grimm in Germany, whose *Deutsches Wörterbuch* had six satisfactory contributors out of eighty-three, and only one of those six could be considered 'ideal'.

It was hard to find good staff in the Scriptorium. And training them took Murray away from important editing. 'You can engage navvies and you can engage assistant schoolmasters', Murray confided to his wealthy friend Gibbs, 'but you can only try men in the hope that they may turn out Dictionary helpers, and in many cases find them of no use; and what becomes, while you are trying them, of the 8 col[umns] a day and two parts a year?' When Murray first moved to Oxford in 1884, he advertised for editorial assistants and wrote to university dons asking for recommendations. One of them was, as Murray put it in a letter to the Secretary to the Delegates (akin to the CEO of Oxford University Press), 'an utter numb-skull' who only lasted a few days. We can almost see the young man, and feel Murray's desperation, when he describes him as 'a most lack-a-daisical, graspless fellow born to stare at existence'.

It was not just some of the Readers and staff who were hopeless, but also some of the Subeditors – those to whom Murray sent piles of quotations for pre-sorting chronologically and into senses of meaning. Murray said that despite the goodwill and diligence of his Subeditors, 'out of nearly 40 who have tried it, it would be difficult to pick out 8 . . . whose help has been appreciably worth the trouble . . . I have had to come to the conclusion that practically the only valuable work that can be done by the average amateur, & out of the Scriptorium, is that of reading books and extracting quotations.' And yet he desperately needed the help of Subeditors because the task was too massive to do alone. Two years into the job, Murray had estimated that he had sent out 817,625 blank slips to Readers. If they returned them with quotations, and if he spent a minimum of 30 seconds reading each one and allocating it to the correct sense of an entry, it would take him three working years to get through a third of the materials gathered.

There were two small flaws in the Dictionary's compilation process: Readers were asked to choose words they considered 'rare' and the choice of these words was random – they were not guided by Murray on what was needed. This resulted in a dearth of quotations for common words which ultimately had to be found by Murray and his assistants. In the first part of the Dictionary alone, 'nearly the whole quotations for *about, after, all, also, and,* in Part I, and for *any, as,* in Part II, have had to be found by myself and my assistants', he explained to the Philological Society. If he had his time again, he said that he would have directed his Readers differently, with the instructions, 'Take out quotations for all words that do *not* strike you as rare, peculiar, or peculiarly used.'

The random selection of words by volunteers often resulted in them choosing the same words with similar dates, and produced gaps in the quotation paragraphs, which Murray and his assistants had to fill by their own manual searching. This must have been like trying to find a needle in a haystack. It was remarkable how successful Murray's small team was at filling those gaps and finding earliest or latest quotations. Murray told the Philological Society that this manual trawling for words had to be done for the majority of words: 'For more than five-sixths of the words we have to search out and find additional quotations in order to complete their history and illustrate the senses; for every word we have to make a general search to discover whether any earlier or later quotations, or quotations in other senses, exist.'

Murray was always quick to seize on and retain good Readers. They were rare and if he received a parcel of useful slips from a new Reader he usually wrote straight back inviting them to read another text which was on his wish list. Miss E. Hilda Taylor lived in Woodbridge, Suffolk, and began contributing as both a Reader and Specialist in 1914. Murray wrote to commend her on her reading of the poems of Matthew Prior, giving rare praise: 'The quotations are excellent and will be very useful.' He went on to ask if she would be willing to read a particular book: 'I do not know whether you have any time or inclination for more reading at present. A French scholar who has printed the Account Rolls of the Revels Of Queen Eliz. which yielded us a number of words, has now sent us in the sheets the [*sic*] similar rolls of the Revels of Edward VI & of Phil. & Mary, which seem as if they would be worth extracting. If you think you would care now or by and by to do these for us, I should be glad to send the work & slips, with some directions. Again thanking you most heartily for your valued help I remain yours very truly James A H Murray.'

Taylor was as keen as Murray. She wrote straight back agreeing to read the book. Murray responded a week later, giving instructions on how to read. This was towards the very end of his life and his instructions to Miss Taylor give rare insight into Murray's reading tips, especially instructions for reading for desiderata, in this case words beginning with S, T, and U–Z: 'I should suggest looking it through and marking with a pencil dot such words as are mentioned in the enclosed note, and any others that strike you as noteworthy, and then go through it copying out from the marked ones those immediately wanted for the letters at which we are working the better parts of S & T, and sending these as soon as ready; then proceed to those in U to Z, and finally the earlier words for our Supplement. I hope you will not find it too tedious; and I should be sorry if it were allowed to interfere with other calls.'

Volunteers like Taylor who could fill gaps in quotations and search out desiderata were invaluable to Murray. They were marked in the address books by numbered D's when desiderata lists had been sent to them, and by a small Star of David sign when a third list had been sent. Desiderata gatherers included Miss Anna Wyckoff Olcott in New York City (she also was responsible for sending in words from the works of Louisa May Alcott); the Revd William Lees, a vicar outside Reigate who sent in a total of 18,500 slips; and Alexander Beazeley, an engineer who specialized in lighthouses and sent in a total of 38,233 slips, many of which were desiderata and did not relate to lighthouses.

The Indian languages Specialist, Edward Brandreth, had D, D4, and D5 beside his name in the address books and spent tireless hours in the British Museum searching for fillers. Murray sent this retired member of the Indian Civil Service a total of 35 lists of desiderata, and Brandreth sent him thousands of quotations in return. When Brandreth died, Murray wrote glowingly of him, 'Among the many volunteers whose work has contributed to making the New English Dictionary what it is, not many have had the capacity and qualifications, the willinghood, and the time to work for it as our honoured friend has done. May his name never be forgotten when the story is told!'

I

for INVENTORS

The year that the Dictionary plans were confirmed and adopted by the London Philological Society was a stinker. Literally, it stank. If you walked down a London street in the summer of 1858 you needed to cover your nose and try to breathe only through your mouth. Temperatures soared and the smell was so bad people thought they could taste excrement. Depending on the direction of the hot wind, the stench flowed into everyone's houses and workplaces. Untreated human waste ran down the middle of the streets and built up on the banks of the Thames. *The Times* reported that in the Houses of Parliament, overlooking the river, politicians 'ventured into the library but they were instantaneously driven to retreat, each man with a handkerchief to his nose'. The problem was that the city, all cities, lacked proper sewerage systems.

It was a Dictionary contributor who helped solve this problem. Dictionary People showed a strong tendency towards innovation, and as well as a pipe for safely and speedily clearing the streets of excrement, they were responsible for an electric tricycle, the net adjuster and the folding umpire's seat for tennis, a combined envelope opener and pencil sharpener, and indelible green ink for printing money. The nineteenth century was an age of invention. By the time Murray wrote the definition for *inventor* in 1901, one who devises or produces something new by original contrivance, he already had quite a few of them in his address book. He was smart enough to realize that inventors and innovative scientists were some of the key specialists and word hunters he needed. The inventors of all these items were contributors to the Dictionary – though Robert Floyd Kerr, Professor of English and Mathematics in Hirosaki, Japan, and later a civil engineer and Professor of Political Economy in Nebraska, USA, who patented the combined envelope opener and pencil sharpener in 1897, might well have belonged in the previous chapter. He was a hopeless contributor who had promised slips on Japanese and American history but instead had 'nothing done' by his name in the address book, his neatly sharpened pencils not doing much work for Murray.

The nineteenth century witnessed the full bloom of the Industrial Revolution and, with it, the rapid growth of cities, overcrowded streets and housing, and the easy spread of disease. People were used to throwing their waste into the streets, which contaminated the water supply. It was not only unhygienic but also foul-smelling, and meant that water-borne diseases such as cholera and typhoid were rife. This prompted the development of proper sanitation systems, and with it, a whole new lexicon: *sewage* and *sewerage* (1834), *sanitary* (1842), *to crap* (1846), *sanitation* (1848), *sanitary reformer* (1850), *sewer water* (1851), *sewer ditch* (1851), *sewer hunter* (1851), *sewer rat* (1851), *sewer man* (1851), *sewery* (1851), *sewerless* (1854), *sewer air* (1859). When the poo problem reached crisis point in 1858 and 'the Great Stink' overwhelmed London, a bill was rushed through Parliament to build a huge new sewer system for the city. Suddenly sewage pipes were in high demand.

In the USA, at the same time in the 1850s, the first

sewage pipes were installed in Chicago and Brooklyn, but other American cities remained smelly for a while longer. In 1878, the city of Trenton in New Jersey was deliberating on how to construct a new sewer and what shape of pipe was best (circular pipes then being the norm). A Trenton civil engineer named Clifford Beakes Rossell had recently invented and patented 'an improved sewer pipe of unusual shape' as one civic report put it. It was elliptical or egg-shaped rather than circular.

Rossell's pipe had a lot going for it. It could 'accommodate minimum as well as maximum flow in a superior manner'. In other words, it could manage high volumes of faeces. It was manufactured locally at the Trenton Terra-Cotta Works, and it cost about the same as a circular pipe of similar capacity. Rossell was an entrepreneurial engineer. Just five years out of college, in 1870, when he was only twenty-five years old, he had become an associate of the James River Manufacturing Company. A year later he had been appointed Superintendent of canals, and in 1880 he was made Treasurer of the state of New Jersey.

By 1880 Rossell was also a contributor to the OED. He read just one book for the Dictionary: John Foster Kirk's two-volume *History of Charles the Bold* published in 1863. It's fascinating to speculate on what interest a land-grabbing fifteenth-century French duke might have held for a nineteenth-century American sewage-pipe inventor, but clearly there was plenty as Rossell produced 200 slips from that book alone, including *suzerain*, a feudal overlord; *perron*, a large block stone used as the base of a monument; and *Dinanderie*, brass kitchen utensils. And he was obviously a good and reliable contributor, as Murray went on to use his skills for two lists of desiderata.

While the 1870s saw the safe removal of faeces from city streets around the globe, it also saw the rise in popularity of a new sport among the middle and upper classes: lawn tennis or 'sphairistike' as it was originally called. Pronounced sfe'ristiki, the name was Greek for 'skill in playing at ball' and had been coined by the man who patented the game in 1874, Major Walter Clopton Wingfield.

Developed out of real (or royal) tennis, not only were national tournaments established – Wimbledon in 1877 and the US Open in 1881 – but every provincial town now wanted its own lawn tennis club. Old words took on new meanings connected with the game – *love* (1880), *chalk* (1886), *volley* (1875), *smash* (1882), *lob* (1890) – and new words emerged as the game evolved and grew in popularity – *grass court* (1875), *first serve* (1878), *second serve* (1878), *centre court* (1883), *hard court* (1885), *doubles* (1894), *ground stroke* (1895). Murray included reference to the game in the very first volume, in 1884, defining the word *ace* as 'a point at rackets, lawn tennis, etc'.

No one was keener on this new craze than Dictionary contributor Robert Charles Hope. Hope lived in Scarborough, Yorkshire, and he quickly founded the North of England Lawn Tennis Association and became Secretary of the Yorkshire Tennis Association. He soon realized that the net dividing the two halves of the court would begin to slump and sag as a game of tennis progressed, as the ball skimmed over it or hit it. His solution: a device to make sure the net could be adjusted to the same height at the beginning of every game, so he invented and patented the net adjuster. He was also keen on fair play and realized that someone needed to rise above the game, literally, to rule on whether a ball had landed in or out of the court; hence he invented the umpire's chair – still used in tennis tournaments today. And for good measure, in 1885 he produced Simple Lawn Tennis Score Sheets.

A man of numerous and enthusiastic commitments,

Robert Hope also loved music and theatre and was described by one biographer as the founder of just about every lawn tennis, music, or drama society within miles of his seaside town. He played the oboe in the Scarborough Amateur Band, nicknamed the Scarborough Band of Hope as a play on his name – and that of a teetotal society of the day.

Hope's other great passion, which he brought to the Dictionary work, was as an editor and antiquarian, and he was a Fellow of both the Royal Society of Literature and the Society of Antiquaries. He wrote on subjects as varied as the holy wells of England, dialectical place nomenclature, medieval music, and lepers, and as obscure as church plate in the churches of Rutland (England's smallest county), and the temples and shrines of Nikko (a small mountain town north of Tokyo in Japan). Murray quoted from Hope's books on medieval music in the entries for *proslambanomenos*, the lowest note in the later scales or systems of Ancient Greek music; and *oration*, a prayer to God. As for Hope himself, his reading for the Dictionary included 200 words from the poems of Felicia Dorothea Hemans and 100 quotations from a 1743 translation and edition of one of the greatest of all Latin epic poems, Virgil's *Aeneid*. He also read Barnaby Googe's *Popish Kingdome* (1570), a book which he was editing at the time and published the following year with a brief memoir of Googe. It provided first quotations for *filching*, pilfering, and *bravely*, in a showy manner, and for two obsolete words which made it into the Dictionary: *mateless*, unrivalled or unmatched; and *to jaunt*, which Murray defined as 'to make a horse prance up and down'.

While inventive Victorians were devising ways of entertaining the middle classes with outdoor sports, and solving the problem of stinky streets, others were trying to prevent counterfeit money. As long as money has existed, the problem of counterfeit currency has too, but it became a particular problem once printed notes went into general circulation. In eighteenth-century North America, Benjamin Franklin – who owned a firm that printed money for several of the colonies – hit on the idea of misspelling Pennsylvania on official currency, on the grounds that forgers would spell it correctly and the notes could easily be spotted as counterfeit, but that only went so far. By the mid-nineteenth century, paper notes were in general use all over the USA, no longer engraved but printed in black ink, making them especially easy to forge.

The man who solved the problem was an American chemist, who also contributed to the Dictionary, Thomas Sterry Hunt. In 1857, he had been teaching at Laval University in Quebec and responded to an appeal by the President of the Montreal City Bank who was battling counterfeit notes. Hunt created a special green ink, using chromium sesquioxide, that was pretty well indestructible. Numerous experiments showed that you couldn't remove it from the banknote without destroying the paper itself – until one chemist succeeded in doing so, and the Canadians dropped Hunt's invention. But the Americans took it up, especially on the back of their banknotes, hence the colloquial term 'greenbacks' for US dollar bills, which was given its own entry in the OED in 1900 and defined as 'the popular name for one of the legal-tender notes of the U.S., first issued in 1862 and so called from the devices printed in green ink on the back', alongside something rather topical at the time but now archaic, *Greenback Party*, defined as 'a party in U.S. politics, which advocated that "greenbacks" should be made the sole currency of the country', and its various derivatives *Greenbacker* and *Greenbackism*.

Like Murray, Thomas Sterry Hunt had left school at fourteen and was self-educated. He taught himself by reading and attending lectures, and doing everything he could to improve his knowledge of science. The chemist also took a keen interest in geology. Of a practical bent, he loved going into the field to classify rocks and understand the chemical forces that had created them. He devised the crenitic theory quoted in the OED as a 'newly proposed explanation of the origin of crystalline rocks, through the action of springs bringing up mineral matters from below'. At the age of nineteen, Hunt had managed to attend the annual meeting of the Association of American Naturalists and Geologists in New Haven by reporting on the event for a New York newspaper. He interviewed the famous chemist Emeritus Professor Benjamin Silliman. Silliman was so impressed by the young man's enthusiasm and intelligence that he arranged for him to become research assistant to his son, Benjamin Silliman Jnr, a professor of chemistry at Yale. After Yale, Hunt moved on to a stellar career with the Geological Survey of Canada and Laval and McGill universities in Canada, ultimately becoming Professor of Geology at the Massachusetts Institute of Technology. But he was an irascible and cantankerous fellow, who fell out with colleagues, and he did not last long at MIT.

Hunt wrote a lot, was enormously industrious, and was showered with academic accolades (he received the Légion d'Honneur in 1855, was made a Fellow of the Royal Society of London in 1859 and of the National Academy of Sciences in 1873), so he was an obvious choice as a Specialist for the Dictionary. He is quoted in the OED over thirty times for geological and chemical terms. The OED records him as the first person to have used the words *metasomatism*, change in the chemical composition of a mineral or rock; *biophysiology*, the scientific study of functions found exclusively in living organisms; *crenitic*, relating to rising mineral matter from subterranean sources through the action of water springs; and several rocks and minerals including *algerite, animikie, anorthosite, leucophanite,* and *loganite.* Murray even included an entry for *huntilite,* named after Hunt, which he defined as 'native arsenide [a compound of arsenic] of silver, from Silver Islet, Lake Superior'.

Despite his confirmed place in the OED within geological and chemical terms, Hunt ended up an isolated figure in the scientific world. He spent the final two years of his life living by himself at the Park Avenue Hotel, New York, where he died of a heart attack in 1892 at the age of sixty-six. His obituarist wrote, rather hyperbolically, that his essays elaborating the crenitic theory 'rise to a high pitch of eloquence, and . . . any one of literary tastes, though utterly ignorant of science, will read [them] with rapt enjoyment'.

Greenback ink, sewer pipes, and tennis-net adjusters – the Dictionary People were an inventive lot! Among the lasting inventions of the nineteenth century were the bicycle and the motor car, so it was inevitable that someone would try to combine the two. In 1881, Dictionary contributor John Perry and his associate William Edward Ayrton vied with a Frenchman, Gustave Trouvé, to create the first electric tricycle. They put two large wheels at the back, and one small wheel at the front. Perry and Ayrton were long-time collaborators, had taught civil engineering together at the Imperial College in Japan and had recently returned to London to teach at Finsbury Technical College from where Perry corresponded with Murray. Their invention was powered by ten lead-acid batteries, and you could change speed by turning the batteries on and off. The tricycle could go up to 9 miles per hour and cover a range of up to 25 miles before the batteries ran out. It was the first vehicle of any kind to have electric lighting. Alas, almost as soon as it was invented, the electrical tricycle fell foul of the 'Red Flag' law which required moving, motorized vehicles to have three operators – a driver, a stoker, and a third who had to precede the vehicle waving a red flag – and to maintain a speed of 4 miles an hour on the highway, 2 miles an hour in a village, town, or city. This law was not revoked until 1896 and meant not only that horses and horse-drawn carriages continued to dominate the roads in Britain but also that France was ahead of the game with motorized vehicles. Undeterred, Perry and Ayrton continued to put their science to practical use, developing the field of electrical engineering. They became consultants to the Faure Accumulator Company and invented a new kind of ammeter and voltmeter. Ever entrepreneurial, they co-founded an electric transportation system, the Telepherage Company, which came to be much used in the USA.

As bicycles and tricycles were becoming more and more popular, Murray came to be well-known in Oxford as a keen cyclist – frequently seen pedalling madly up and down the Banbury Road and through Jericho, his white hair, white beard, and black gown flowing in the wind as he delivered copy to the University Press. He was also known to fall off it quite regularly, as the wheel would easily buckle on turning, and his signature method of dismounting was simply to fall sideways with a clash and a clang. Exercise and physical activity were passions for Murray – he would rise at sunrise and cycle to the nearby village of Kidlington and back before breakfast – so we can be assured that, while he would have been interested in the invention of such a thing, he probably would not have been Perry's target audience. The notion of not having to pedal might have helped him on one occasion when he took the etymologist Walter Skeat, who was visiting from Cambridge, for a tandem ride in the nearby town of Eynsham. As told by Murray's granddaughter in her biography of him, they returned home totally worn out. Skeat told Ada that Murray had left most of the pedalling to him, and Murray whispered to her that in fact Skeat had barely helped at all. Ada suspected what had happened and went outside to discover that, sure enough, they had left the brake screwed on the entire time.

We don't know whether it was John Perry's role in developing the electrical tricycle or something else that sparked Murray's interest in his work, but we do know that Perry was a trusted Specialist and Murray wrote to him at the Royal College of Sciences in South Kensington. None of their correspondence survives but Perry's interests were vast, ranging from spinning tops and gyrocompasses (he patented the latter) to the age of the Earth and the question of thermal conductivity in the Earth's core, so he could have advised Murray on many subjects, most probably in the area of engineering.

Murray ensured that new inventions in the cycling world were included in the OED: *velocipede*, the generic name in the 1850s for 'a travelling-machine having wheels turned by pressure of the feet upon pedals; esp. an early form of the bicycle or tricycle, a "bone shaker"', which was considered 'rare' by the time the letter V was published in 1916; *bicycle* and *tricycle*, both invented in 1868; *dicycle*, a bicycle invented in the late 1880s with two parallel wheels rather than one behind the other; and *the Otto*, a dicycle invented by Edward C. F. Otto and very popular in the 1880s. By the time Murray wrote the entry for *tricycle* in 1914 he had been recklessly riding one through the streets of Oxford for thirty years. It is unlikely that he needed any advice from the inventor when he included Perry's motorized version in the definition: 'a velocipede with three wheels (now usually one in front and one on each side behind), driven by treadles actuated by the feet, or (motor tricycle) by a small motor attached'. But I do wonder what Perry would have thought of Murray's choice of quotations, the second of which refers to his inventor-rival, Monsieur Trouvé, 'riding at ease through the streets of Paris upon a tricycle driven by stored-up electricity'.

J

for JUNKIE

I admit that it is anachronistic to call this chapter Junkie when the word did not even exist until 1923, by which time our Dictionary volunteer, Eustace Bright, had already been dead thirty years. But junkie, someone with a compulsive habit or an obsessive dependency on drugs, seems the closest adjective beginning with j to describe Murray's former student who became a cocaine and morphine addict and was found dead in a railway station lavatory at the age of twenty-nine.

Eustace Frederick Bright began sending in slips, advising Murray on medical terms, and finding desiderata, in 1880, as an eighteen-year-old student. Like many Old Millhillians, he had enthusiastically answered the call of his former teacher to gather quotations for the Dictionary. Bright by name and bright by nature, Eustace was a top student and went on to medical school, passing all his examinations with flying colours, and graduating as a doctor in 1887. A good-looking young man, he had an engaging and outgoing personality, and many friends.

It was while he was a medical student that he started contributing to the Dictionary by answering Murray's queries about medical terms such as *agamogenetically*, in an asexual

manner, by asexual reproduction. His reading for the Dictionary reflected both his medical studies and his personal interest
in zoology. He sent in an impressive 1,400 slips from Hogg's
The Microscope which gave the world-first citations for *oogonium*,
the female gametangium of certain algae and fungi containing oospheres (female gametes); *oosporange*, a receptacle containing spores of brown algae; *flabellum*, a fan-shaped part of
anything; *lamellibranch*, belonging to a group of molluscs with
lamellate gills; and *microspectroscope*, an instrument combining a
microscope and spectroscope, used for spectroscopic examinations of microscopic objects. He sent in a further 250 slips
full of original animal names from reading a book on animal
habitations called *Homes Without Hands*: *chelodine*, a genus of
river tortoise with a very long neck and flat head; *cuckoo-fly*,
a species of hymenopterous insects; and *indigo-bird*, a North
American species of painted finch, the male of which has the
head and upperparts of rich indigo blue. Bright's younger
brother, Percy, also read for the Dictionary and sent in hundreds of words from Thomas Henry Huxley's *Physiography* and
James Ferguson's *Electricity*, which exemplified words such as
anode, cathode, electric, and *electrodynamics*.

As a young doctor, Eustace Bright took placements
at University College Hospital and St Pancras Infirmary.
He won the confidence and esteem of his colleagues as a
conscientious and energetic practitioner who got things
done with precision and competence. In 1889, he was appointed as a general physician back in his home town of
Bournemouth, where his prospects of success as a doctor
seemed assured.

Bright had, however, developed a habit of experimenting with drugs. It had started when he was a student with the
inhaling of chloroform, and he soon progressed to stronger
stuff. We now think of a junkie as someone addicted to
heroin, and if heroin had existed in Bright's day (it wasn't

available until 1898), he probably would have tried it. As it was, cocaine was relatively new, and regarded as something of a wonder cure for ailments from hay fever to toothache, melancholia, and seasickness. Sigmund Freud thought cocaine therapy could treat syphilis and asthma. Famously, the fictional detective Sherlock Holmes took cocaine to stimulate the mind in moments of idleness.

Bright used cocaine regularly, along with morphine. Both drugs were legal and could be obtained by him in the hospitals where he worked, or bought at a pharmacy – their addictive qualities were not yet understood. We do not know how long he had been addicted to the drugs but a few months before his death, his colleagues were concerned about his behaviour. In early August 1891, Bright had been visiting London for an International Congress of Hygiene where he stayed at St Pancras Infirmary. He rushed into the room of his colleague Dr Cooper, asking for morphine. He told his friend that he had a toothache and had taken cocaine to alleviate the pain but, worried he had taken too much, he said that he needed morphine to induce vomiting.

Two months later, on a clear autumn evening, Bright, dressed in a dinner jacket and black bow tie, joined friends for the University College Hospital dinner. He was in unusually good spirits, and everyone wanted to be in his orbit. He partied with his medical friends until late, and made plans to meet them at a smoking concert (popular musical performances for men only, where smoking was allowed) at the Brompton Hospital the following evening. Bright stayed the night with a friend in Bloomsbury Square. He woke quite early and, on the spur of the moment, decided to visit another friend, Dr Rushbrook, at Walthamstow. His Bloomsbury host later said that before leaving the house, Bright 'was in the highest spirits and talked cheerfully about his professional prospects'.

Bright made the 8-mile journey by train to Walthamstow, but Rushbrook was out when he called. Around lunchtime, Bright returned to the railway station and went into the lavatory to take cocaine. He drank a phial of liquid cocaine and took several tabloids of the drug, followed by morphine. He began to vomit, then collapsed and, lying on the toilet floor, he died. His body lay there until someone reported the locked cubicle to the stationmaster at seven that evening. They broke open the door and found Bright's cold body with two uncorked phials beside him. Four more phials and corks were found in his hat, and more in his coat. In total, Bright was found in possession of twelve small phials containing morphia as well as cocaine tablets, tabloids, and liquid.

At the inquest into his death, Bright's father, who was a bookseller, testified that his son was 'in the habit of carrying drugs that he might need in his profession'. The court heard that Bright had been suffering from toothache, and the jury found that his death was due to an overdose of cocaine taken inadvertently for the purpose of relieving pain.

The *Lancet* medical journal used his death as a warning to other medical men treating themselves with powerful drugs. 'Dr Bright had unfortunately been fond of experimenting on himself with dangerous remedies; twice he had incurred serious danger by inhaling chloroform, and only last August he had produced alarming symptoms by injecting an overdose of cocaine for toothache, and he had then used morphia freely as an antidote.' The *British Medical Journal* also featured an obituary of the young, promising doctor: 'A more tragic termination to a career most successful in the past and most promising for the future it is difficult to conceive.' His death notice in *The Times* mentioned none of the controversy, and simply read, 'On the 2d Oct, Eustace Frederick Bright, M. D. Lond., of Woodleigh Tower and Roccabruna, Bournemouth, aged 29. No cards.'

Murray, as a teetotaller, would have been shocked and saddened by the demise of one of his most promising students and volunteers. News of Bright's overdose came at a difficult time for him. Life in the Scriptorium was particularly stressful. He was feeling pressure and competition from America because of the successful publication of the *Century Dictionary* and the generously funded progress of another, Funk and Wagnall's *Standard Dictionary of the English Language*, whose budget of nearly $1 million severely dwarfed that of the OED. He worried that progress on the Dictionary was too slow; even reviewers were beginning to comment, 'Will any of our grandchildren live to see it reach Z?' He had also just published a portion of the letter C, containing the word *cock*, in which one definition was slang for penis, and, as John Stephen Farmer's obscenity court case was nearing its verdict, Murray feared that the Dictionary might attract criticism. He had already learned that it was important to keep sensitive Dictionary matters out of the public eye.

K

for KLEPTOMANIAC

A year into Murray's Editorship, in 1880, a slightly scurrilous article about the Dictionary volunteers was written by someone in, or close to, the Scriptorium under the pseudonym 'Curiosus'. The piece, entitled 'The Literary Workshop', gave an update on Dictionary progress and in the process managed to ridicule several volunteers by sharing their silly comments and misguided contributions to the project thus far.

The article appeared in *Notes & Queries*, a quirky journal that still exists today for literary scholars who write 'notes' on miscellaneous discoveries in their reading and research, and ask 'queries' relating to the same. Over the many years of his Editorship, Murray regularly asked questions and successfully sought help on lexical quandaries via the journal. It functioned as the equivalent of an internet forum, the Reddit of nineteenth-century antiquarian London, and was one of the main sources of engagement between Murray and the Dictionary People.

We do not know for certain who wrote the piece. Nor do we know how Murray reacted to it, or whether in fact he knew about it before it went to print. It is doubtful that he wrote it. It was not a Murray kind of article; it sounded more like the talk of Dictionary staff at morning tea – having a bit of a laugh at the volunteers' expense. We know from Murray's letters that he could be forthright and critical in his views of people. I am thinking especially of his comments about Furnivall to the Secretary of the Delegates at OUP in June 1882, when he complained that Furnivall 'has an itching for annoying people . . . There is no saying what he may do in one of his mad fits . . . I do not believe in the soundness of his judgment or the sufficiency of his scholarship . . . He speaks of himself as a former "Editor"; he never "edited" one word – only superintended the Reading.' But it was not Murray's style to do this publicly.

Whoever wrote the piece was terribly indiscreet about the volunteers. 'Some Readers are a constant source of amusement and vexation', wrote Curiosus. 'Readers may be divided into four classes – the good, the bad, the indifferent, and the dishonourable.' The 'dishonourable' were those who borrowed books to read, but who neither did any work nor returned the books, even after repeated requests. The number of these was 'almost infinitesimal'.

It was the 'indifferent' volunteers that Curiosus most despised. 'Many do not seem able to grasp the idea of what an English dictionary should be. Some appear to assume that it is only to be a storehouse of rare and obsolete terms.' He then went on to criticize someone he refers to as 'he', who had read Layard's *Nineveh* (1850) and had said he could not find one word worth quoting because of 'the style being modern, and the words in general use and spelling'.

Looking through the address books there is only one person who read Layard's *Nineveh*, and it was not a 'he', but rather twenty-four-year-old Miss Annie Shaw Petrie of Rochdale. Six months before the article came out, she had actually sent in 200 slips from her reading of *Nineveh*, so it is puzzling that she is criticized in this way. Miss Petrie contributed to the Dictionary for nine years, sending in a total of 1,400 slips, until her marriage in 1889 to the barrister Lancelot Charles d'Auvergne Lipscomb. Her reading interests also included vegetables, and she sent in 300 quotations from William B. Carpenter's *Vegetable Physiology* (1858), giving the world-first citations for *unicellular,* having one cell; *basidium,* cells of the fructification in some fungi; and *cystidium,* one of the projecting cells among the basidia of hymenomycetous fungi. Although we have evidence that she kept in correspondence with Murray until 1889, her last bundle of slips was sent in July 1880. In other words, it may have been coincidence, but once Curiosus's article was published she did not send in any more slips. She may have seen it and been offended.

Curiosus did not stop there. He also ridiculed another volunteer who, he said, did not think Sir John Lubbock's *Insects and Wild Flowers* a suitable book 'as the bulk of the book was descriptions of flowers'. The address books reveal that two people read this book – William Douglas who sent in 200 slips and Miss Frances E. Scott of Leamington who sent in many slips for other books but nothing for this one. Douglas was one of the top contributors so we can guess that Curiosus was referring to Miss Scott, a faithful contributor who began reading for the Dictionary right at its inception and sent in 3,300 slips over twenty-three years. The address books show that after Curiosus's article, Miss Scott only sent in one more bundle of slips. Her final 550 slips from George Payne Rainsford James's *The Life and Times of Louis XIV* (1839) arrived at the Scriptorium on 12 February 1881, a mere five months after the article appeared. One wonders whether she saw the article and was discouraged from contributing any more?

Volunteers with peculiar notions, or 'crotchets', were particularly annoying to Curiosus, especially those who wished to impress on the editors the fact that 'all English words are derived from Gaelic'; 'another objects to any Freemannic jargon about calling Anglo-Saxons (i.e. Germans) by the name of Old English'; another insisted on the editors using his own invented spelling system; 'but each alike prophesies the inevitable failure of the work if his particular crotchet is not adopted'.

Curiosus gave an update on Dictionary progress, which echoed Murray's voice when he gave updates to the London Philological Society: 'no fewer than 1,800 books have been undertaken by 760 Readers', resulting in a total of 445,000 quotations sent to the Scriptorium in the first eighteen months. One hundred of these Readers were American, Curiosus mentioned, while many others hailed from Germany, India, Ceylon, Russia, Japan, Egypt, Jamaica, Madagascar, and South Africa. Curiosus was cautiously optimistic about an end date of 1892, 'but in a task of such magnitude it is impossible to foresee events, and we can only hope that nothing may happen to prevent the editor from bringing to a successful finish this great national undertaking'.

Curiosus had an ear for gossip and name dropping, mentioning that the Prime Minister, Mr Gladstone, then seventy-one years old, had visited the Scriptorium frequently that summer 'though he expressed his sorrowful conviction that he would never see its [the Dictionary's] completion'. The piece ends with an anecdote about a recent German visitor to the Scriptorium who was entertained by the notion of a building devoted solely to the task: 'How thoroughly English! You English, when you have a work to do, build a house to do it in: a German scholar would sit down and do it in his garret.'

Curiosus may have thought these quips were humorous, and they probably were amusing, but they ran the risk of damaging the goodwill of the project. The tone was cocky, condescending, and conceited, and could not have done the project any favours. Many of the contributors were readers of the journal, and knowing that the quality of their work might

be scrutinized publicly in this fashion could have been damaging to the whole enterprise which depended so completely
on the generosity and loyalty of volunteers. To put it bluntly,
the volunteers were the life and soul of the Dictionary – to
criticize them in this way was potential dynamite.

So who was Curiosus? If it was not Murray, it had to
be one of the other four staff in the Scriptorium during
that first year of his Editorship: two women who sorted the
slips, Miss Skipper and Miss Scott; Ada's brother, Herbert
'Fred' Ruthven, who started out as the carpenter of the 1,000
pigeonholes and then moved on to clerical work; and Sidney
Herrtage, an intelligent editorial assistant who had been
recommended to Murray by Furnivall and had previously
contributed to *Notes & Queries* under his initials 'S. J. H.'.

It was unlikely to be either Miss Skipper or Miss Scott
because they were women from the local village who probably
did not have access to *Notes & Queries*. Since Fred Ruthven
was Ada Murray's brother and probably had a degree of loyalty to Murray which precluded him from going behind his
back with such a potentially controversial piece. But before
I pointed the finger at Herrtage, I decided to dig a little
deeper to interrogate how far the charge was likely to be true.

Sidney John Herrtage was the first editorial assistant on
Murray's staff – the first of forty-four, if you count the names
mentioned in the prefaces to the Dictionary fascicles – but
there were probably many more over the lifetime of the
project. Some, like Miss Eleanor Bradley, Charles Balk, and
Walter Worrall, stayed for decades. Others, such as the 'utter
numb-skull' who was recommended to Murray by the Rector
of Exeter College when he moved to Oxford, were out in a
matter of days. Herrtage lasted three years, but he left under
tricky circumstances.

Born in Ireland in 1845, Herrtage was a literary scholar
who had given up a career in civil engineering to spend his

time editing Middle English manuscripts for the Early English Text Society. He began working for Murray in 1879 as soon as Murray became Chief Editor. He moved with his wife, Jane, and their four children to the Laurels Cottage, two houses down from Murray and his growing family on Hammer Lane, Mill Hill. The Herrtage children played with the Murray children while their fathers worked in the Scriptorium.

Herrtage's initial work for Murray involved reading at the British Museum Library each day, and extracting quotations from Middle English texts. He soon moved on to drafting and constructing entries. This involved taking all the slips which Miss Skipper and Miss Scott had sorted alphabetically, and sorting them chronologically for each word according to the word's part of speech and senses of meaning. If there were gaps in the dated quotations – keeping in mind the importance of finding the earliest citation and ensuring a good spread of dated quotations across the life of a word – Herrtage needed to search more books published at the necessary date to fill those gaps. Drafting a definition came next, before he pinned the slips together and passed the bundle on to Murray who checked and perfected Herrtage's work, and added the etymology and pronunciation, before sending it to press. This system established by Murray and Herrtage proved a good one, and continued unchanged from 1879 until the Dictionary was completed in 1928. It remains to this day – a team of quotation scouters collect examples of words, which editors supplement with their own searches and craft into entries according to parts of speech and nuances of meaning; a team of etymologists research the origin and history of the word before it goes to a pronunciation expert, and is finally checked by the Chief Editor.

Two months before the Curiosus piece appeared in *Notes & Queries*, Herrtage had published an article in the journal under his own initials. There was no evidence of grievance but what was in the article? I took a closer look. His subject was 'Blunders in our English Dictionaries' in which he revealed errors in the famous dictionaries of the past. In closing the piece, he offered a correction to a competitor's dictionary, *Cassell's Encyclopedia Dictionary* by Robert Hunter, which had misread a Middle English form. What happened next is telling. Robert Hunter responded as any smart project leader might: he asked Herrtage to work for him. Herrtage took up Hunter's invitation, but he made the strange decision to keep working for Murray at the same time and not tell him about his work for Cassell's. While the scandalous article by Curiosus would not have helped Murray's view of Herrtage, it was actually this greater betrayal which would lead to his downfall.

Working for both dictionaries, Herrtage used the resources of the Scriptorium, and smuggled information, slips, and books to Cassell's. One day a volume of *Annals of the Reformation* by the seventeenth-century historian John Strype, an important Protestant history of the period, was sitting on Murray's desk in the Scriptorium. The next day it was gone. The same with another seventeenth-century volume, *Anglia Rediviva* by Joshua Sprigge. Murray knew it could only be Herrtage who was stealing the books, and when he discovered that Herrtage was surreptitiously working for Cassell's, Murray fired him.

He wrote to Furnivall who had recommended Herrtage in the first place. Furnivall confessed to knowing something of his traits: 'I do believe in partial insanity in him, a kind of kleptomania for books.' But he slightly took Herrtage's side, pleading for Murray to go gently on him because 'the position is a very difficult one for me, as H has work in hand [at Furnivall's Early English Text Society], & I feel bound to help him as much as I can'. He likened Herrtage's kleptomania to 'dipsomania', a craving for alcohol (*dipso-*, thirst + *-mania*, madness), and ended the letter by conceding that Herrtage would have to be removed from the Early English Text Society Committee.

Furnivall took it upon himself to go to Herrtage's house and try to retrieve the stolen books. On Sunday 6 August 1882, he knocked on Herrtage's door and was greeted by his wife, Jane. Herrtage was not home, and Furnivall explained the situation to her. 'My impression is that she knew nothing of his conduct', Furnivall later told Murray.

Furnivall and Herrtage's wife looked for the books but could not find them. Before Furnivall left, she said that they might be in her husband's 'best book case' and that she would find a way in the coming days to get the key and search for them. 'Whatever is the cost of Strype & Sprigge', wrote Furnivall to Murray, '& any other book you can trace to him pray deduct it from what you owe him, if his wife cannot find the books, & buy new copies. This restitution can at any rate be made & I will be responsible for it.'

A few days later, Herrtage's wife returned Strype and Sprigge to Murray. He had his precious books back, but he now needed to find reliable Readers for these books and a new editorial assistant. He recruited a vicar, the Revd Thomas Wimberley Mossman, in Wragby, Lincolnshire, to read Strype and the book is quoted over 500 times in the Dictionary. Had it not been read, we would not have first quotations for *archpresbyter*, a chief priest; *alterance*, alteration; and for words which were out of use but still included in the Dictionary such as an obsolete sense of *adjuring* meaning 'the action of causing someone to recant'; an obsolete sense of *circumcised* meaning 'cut short, curtailed'; and *to collate* meaning 'to confer a benefice on a person'. The other restored volume, Joshua Sprigge's *Anglia Rediviva*, was read by Miss Grace Saunders who lived with her sister, Emily, and a servant in Addlestone, Surrey. In addition to 300 slips from Sprigge, the sisters sent in over 8,000 slips from James Heath's *Flagellum: the Life and Death, Birth and Burial of Oliver Cromwell* (1663), Swift's *Gulliver's Travels,* and sixteenth-century Roman Catholic writers Thomas More and Edmund Campion.

Furnivall conceded to Murray that he had already known that Herrtage had 'a tendency to insanity' and kleptomania. He had stolen books from Furnivall when Furnivall was the Editor of the Dictionary. 'As to the offences touching me personally', Furnivall wrote to Murray, 'H has had & has more valuable books of mine than of yours. You don't know of a nearly parallel case during my editorship which was forgiven without one hard word . . . I've found some of the Publicans [tax collectors] better fellows than the Pharisees.'

Furnivall showed compassion towards Herrtage and tried to safeguard his professional reputation: 'If folk ask why he has left', Furnivall told Murray, 'surely the whole facts needn't be stated. It is enough to say that you had good reasons for parting with him and that he was and is getting more from Cassells than you gave him . . . I do think he has had licking enough for his fault.' Furnivall summed it up thus: 'While officially and personally I condemn certain acts of his, he is a man with 2 sides to his character, & to one of these I hope to hold.'

Murray was enraged that Furnivall should have recommended a known kleptomaniac for his first editorial assistant, but he had no time to dwell on the situation. He quickly replaced Herrtage with a superb editorial assistant, Alfred Erlebach, a former teacher at Mill Hill, who proved so good that Murray wanted him instead of Henry Bradley as his co-Editor, but OUP made an arbitrary rule that only external candidates could be co-Editors. Erlebach ended up leaving after three years to be Principal of Woodford House School in Kent, but he remained a staunch supporter by proofreading, subediting, reading (he sent in 3,300 slips), and frequently returning to the Scriptorium to sub for Murray when he went on his annual summer holiday to the Lake District.

The klepto-inclined Herrtage moved to Cassell's in mid-1882. Furnivall stayed in touch with him, and kept Murray updated on his mental health: 'He has gained a new and kind-hearted friend or two, who do kind acts as well as say kind words. Cassells have made a fresh arrangement about the Dicty, & I do sincerely trust that a new start has been made which'll turn out well. I am cheered by the turn matters have taken, & I hope for the best. His house is far nicer than the M. H. [Mill Hill] one & in a healthy place.'

Herrtage stayed at Cassell's for the next ten years. He died in 1893, aged forty-eight. His name appeared in Volumes 3 and 4 of *Cassell's Encyclopaedic Dictionary*, but not in the OED. The three years he had spent working as Murray's first editorial assistant were never officially acknowledged and his name never appeared in the OED prefaces.

We can imagine that when Murray was crafting the definition of *kleptomania*, in 1901, he had someone in mind when he wrote, from the Greek *klepto-*, thief + *-mania*, madness, 'an irresistible tendency to theft, actuating persons who are not tempted to it by necessitous circumstances, supposed by some to be a form of insanity'.

If Herrtage's kleptomania was a form of insanity, it was nothing as compared with the insanity suffered by other Dictionary People.

L

for LUNATICS

It was a foggy day in January 1907 when thirty-five-year-old John Dormer, one of Murray's most faithful Subeditors and Readers, was delivered by horse-drawn wagon through the red-and-cream brick gates of an asylum in Warlingham, Surrey. The bell in the tall clock tower struck three as the new inmate was ordered to get out, and taken through the arched sandstone portico into a dimly lit reception hall. The heavy door was closed shut behind him. He was led in deathly silence down a long corridor to the cold interview room of Croydon Mental Hospital.

Dormer was not the first OED contributor to be committed to a psychiatric institution. Dormer aside, all of Murray's top four contributors had connections to mental asylums – one as an administrator and three as inmates. At the time, a person who was mentally ill was called a 'lunatic' – a term added to the final column of the census in 1871, alongside 'Deaf and Dumb or Blind, Imbecile or Idiot'. The meaning originally lacked offence, and when it was added to the Dictionary in 1903, it was simply defined as 'a person of unsound mind, a madman'. Was it their madness that drove them to do so much Dictionary work, or was it the Dictionary work that drove them mad?

For John Dormer, it was a combination of the Dictionary

work and personal grief that led to his breakdown. He first volunteered for Murray as a sensitive and intelligent teenager. I do not know how he discovered the Dictionary project, but I do know that he started as a Reader of novels and sent in 2,000 slips in his first year. Looking through many of these, it is clear that the young Dormer took pride in his work. He had had a rubber stamp made up with 'J. Dormer' on it, which he dipped in purple ink and stamped on the top right-hand corner of each slip. No one else did that.

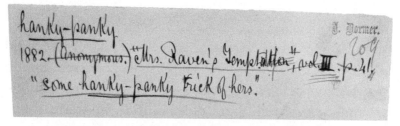

John Dormer took pride in his work and stamped each
slip with his name, as seen here for hanky-panky.

When choosing quotations, he had an eye for the quirky, fun, and quaint. His reading of Mayo's *Mrs Raven's Temptation* gave the Dictionary evidence for *humbug*, to hoax or cajole, 'Does she humbug herself into that belief, as neatly as she humbugs you?'; *hanky-panky*, trickery, double dealing, 'Some hanky-panky trick of hers'; and *minx*, a pert, sly or boldly flirtatious young woman, 'We shall be sorry if this young minx brings more trouble on the Agates'. His reading of *Poor Nellie* gave evidence for *jolly*, 'By Jove! But it is awfully jolly out here!'; *flutter*, agitated condition, 'No wonder poor Adela's pulse was all in a flutter'; *fig*, 'Charlie does not care a fig about it'; *matchmaking*, 'Perfect matchmaking requires experience and practice'; and *squeamish*, 'You're feeling squeamish, I see, so take my advice and have a brandy-and-soda'.

Murray immediately spotted the teenager's agile and quick intelligence. By the time Dormer was in his early twenties, Murray had him not just reading books but also sub-editing. Dormer would receive parcels of slips from Murray and be asked to sort them into senses in preparation for the editors in the Scriptorium who would write the definitions. He was fast and conscientious. Murray knew how rare it was to find a young volunteer who shared his work ethic. He asked Dormer to search for desiderata and to perform more complex editing tasks. Just as important to Murray, who was struggling financially, was that Dormer was a young man of independent means. He did not cost a penny. When Murray's assistants let him down, he confided in Dormer, writing to him as hard worker to hard worker, as a way of bringing the young volunteer into his confidence and making him feel special. Dormer admired Murray greatly, and kept letters from the Editor in a pocketbook which he carried in his jacket.

Dormer's speed, patience, and attention to detail were perfectly suited to lexicography. If there was a tricky or painstaking task to do, Dormer was the man for it. Perhaps his greatest single contribution to the Dictionary programme was made when he was twenty-four years old. Murray asked him to identify missing quotations in the Dictionary, and to create 'Lists of Special Wants'. These were lists of Dictionary entries which lacked quotations for certain dates.

It was an immense undertaking: Dormer had to examine over 200,000 slips; sort them into senses; order them chronologically; and identify any gaps in the quotation paragraphs that needed filling. It was a mentally challenging process, but one that lies at the heart of writing a dictionary – teasing out the nuanced senses of a word via written examples. This is what all those slips were for!

Take the verb *to drive* and its 322 slips of quotations. In his left hand, we can imagine Dormer holding two slips: Shelley's

Queen Mab, 'Religion drives his wife raving mad'; and Robinson's *Coward Conscience*, 'It's enough to drive one out of his senses'. In his right hand, a slip from Stowe's *Uncle Tom's Cabin*, 'A strange hand about me would drive me absolutely frantic.'

He would have to ask himself, *Are these three quotations for the same sense of the verb?* They are, but two of them form a subsense of the other. The Robinson quotation demonstrates the sense 'to impel, force, or bring forcibly into some state or condition'. The other two also mean this, but if Dormer were able to hold these quotations in his memory while looking through the 319 others, he would recognize a pattern: this particular sense of *drive* always occurs with an adjectival complement, 'absolutely frantic' and 'raving mad', requiring the first and third quotation to be grouped together into their own subsense.

This task was complicated and time-consuming. Even Murray struggled with it, as he had told members of the London Philological Society and wrote in his notes in 1887, 'You sort your quotations into bundls on your big table, and think you ar getting the word's pedigree riht, when a new sense, or three or four new senses, start up, which upset all your scheme, and you ar obliged to begin afresh, oftn three or four times.' After sorting them into the correct senses, Dormer had to inspect the dates of the quotations in each paragraph, and ensure a good spread across centuries and decades. Most quotation paragraphs had between three and six quotations spanning the life of a sense. When there was a gap, Dormer recorded it on his List of Special Wants, which Murray could then take to other Readers as desiderata and ask them to find.

The process would have been a mental strain on any one person, but Dormer rose admirably to the challenge, his diligence earning him a special mention by Murray in the preface to part of the letter D (Depravative to Distrustful).

He continued to work hard for Murray as a Subeditor on the letters D and S. His reading contributed 20,665 slips.

John Dormer began to hear voices at the age of thirty-five. He had been working for Murray for seventeen years. It was Christmas. He lived alone and was working on the letter S. He had been subediting the letter S for three years, and was up to words beginning with *So-*. Only a month earlier, he had lost his wife to a long illness. They had no children. In his grief, Dormer had found solace in a letter from Murray which told him that, before Ada, he had been married to a woman called Maggie. They had had a baby daughter who died at six months old. Maggie died a year later, and Murray had been left a widower at the age of twenty-eight.

Murray's story consoled Dormer. Immediately after his wife's funeral, he wrote to Murray, 'How can I thank you for your letter? I find it on entering this lonely house, utterly despondent, feeling that now there is no one to care for or that cares. To learn that you have passed through a like trial and understand comforts me in some strange fashion; and I am indeed grateful to you for writing.'

Dormer was deep in the *So-* words when he heard noises between his house and the one next door. *Soulful, soul-heal, soul-health, soulical, soulify.* The noises were disrupting his concentration. *Souling, soulish, soul-knell, soulless, soul-like.* The neighbours were boring holes in the walls and shouting at him. *Soul-mass, soul-priest, soul-saving, soul-searching, soul-shot.* He took out his revolver and placed it on his desk. *Soul-sick, soul-sickness, soul-sickening.* He was convinced they were trying to shoot him. *Soulx, souly, soum, soumer.* He carried the gun with him whenever he left the desk. *Sound, soundable, sound-age, sound-board, sound-boarding.*

Maybe Dormer left the house with the gun? Maybe he confronted the neighbours? On the 14th day of January, we do not know exactly what happened, but the police arrested him and took him to an infirmary. A few days later, he was transferred to the asylum. The police searched for clues to Dormer's identity and next of kin, and found the letters from Murray in his jacket pocket. They wrote to Murray at the Scriptorium to notify him of the situation.

John Dormer sat quietly and stared straight ahead as the doctor at Croydon Mental Hospital filled out the form. This was one of Britain's more progressive psychiatric institutions which had only been open a few years. It was one of the first to use the title 'mental hospital' rather than 'lunatic asylum'.

Of average build (Weight on Admission: *11.1*), Dormer had hazel eyes, a neat beard, dark brown hair and a slightly receding hairline. He was still dressed in his tidy civilian clothes of grey double-breasted suit, white shirt, wing collar, and spotted tie.

He explained to the doctor that his next-door neighbours had bored holes through the wall separating the two houses.

'They shot at me with poison needles.' His lips and tongue tremored slightly as he spoke. 'I had heard them conspiring to murder me. They fired shots into my house which broke my furniture.'

After listening to Dormer's story, the doctor noted: 'Patient is somewhat depressed in manner & speech, answers questions readily but is somewhat confused as regards time & place. He appears to have delusions of suspicion & identity & will not deny that the fact of his being brought here may be due to a plot on the part of some people. Denies any hallucinations. Has marked tremor at times of the lips when speaking suggesting general paralysis.' (In 1907, the term 'general paralysis' was code for 'General Paralysis of the Insane', a form of tertiary syphilis which at the time was untreatable and usually terminal.)

The doctor checked the patient's vitals: 'Pulse regular, respiratory nothing abnormal, marked tremor of tongue, teeth defective, tongue furred. Patient is in fair condition & is well nourished. Has old healed scar on right leg.'

What the doctor wrote next may come as no surprise to those of us who appreciate Dormer's efforts for Murray.

Cause of Insanity: *Overwork*

This doctor left the room. A different doctor arrived. His notes paint a picture of a very distressed Dormer: 'He had delusions that people were going to shoot him through the roof & that they blew poisoned pin points at him. He says that his annoyance occurred when he was at home & that he had to carry a revolver for protection. He also says he hears people calling out about him & threatening him & screaming.'

Epileptic: *No*
Suicidal: *No*
Dangerous: *Yes if thwarted*
Diagnosis: *Delusional insanity*
Prognosis: *Unfavourable*

The doctor steadied the camera. Dormer sat still and stared with glassy eyes slightly right of the lens. The bulb flashed. He stood up and was led by a nurse to another wing of the building.

Doors were unlocked and locked. Another long corridor, and Dormer suddenly found himself surrounded by men wandering aimlessly about. One came up asking for tobacco. Another made hideous snatchings at him as though he wanted his jacket. Others stared and surrounded him with curiosity. He was led past a sick ward with patients moaning and crying out in distress. More doors were unlocked and locked. He was being led to his dormitory, but first he was given a bath. As he followed the nurse to the bathroom, the

Photo of John Dormer taken on admittance to
Croydon Mental Hospital in 1907.

door of a padded room was open and a naked man lay on the
floor. The smell of faeces was poorly masked by disinfectant.
Dormer was stripped, washed, and given another person's
garments to wear.

The asylum had 475 inmates of all ages: 209 men and
266 women. They were a mix of every social class and condition: some merely suffering from nerves; others suffering
from the most acute forms of madness. Dormer and the men
were separated from the women. He ate meals of boiled pork
or cold beef, potatoes and pickles, and slept in a crowded
dormitory with large windows and dozens of metal beds side
by side, which clanked and squeaked through the night.

Rest was difficult because noise was constant in the
asylum – whether the voices of inmates; the rowdy dining
hall; the clatter of washing-up for five hundred patients; or
strains of 'The Maiden's Prayer' and ragtime being played on
an inferior piano in the nurses' messroom.

Inmates were allowed out once a day to walk around an 'airing court', a very small part of the eighty acres of grounds. Fifty-one people died in Croydon Mental Hospital that year, ten from *phthisis*, a word from the Ancient Greek for 'wasting away'. Back at the Scriptorium, this was a word Murray happened to be preparing for publication, defined as 'a progressive wasting disease, spec. pulmonary consumption'.

The male night nurse reported that Dormer thought his food was poisoned and had warned him 'to take his uniform off as he made himself a target for the bullets when the people fired at him'. Another hospital attendant reported that Dormer was 'very noisy at night, imagining that people anxious to murder him are upstairs'.

James Murray had been following Dormer's situation from afar. A nursemaid called Mrs Griggs, who had nursed Dormer's dying wife and provided general care for him after her death, visited Dormer each day and wrote to Murray with updates on his progress.

Murray had been expecting Dormer's subedit of his section of the letter S. When the police had notified him of Dormer's situation, he had written Dormer a sympathetic letter asking for the materials back.

Dormer was in no state to organize the return of the slips.

Murray found a way to retrieve the slips by enlisting the help of Nurse Griggs and Dormer's solicitor, who collected the slips from Dormer's house and sent them on to Oxford.

While Murray was negotiating the return of the slips, the patient was gradually recovering. His delusional thoughts were easing and doctors at the mental hospital reported: 'Patient is well contented & no delusions elicited now. Has rather an excessive air of contentment & well being.' Two weeks later: 'Patient continues well behaved, quiet, & denies all delusions or hallucinations. He has very contented manner &

sense of well being & does not quite seem to realize his position. Eats & sleeps well.'

The slips were safely back in the Scriptorium. Murray was receiving regular updates on the patient's progress from Nurse Griggs. 'He is as right as I am. I went to see him on Sunday . . . he still talks about his work.' The doctors recorded in the patient notes: 'Continues the same, takes little interest in his surroundings. Does not appear to have any ambition to leave the asylum, is too contented. Has tremor of tongue and lips.'

Nurse Griggs first asked Murray to help them get Dormer out of the mental hospital four weeks into his stay. She suggested that she and her husband would care for him. 'Dr Passmore at the Croydon Mental says he could come out if he had someone responsible for him. Sir perhaps if you could come or write to Dr Passmore it would make a great difference.'

She wrote again the following week. 'Mr Dormer was bright and cheerful to me, and ask me for more tobbaco [*sic*] before Sunday as they share in the Ward . . . Dr said he was not bad enough to be there nor was he satisfied so he could be discharged . . . Sir my husband and myself promises if we could get him out on a months trial we would do our duty by him and look after him . . . Sir should you feel inclined to speak on our behalf if Mr Dormer should come out, I should be thankful.'

There is no record that Murray wrote to the doctor. We do know that Dormer stayed in the mental hospital for a total of four months before being released on 25 April 1907, weighing six and a half pounds heavier, and described as 'Recovered'.

The bulb flashed. Dormer's image was taken again, looking not much different from when he entered. He walked out of the gates a free and well man.

The first person John Dormer contacted upon his release was Murray. The unreturned slips had worried the assiduous Dormer – until a month before his release, no one had told him that Murray had got them back.

A letter from Dormer, written the day after his return home, gives an insight into his devotion to Murray and the Dictionary. He apologized for not answering Murray's letter of 17 January, and wrote, 'Let me . . . express my regret at the trouble caused by that box of So- material, which I hope you found complete.' He told Murray that he had spent nearly four months in the mental hospital. 'The cautious hospital doctors then thought that another tedious month in their pleasant (!) haven of rest would do me no harm, and hence it was not till yesterday that I regained my liberty. I now find that a small collection of quots. for S–Z and supplement was returned, or rather sent [to you].' He only made one reference to his treatment in the hospital: 'I will not tax your patience by speaking of the blunders which initiated my recent detention though the treatment I received on 14 Jan last still appears to me and to those fully aware of the circumstances to be both arbitrary and inhumane.'

Now that he was out of the asylum, he told Murray, 'I am going to "laze" industriously for a couple of months or so; and neither know whether at the end of that time I shall be able to offer to do more Dict. Work, nor even my whereabouts then.'

That was his last letter to Murray. John Dormer never worked for the Dictionary again.

*

John Dormer was not the only volunteer to suffer psychological distress. Thomas Austin, the 'best contributor' who read more books and sent in more slips than anyone else, spent time in institutions and suffered from a combination of overwork, delusions, and paranoia. His mental state was summed up in Henry Bradley's comment to Murray, '[Austin] mentioned his having formerly been insane; he added that he was now recovered, and there was no fear of the danger which I apprehended. I was a good deal taken aback by this; somebody had told me he was considered "rather crazy", but I did not know that this was meant literally.'

Not far behind Austin's lifetime contribution of 165,061 slips was William Douglas of Primrose Hill, London, who sent in 151,982 slips. From the address books, you would not know that William Douglas was classified on the census as a 'lunatic'. Well, not until you really looked at his reading habits. Across the twenty-two years that he read for Murray, a pattern emerged: he had obsessive runs on certain topics.

1879 was the year of the novel – Walter Scott's *Woodstock*, Mrs Wood's *The Channings*, and Mary Elizabeth Braddon's *Lady Audley's Secret*.

1880 was the year of science – Douglas asked Murray to buy him five volumes by Darwin (Murray sometimes bought books for Readers, taking the money out of his meagre salary from OUP), including Darwin's *Descent of Man*, and thereafter begins an obsession with books on the human body and its ailments: Richard Owen's *Skeleton and the Teeth*, Herbert Spencer's *Biology*, and H. Charlton Bastian's *The Brain*, to name just a few.

1881 was his year of disease – Edmund Peaslee's *Ovarian Tumours*, Louis Duhring's *Diseases of the Skin*, D. B. Roosa's *Diseases of the Ear*, Samuel D. Gross's *Diseases of Urinary Organs*, J. Solis Cohen's *Throat Diseases*, Henry Fuller's *Diseases of Lungs*, Henry Walton's *Diseases of the Eye*, Samuel Habershon's *Diseases of the Abdomen*, T. G. Thomas's *Diseases of Women . . .*

Thousands of anatomical marvels tumbled out of these books onto Douglas's slips, his large slanted handwriting patiently copying each one – *cilia*, the eyelashes; *gingival*, of the gums; *fauces*, a cavity at the back of the mouth; *utricle*, a small cul-de-sac in a man's urethra – until the Dictionary became a veritable treasure chest of maladies: *cephalalgy*, a headache; *anosmia*, the loss of sense of smell; *micturition*, an intense desire to urinate; *glossitis*, the inflammation of the tongue; *chancre*, a syphilis lesion; *chemosis*, a swelling of the eyeball; *enteritis*, the inflammation of the intestines; and *condyloma*, syphilitic warts.

As though he were working his way along a library shelf on disease, Douglas's obsession ran until June 1882 when he sent in 150 slips from Henry Thompson's *Diseases of the Prostate*. And then nothing. William Douglas went silent for three years.

It was difficult to find out anything about William Douglas, as no one with that name shows up in official records. I went back to study the address book to see if Murray left us any clues to William's identity. And sure enough, the clue lay in his address: 3 St George's Square, London. This is the same address as that of Frederick Furnivall, the second Chief Editor of the OED, the man who had held the reins between Herbert Coleridge's death in 1861 and Murray taking over in 1879.

Why was the second-highest contributor to the OED living with Frederick Furnivall, and why has no one realized this before, not even Furnivall's biographers?

A search for William Douglas's birth certificate revealed that Douglas was not his real surname. He had been born 'William Furnivall' in 1842, the first son of Frederick Furnivall's cousin. Frederick Furnivall was seventeen years old when Cousin William was born. Tracing their relationship is complicated by the fact that they both have fathers called George Frederick who were cousins – Frederick's father was a surgeon born in 1781, and William's father was a military publisher born in 1814.

William was eight years old when he was first classified as 'Deaf and Dumb or Blind' in the final column of the census.

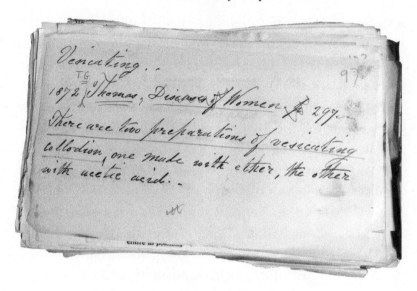

One of the 151,982 slips written out by
William Douglas.

He was twenty-nine years old when 'Lunatic, Imbecile and Idiot' were added to the census, and thereafter he was described as 'Lunatic'. It is difficult to understand why. It may be that in Victorian Britain he was misunderstood. Perhaps he had difficulties with social interactions? Perhaps his remarkable focus and persistence in reading for Murray were mistakenly viewed as obsessive and compulsive monomania? Perhaps he suffered, like John Dormer, from some sort of psychosis with 'grandiose' delusions that took the form of having a 'mission' such as writing out thousands of slips? Perhaps his all-consuming interests made it difficult for him to live in the world and mix with people or to go out in public? Perhaps he had a desire for sameness which manifested itself as an extraordinary aptitude for repetitive action or speech? Perhaps he was hypersensitive to sounds or tastes? Perhaps he was non-verbal or had difficulty with conversations? Perhaps he was clumsy or moved his limbs uncontrollably? Perhaps he suffered from anxiety or depression? These are all big 'if's, but I can't help thinking that quite a few of us who are neurodiverse, or who present on the autism spectrum, might have been labelled in the same way as William Douglas in the nineteenth century.

And what about William's host, Frederick Furnivall? Madness and asylums had played an important role in Furnivall's own life and his private wealth. His father had been a surgeon and owner of the lucrative Great Fosters Asylum in Egham, Surrey, and it was here – in a sixteenth-century mansion – that Furnivall was born in 1825. He and his brother inherited the asylum, along with £20,000 in effects, which they sold on their father's death in 1865.

The fortune changed Furnivall's life instantly. He and his wife, Eleanor 'Lizzy' Dalziel, were able to buy a large house on fashionable St George's Square in London. Sadly, their baby daughter died soon after but, two years on, life was looking brighter with the birth of a son, Percy. It seemed for a little while that Furnivall, now forty-two years old, was living the dream: he had a wife, a healthy baby son, a handsome house in a stylish part of London, and independent wealth that enabled him to stop working as a barrister. He could devote his days to what excited him most: enthusing volunteers for the fledgling OED; helping to organize the Working Men's College with the Anglican priest and theologian F. D. Maurice; attending meetings of the London Philological Society (he would be Honorary Secretary for fifty years); setting up literary societies; and rowing on the Thames.

This good fortune did not last long. A few months after Percy's birth, the Overend, Gurney & Company bank collapsed, and Furnivall lost most of his wealth. Suddenly his independence seemed precarious.

It was at this time that Cousin William, by then in his mid-twenties, came to live with Furnivall and Lizzy. As the oldest son in his family, William brought with him substantial personal wealth and was listed on the census as 'landowner' and 'living on own means'. Furnivall's upbringing around Great Fosters Asylum may have been why he decided to care for William at home rather than put him in an institution. It seems that Furnivall never talked or wrote about William. There is no mention of him in any of the biographies or memoirs, and yet he is listed in the address books at Furnivall's address, so Murray and his team in the Scriptorium must have known about him.

William and Furnivall lived together for the rest of their lives, another forty years. I'd like to hope that the living arrangements were mutually beneficial. Furnivall provided care for William with his mental illness, and William funded Furnivall's exuberant lifestyle and entrepreneurial enterprises. Furnivall was one of those big Victorian characters. Larger than life, he seemed powered by a supernatural energy. In addition to starting the Early English Text Society in 1864, he founded the Chaucer Society (1868), the Ballad Society (1868), the New Shakspere Society (1873), the Browning Society (1881), the Wyclif Society (1881), and the Shelley Society (1886).

Although his literary interests were highbrow, there was nothing snobbish about Furnivall. His democratic principles and all-embracing attitude to the Dictionary were mirrored in his eclectic friendships. He was a generous soul who took delight in connecting people. He brought hundreds, if not thousands, of volunteers to the Dictionary project. But it came at a price, especially for Murray who was often annoyed by his bossy, impetuous, outspoken, gossipy, and wildly indiscreet predecessor.

Furnivall was always up for a party even though he was a teetotaller. When he died, a book of remembrances included tributes from the great, the good, and a waitress from his favourite ABC tea shop on Oxford Street where he always sat at the same table and took a meal after a long day's work at the British Museum Library.

His friends described him as a boy at heart with rollicking spirits who delighted in using slang and phonetic spelling. Although his editing and scholarship were not always commended by his colleagues, they all recognized that he displayed the wisdom, concentration, and learning of a gifted and industrious man. It was a very Victorian combination.

Women, usually young women, were of particular interest to Furnivall. Some critics have called him 'an old letch', others have called him a feminist, taking account of his context in which women were denied access to education, scholarship, and membership of clubs and societies, all of which he fought against. He recruited female volunteers for the OED, and his societies boasted many women members. Young female scholars especially benefited from his patronage, as did young women athletes – he founded the world's first female rowing club, Hammersmith Girls' Sculling Club, known today as Furnivall Sculling Club. The American medievalist Edith Rickert visited Furnivall at the boathouse in 1896 and wrote in her diary, 'There we found a large party of young people – the boys rather sheepish in the corner with cigarettes – the girls dancing with one another & in their midst Dr. F. with red necktie & handkerchief (is he a socialist?) the gayest of the gay.'

William's work on the Dictionary ebbed and flowed according to what was going on in his family life. He had a troubled younger brother, Penn, who studied medicine and trained as a surgeon, but liked to party and was often seen, fashionably moustachioed, in his black felt hat and smart dark suit drinking at the popular Arundel and Caledonian Hotels on Victoria Embankment. Penn married a beautiful artist but soon got into trouble with the law. He was drinking at a hotel in the market town of Farnham when he cheated two men out of £5, and absconded. A warrant was issued for his arrest and he was described in all the newspapers. Penn went on the run but was eventually found and sentenced to five years of hard labour in Pentonville Prison.

The address book showed that William stopped sending in slips for a period and I wondered whether it had something to do with his feckless brother. It seems to have come after Penn's release from prison, the birth of three children, his bankruptcy, and his disappearance and desertion of his wife. I wondered whether William had gone to stay with Penn's abandoned wife, or had taken her and the babies in at 3 St George's Square? This all happened between 1882 and 1885 – the exact same years that there were no entries for William in the address book. These were not census years so I had no way of finding out from official documents. Another possibility of course was that he had had a stint in a psychiatric hospital. I was contemplating all these possibilities when

Furnivall pictured with the world's first female rowing
team at the club he founded, Hammersmith Girls'
Sculling Club, now called Furnivall Sculling Club.

I discovered something else even more intriguing than the escapades of a rogue sibling – this time relating directly to Frederick Furnivall but having an impact on William's domestic life.

In the summer of 1882, at the same time that William was writing out his last set of slips for a while – for *ejaculatory*, *gonorrhoeal*, *urethral*, and *verumontanum* from *Diseases of the Prostate* – Furnivall was having his own problems of the romantic kind and this had an impact on life at home.

The fifty-seven-year-old Furnivall fell madly in love with a brilliant young woman called Mary Lilian 'Teena' Rochfort-Smith who had edited a *Four-Text Hamlet* and helped him with edits of *Old-Spelling Shakspere* for the New Shakspere Society. Thirty-six years his junior, Teena had a fierce intellect and a photographic memory, and Furnivall had come to rely on her assistance with everything that he wrote. He referred to her as his 'greatest helper and friend'.

In addition to Teena's exceptional mind, many remarked on her beauty. She had deep brown eyes, pale skin, and long golden-brown hair that reached to her knees. She also had a rich mezzo-soprano voice. When asked to sing she would stand to her full 5 foot 4 inches and perform for three hours straight – Mendelssohn, Schubert, Mozart, Gluck, or Beethoven.

Teena moved in with Furnivall in summer 1882. Controversially, Furnivall's wife and son were still living in the house at the time, and they did not move out until the marriage was legally dissolved nine months later.

London's literary and philological circles were all a-flutter with the Teena scandal. Murray received a letter from a disgusted Lucy Toulmin Smith, a loyal Specialist and Reader, who wrote to him:

> *You asked me the other night why I did not continue to subscribe to the New Sh[akspere] Soc[iety]. I do not feel*

satisfied with its management this year, in one particular,
which seems to me dishonest. But, there is a much worse
thing which I must tell you, tho' odious to me. Furnivall
is being separated from his wife, at his own desire, as he
has become infatuated with a young girl. He is selling his
books & breaking up his house on 24 June. I tell you this
for the sake of the poor innocent wronged wife, to whom
he owes much. She needs all the manly and womanly sym-
pathy of her friends . . . Good heavens, what desecration!
Pardon me I feel it deeply.

The silence – no slips for three years – from William
during this period may have been because there was so much
going on at home. Or it may have been a sign that he was
'removed' just before Teena moved in, conveniently placed
in an institution for a rest cure, perhaps? It happened frequently in the late nineteenth century, though usually with
women who would not bend to their husband's will, or did
not fit conventional expectations of conduct, or (as perhaps
in William's case) for matters of 'domestic convenience'.

If Furnivall and Teena were affected by the gossip,
they did not show it. She joined him for soirées among
the literary set and accompanied him to meetings of the
Philological Society. He introduced her to Murray and the
Glossotypists – Henry Sweet, Prince Lucien Bonaparte, and
Alexander Ellis. Her name does not appear in Murray's
address book, but, according to Furnivall, she read for the
OED in the British Museum and sent in the earliest quotation
for the word *airtight*.

The prodigious Teena gave a paper on *Hamlet* to the
New Shakspere Society. She joined Furnivall for tea each day
at the ABC tea shop. He arranged for her to meet the poet
she most admired, Robert Browning, at whose house she
lunched several times. It was in Browning's drawing room

that Furnivall looked on as Teena sat on a green velvet sofa, beside the grey-haired seventy-year-old poet, who read to her a set of poems.

Not long after Furnivall's marriage to Lizzy was legally dissolved, and he and Teena were finally in domestic bliss (but not yet married), Teena left London for a short break with her family in Yorkshire. It was a summer's day in August 1883 when she joined her parents and sister on a visit to an uncle in the village of Goole. Someone suggested taking a walk, but she declined and said she was going upstairs to write. She had a habit of burning her letters after she had read them. As she struck a match, the head flew off and set fire to a needlework mat. Teena threw it down and stamped on it. She put out the mat but did not notice that the bustle of her dress had caught fire, and, as she moved, it lit the lace curtains. She first tried to put out the curtains, and then her own dress. When this failed, and being unable to undo her corset, she raced downstairs and ran outside. She was fully alight and her dress was melting into her skin and flesh. When the flames were eventually extinguished, despite her anguish, Teena made herself walk upstairs. A surgeon examined her, and declared that nothing could be done for her scorched and charred body. She suffered fits of delirium and agony for six days. Her family tended for her but she died on 4 September 1883. She was buried in Goole cemetery two days later.

After her death, Furnivall wrote a memoir of Teena for her old school, Cheltenham Ladies' College, in which he described her intellect: 'Compared with the surface turquoise minds of so many girls, hers was as the sapphire depths of the infinite heaven, lit by the multitudinous stars.' He recounted stories of her impressive memory: 'Her knowledge of the Elizabethan dramatists was such, that she could from memory quote from Peele and Greene parallel passages to lines in 2 and 3 Henry VI, which had evaded the search of even such an exhaustive commentator on these plays as Miss Jane Lee.' He summed up his admiration thus: 'Those who have known women of the type of Harriet Martineau, Mrs Gaskell, George Eliot, and Cristina Rosetti [*sic*], can yet say with truth, that so sweet, unselfish, and self-forgetting a nature as Teena Rochfort-Smith's, or one so rich, from which they hoped higher things, they have never come across. The glance of her eye, the smile of her lip, the tone of her voice, her sweet, bright, gentle ways, her wealth of sympathy and love, are still in memory with them.'

It was sixteen months after Teena's death when William resurfaced, with a whopping 1,000 quotations from Ellis's *Anatomy* and 1,600 slips from Knox's *System of Human Anatomy*. His slips now displayed a penchant for the brain with words such as *amnesia*, loss of memory; *aphasic*, having lost the power of speech; *convolution*, each of the folds of the brain; *cineritious*, the ash-colour of the brain; and for obscure muscles: *occipitofrontalis*, a muscle of the scalp; *omohyoid*, a shoulder muscle; and *buccinator*, a muscle of the wall of the cheek.

Later that year, we might imagine that he was trying to get away from his obsession with diseases and the human body when he read Elizabeth Raffald's *Experienced English Housekeeper* (1769), and found first instances of the words *pikelet*, a type of round teacake; *gofer*, a waffle cake; and *ozyat*, an obsolete drink of almond and orange-flower water. But soon after we see him return to a disease or two with John Forbes's *Diseases of the Chest*.

1886 and 1887 were travel-writing years for William with Connop Thirwall's *Greece*, John Stephen's *Travels in Greece*, William Spalding's *Italy*; and Mountstuart Elphinstone's *History of India*, John McCulloch's *British Empire*, Wilson's *British India*; but still a few diseases with John Thomson's

Inflammation and William Buchan's *Domestic Medicine*. His interest in dental health continued with L. P. Meredith's *Teeth* in 1887.

William was back in his stride. Again, 1888 and 1889 were years of the novel – Mary Elizabeth Braddon, Edward Bulwer-Lytton, George Payne Rainsford James, and Charles Dickens. He worked at incredible speed – some weeks sending in an average of 500 slips a day. From his letters we know that he often did his reading in a library (though we don't know which one) that only opened at 1 p.m. each day. He sent in 210 slips from Maria Grant's *The Sun-Maid*, and then there was another silence again, this time for ten years.

William remained living with Furnivall and was now listed for the first time officially as 'William Douglas', rather than William Furnivall, on the 1891 census, even though he had been known by that name in Murray's address book since 1879.

During this period of silence, the hopeless Penn, although still legally married, appears to have declared himself 'widowed', but a search of the censuses shows that he moved to Oldham in the north of England where he married again and lived as a bigamist. Penn's abandoned first wife was desperate for money to support her children, and Furnivall appears to have come to her rescue by finding her transcription work among his scholarly contacts. She made a living from transcribing a manuscript of pre-Shakespearean drama for the Chicago-based Professor John Matthews Manly (she is thanked as 'Mrs Furnivall' in the preface of several of his books). William forged a friendship with his niece, her daughter Agnes Mary, now fourteen, who visited him frequently in Primrose Hill.

William's reading for Murray started up again briefly in 1901. The final books he read were predictably medical: John Bristowe's *Medicine* and Robert Semple's *Memoirs on Diphtheria*. On 20 and 26 February 1901, he sent in 1,200 slips and 400 slips respectively. It was in the census of this year that William was again listed as 'Lunatic' and strangely he also declared that he was born in 'Malta' when in fact his place of birth was Battersea, Surrey.

By this time, it was only William and Frederick and two servants, Rose and Dora, living in the big house on St George's Square. Even in his eighties, Furnivall showed no sign of slowing down. He still rowed, he still frequented the ABC tea shop, he still attended meetings of the Philological Society, he still sent Murray newspaper clippings, and he still had an eye for the ladies.

It was a cold February day in 1910 when doctors told the eighty-five-year-old Furnivall that he had cancer of the bowel and only a short time to live. He wrote to Murray, 'I am to disappear in 6 months . . . It's a great disappointment, as I wanted To see The Dict. finishd before I die. But it is not to be. However the completion of the work is certain. So that's all right.' Murray did not reply with any degree of sentimentality, but, with his mind fixed only on the Dictionary, asked Furnivall if he would like to see the proofs for a particular word: 'Would it give you any satisfaction to see the gigantic TAKE in final? Before it is too late?' He did however confide to his daughter, 'The news from Dr F quite upset me and made me feel that my end might also come soon; esp. when he wrote that his great disappointment is that he is not to see the Dictionary finished; I asked myself "And shall I?" Alas! My friends seem to be dying daily, & younger than me too.' It was true; Murray had lost most of his friends in recent years.

Upon Furnivall's terminal diagnosis, William was moved into Wyke House, a private asylum in Brentford for fifteen men and fifteen women, which was described by the Lunacy Commissioners in 1910 as 'in a very shabby condition'. His favourite niece had married an older man, a tourist agent, Andrew Reed, and was now known as Mrs Agnes Mary

Ackroyd Reed. I like to think that she continued to visit her uncle William at the asylum as she had when he lived with Furnivall.

William Douglas died in the asylum on 21 June 1910, aged sixty-eight. Agnes Mary inherited his fortune of £9,634 (the equivalent of £300,000 today). She lived a quiet life in a picture-perfect Tudor farm house in Hemel Hempstead, Hertfordshire, where she died in 1974 leaving £39,930 in her will, which – taking inflation into account – was roughly the same amount that she had been left by William.

Furnivall died ten days after William, at 3 St George's Square. He was conscious until fifteen minutes before his death. In sharp contrast with the fortune William left to Agnes Mary, Furnivall left a mere £796 to his son, Percy, who by then was a well-known surgeon like his grandfather.

Despite Murray's best efforts to finish the gigantic verb *take* in time, Furnivall died three months before it was published. It took up forty columns and was the longest entry in the Dictionary at the time. (Though it was overtaken by *set* which was published two years later; and today, at 586 senses, *take* ranks as the third-longest entry after the verbs *go* (603 senses) and *run* (654 senses).) Murray had done a remarkable job at describing the word's semantic progression from meaning 'touch with the hand' to 'lay hands on' to 'seize' to 'remove from a particular place'. Furnivall would have appreciated more than anyone the exceptional skill with which Murray had shown the contradictions held within the word, meaning its opposites: 'give' ('you took him a smack in the face for that'); 'go' ('he took across the field'); or 'make' ('he took a leap').

Looking at the preface of the fascicle containing the verb *take*, I was surprised that there was no special mention of Frederick Furnivall's death, or indeed that of his cousin William Douglas. I would have expected at least a few sentences

in memory of the man who had kept the Dictionary in existence for twenty years before Murray took over, who founded
societies dedicated to the literature that supplied the quotations, whose daily reading of the *Daily Telegraph* kept the
Dictionary in constant supply of newspaper quotations, and
who recruited so many helpers to its creation, including his
own industrious cousin William. It was Henry Bradley who,
three years later in the preface of the section S–Sh (not the
main volume, merely a section), made a brief mention of
Furnivall's death: 'Dr Furnivall and Professor Skeat, whose
constant help has been acknowledged in the preface to every
volume of the Dictionary, lived to see the publication of some
of the sections of this half-volume.' We know Furnivall had annoyed Murray so maybe this was all that he and the other Editors could bring themselves to say? Similarly, once I knew the
story of William Douglas I was disappointed to discover that
Murray had only mentioned his name, like that of Thomas
Austin, in a footnote in part I A–Ant and in an appendix to
the preface of Volume I.

*

Ranking below Thomas Austin, who sent in 165,061 slips,
and William Douglas, who sent in 151,982, there is a big drop
to the third-highest contributor Dr Thomas Nadauld Brushfield, who sent in 70,277 slips. He was also closely connected
to the Victorian mental health system, but worked on the
other side of the locked doors – as a psychiatrist, notable
in the late-nineteenth century for his humane treatment of
those with mental health issues.

There were two approaches to the treatment of patients
in psychiatric hospitals at the time: a humane consideration
for their well-being and possible recovery, or the opposite –
an inhumane disregard for their personhood and possible

recovery. These different approaches were championed by two Dictionary volunteers who sat on either side of the debate: Thomas Nadauld Brushfield and George Fielding Blandford.

Brushfield was a young doctor, recently graduated from St Andrews, when he first worked at Bethnal House Asylum in London. He was only twenty-four years old when he was appointed house surgeon at Cheshire County Lunatic Asylum, and thirty-three when he was put in charge of the new Surrey County Asylum at Brookwood. As well as pioneering the non-restraint treatment of mentally ill patients, he advocated the use of activities and entertainment to stimulate them. His argument was that fewer cases would be admitted to asylums if doctors considered insanity to be the same as any other treatable disease, whereby 'the early symptoms would be discovered by medical men long before the patient became, to the outside world, palpably insane, and whilst in the early stage would be treated successfully'.

In 1880, he wrote an article in the *Lancet* suggesting improved questions on asylum admission forms to take account of the name and address of a friend of the patient, the menstrual cycles of young women, the state of a patient's bowels, and histories of addiction or alcoholism. He warned against rashly judging someone as 'insane' on admission when sometimes all they required was 'a warm bath and a purgative'. Looking at John Dormer's admission form, it is clear that Brushfield's sensible suggestions were not implemented by the profession, or at least that asylum. His humane and thoughtful approach to mental illness was way ahead of his time.

Over a thirty-year period, Brushfield's reading for the Dictionary varied greatly and was not confined to his specialism of mental illness. He retired to Devon in 1882, at the age of sixty, and devoted the rest of his life to reading for Murray and collecting 'Raleghana' – paraphernalia related to the Eliza-bethan statesman and writer, Sir Walter Ralegh. He chose a retirement home in Budleigh Salterton, the coastal town in Devon close to where Ralegh had lived. Brushfield's letters to Murray show that he was keenly aware of the progress of his slip tally. In 1888, he wrote, 'I am afraid that in my hurry to complete my 50,000 I sent off one packet not quite finished.'

Brushfield and Murray forged a strong friendship over the years and their letters are a combination of discussion of reading and the personal: 'Considering my age (78)', wrote Brushfield, 'I am told that I am a "wonderful" man to have recovered so well.' They were both good friends of the anti-quarian and sheep-farm owner Frederick Elworthy and often holidayed at Foxdown together. Brushfield died in 1910, a few months after Furnivall and William Douglas, adding to Murray's lamentation that the friends of the Dictionary were leaving him.

The psychiatrist George Fielding Blandford was a contrast to Brushfield. His attitude to mental illness was not entirely 'old school' – in fact he shared many of Brushfield's approaches to care for the mentally ill – but he sometimes acted in ways that were questionable by our standards today. He started his career at Blacklands House, a private asylum in Chelsea known in the early nineteenth century for employing 'the bath of surprise' (cold baths) and using handcuffs rather than straitjackets to restrain patients because they 'kept the patient cool and com-fortable'; it was the hospital where Charles Wesley's son Samuel was unjustly detained for a year in 1817. He moved on to take charge of Devon County Asylum, and eventually owned his own hospital, Munster House Asylum in Fulham, London. His series of twenty lectures on *Insanity and Its Treatment*, published as a book in 1871, informed a generation of psychiatrists.

Fielding Blandford read books for Murray relating to mental illness but did not necessarily choose words relating to mental illness. His reading of Timothy Bright's sixteenth-century *Treatise of Melancholie* (1586) resulted in the words *hotness*, the state of being hot, and *heartspoon*, the slight hollow overlying the lower end of the breastbone. From Thomas Arnold's *Observations on the Nature, Kinds, Causes, and Prevention of Insanity, Lunacy, or Madness* (1782) he gave the world its first use of the word *nostalgic*: 'A variety of pathetic insanity, to which, from nostalgia its most usual appellation, I have given the epithet nostalgic.' Nevertheless, Murray sought his advice on certain words related to the field. Blandford wrote to him that *aphrodisiomania*, an abnormal enthusiasm for sexual pleasure, was a word coined by an Italian professor and 'doubtful whether it can rank as English'. (Murray did not put it in the Dictionary.)

Fielding Blandford's views on women, sexuality and mental illness were striking, though not untypical for the time. Masturbation when indulged in by the female sex, he thought, was 'practised by nymphomaniacal and hysterical women'. Furthermore, he wrote, 'We see other effects of sexual excess every day in ordinary practice, such as lassitude, dyspepsia, giddiness, dimness of sight.'

According to Fielding Blandford, insanity was most likely to recur in women when they were pregnant or in the throes of nuptial intercourse, and he warned against unstable women marrying:

> *Where a woman has been insane, her insanity is so likely to recur during pregnancy, or after parturition, or even during the first excitement of nuptial intercourse, that I never could bring myself to consent to the marriage of such a one; in addition, her children would run a great risk of being insane, nervous, epileptic, or idiots. A man is not exposed to so many causes of insanity as a woman, but his children are also liable to be affected with the inherited*

taint. Of course if a woman is past child-bearing, there is far less objection to her contracting marriage. It is for the husband only to say whether he chooses to encounter the risk of marrying one who has already shown symptoms of the disorder.

Fielding Blandford hit the headlines in 1895 when he forcibly committed to an asylum a well-connected feminist socialist called Edith Lanchester. Edith was a young upper-middle-class woman who was educated and totally sane. She mixed in feminist and socialist circles, and she was living with (and decidedly not marrying) her partner, an Irish Catholic railway clerk. Her upper-middle-class English family objected to the love match and her insistence on living with him out of wedlock. Fielding Blandford colluded with the family and argued that her opposition to matrimony made her unfit to care for herself.

Very early one chilly morning in October 1895, Fielding Blandford stepped into a horse-drawn carriage with Edith Lanchester's father and two brothers. The four men arrived at Edith's rented lodgings in Battersea. They woke the whole house with heavy banging on the front door, and Fielding Blandford forced his way in to 'examine' Edith. He ordered that she be taken to an asylum because she was committing 'social suicide' by insisting on living with her working-class lover without marrying him. He justified this by arguing that under the Lunacy Act 1890 he would have certified her had she attempted (normal) suicide.

Edith tried to run out of the house but one brother grabbed her around the shoulders, the other by the legs. They carried her to the waiting carriage and tied her up with rope. The blinds of the carriage were pulled down so she had no idea where they were taking her. When she arrived at the Priory Private Asylum, she tried to reason with the doctors but they were legally powerless because of Blandford's certification. The cause of her insanity was recorded as 'over-education'.

Edith Lanchester was a member of the Social Democratic Federation and good friends with one of Murray's most hopeless contributors, Eleanor Marx, having at one time been Marx's clerical assistant and personal nurse. In fact, one of Eleanor's final letters before her suicide was to Lanchester: 'I am so worried in all ways (material as well as others) that I hardly have the heart to write. Edward is very ill. I fear hopelessly. You will understand . . . I often wonder why one goes on at all with all this fearful suffering. Of course I could not say so to my poor Edward but I often think it would be easier to make an end of it.' Upon her death, Lanchester received Marx's writing pen.

Through her associations with Marx and the Social Democratic Federation, Edith had powerful friends who, immediately upon her incarceration in the asylum, helped bring the case to public attention. Within four days, she was freed.

Lanchester's kidnapping and committal, and Fielding Blandford's role in it, gained widespread international attention from London to New York. Edith's father wrote an unapologetic letter to the editor of *The Times* on 31 October 1895: 'My opinion, and that of the family is that the girl is, for the time being, not of sound mind, and that the effects of overstudy have predisposed her naturally impressionable temperament to be abnormally acted on by her self-imposed surroundings.' The family never gained control of Edith again. She and her Irish working-class lover went on to have two children and lived together until his death in 1945. Most of the newspapers concluded that Fielding Blandford, a respected physician, had lent himself to what was in effect a family conspiracy.

Following the incident, Fielding Blandford stopped contributing to the Dictionary. His reputation did not suffer unduly, and he remained in private practice in London until 1909. He was an active member of the Royal College of Physicians for forty-four years, sitting on educational and parliamentary committees where he fiercely protected the interests of private asylum owners.

*

That's not all when it comes to mental illness, asylums, and the OED. Our fourth-highest contributor, Dr William Chester Minor, also lived in an asylum. His case is particularly intriguing because Murray assumed that the learned Dr Minor who wrote to him from Broadmoor Criminal Lunatic Asylum for the Criminally Insane was – like Brushfield and Fielding Blandford – a doctor working there. It wasn't until he had been corresponding with him for several years that Murray discovered Dr Minor was in fact an inmate who had killed a man. He was one of three murderers that I found among the Dictionary People, but he was the only one who went to prison.

M

for MURDERERS

William Chester Minor had an unusual way of volunteering for the Dictionary. As though he were a remote member of the Scriptorium, he preferred always to work on the same part of the alphabet as Murray. It suited Murray as he and his assistants often found themselves scrambling around at the last minute trying to find quotations to fill gaps in the section they were working on. Murray knew this helped Dr Minor 'feel that he is in living touch with the making of the Dictionary as it goes on', as Murray put it. By the time Dr Minor stopped sending in slips in 1906, he had produced a total of 62,720, ranking him fourth-highest contributor behind Austin, Douglas, and Brushfield.

William Minor was something of a mythical figure when I first encountered his slips. As a young lexicographer in the 1990s I had read academic articles about him as well as Simon Winchester's famous book. When I was working as an editor on the Oxford English Dictionary, I shared responsibility for words entering English from outside Europe. Over the twenty-three years that Minor had sent in slips to the Scriptorium, he mainly read travellers' tales and medical texts from the sixteenth and seventeenth centuries. It was the travellers' tales that interested me because they brought thousands of words from indigenous languages around the world into the English language. Many quotations for these words were written out on slips in Minor's distinctive handwriting.

Minor had spent his childhood in Ceylon (now Sri Lanka) with missionary parents, which may have given him an eye for foreign words that deserved a place in the Dictionary. To name just a few of the thousands he sent in: *kajawah*, a large pannier carried on a camel, from Urdu; *curricurro*, a boat used in the Malay Archipelago; *pagoda*, a Buddhist temple; *pilau*, a rice dish of South Asian origin, from Persian; *cockatoo*, a large white, grey, or black parrot with an erectile crest native to Australasia and eastern Indonesia, from Malay; *khan*, a title commonly given to rulers and men of rank in central Asia, from Persian and Arabic.

When I was editing these words, I sometimes needed to check something on the original slip from the first edition, so I would walk down to the basement where the slips were stored. Dr Minor was probably the contributor who sent in the most words from languages outside of Europe, and, because it was my task to edit these particular words for the OED, most of the slips that I checked in the archives came from him.

It was not Minor's slips that stood out per se – they looked pretty normal. It was his concordances, or lists of words contained in a book alongside their page numbers, which were striking in their appearance and made me think he was a little unusual. His handwriting was tiny and impossibly neat. He would squeeze a few handwritten lines into what normally was a single line.

Dr Minor would read a text not for its meaning but for its words. It was a novel approach to the task – the equivalent of cutting up a book word by word, and then placing each in an alphabetical list which helped the editors quickly find quotations. Just as Google today 'reads' text as a series of words or

One of the 62,720 slips sent in by Dr William
Chester Minor.

symbols that are searchable and discoverable, so with Dr Minor. A manual undertaking of this kind was laborious – he was basically working as a computer would work – but it probably resulted in a higher percentage of his quotations making it to the Dictionary page than those of other contributors.

Dr Minor was not the only volunteer to send in concordances of this kind. A recluse in Suffolk named Fitz-edward Hall, whom we will meet in O for Outsiders, did it with a better editor's eye for which words were worth indexing. Regardless, the editors in the Scriptorium were grateful for anything Dr Minor sent them because his lists were in complete sync with the entries they were preparing week by week.

There *was* something up with the brilliant Dr Minor. He had suffered from paranoid schizophrenia since his teenage years, and had displayed signs of sex addiction. This was not evident in the words he sent in to Murray, but rather in his life choices, or rather consequences.

When he was thirteen years old, Minor's missionary father (his mother died when he was only two) had sent him on a ship from Ceylon to America, to stay with relatives and to attend school in New Haven, Connecticut, because he was worried that his son was too interested in the local girls. After Minor graduated from Yale Medical School in 1863, he served as a surgeon with the Union Army during the American Civil War. He worked on the front line and was traumatized by combat, which, according to his half-brother George, included being ordered to brand an Irish deserter on the cheek with a hot iron. The smell of burning flesh is not easy to forget.

Dr Minor's work in lexicography began in America. As a student at Yale and while serving in the military, he had contributed to the 1864 edition of *Webster's Dictionary* by helping with words related to geology and natural history. After the Civil War, he was posted to New York, but was admonished for visiting brothels on a daily basis. He was sent to an outpost in Florida, where he alleged that his fellow officers were persecuting him. His first stint in an asylum came at the age of thirty-four, six months after his father died. He was diagnosed with delusional monomania and was committed to the Government Hospital for the Insane, now St Elizabeth's Hospital in Washington DC. Three years later, in 1871, he was discharged from the asylum and from the army, and his family sent him to London to convalesce.

Dr Minor rented a room at 44 Tenison Street in Lambeth, a seedy part of London bustling with street stalls, butchers, hatters, stout and whisky dens, the Canterbury Music Hall, the Grove Clothing Factory, the Red Lion Brewery, and prostitutes – plenty of prostitutes. His landlady later told an inquest that he had taken to walking the streets at night, perhaps to find sex or to quieten the voices in his head, or both. She said that on the night in question, Saturday 17 February 1872, her lodger had left the house just before 2 a.m.

At the same time, a few streets away, a man named George Merrett, a coal stoker at the Red Lion Brewery, left his pregnant wife and six children sleeping soundly at home and made his way to the night shift. Just before he reached the brewery gates he was stopped by someone who fired a gun at his head. He managed to turn and avoid being hit. He ran up Belvedere Road and called for help. A second shot was fired, which also missed. But the third shot struck him in the neck. One newspaper reported that after shooting the victim, the murderer ran up and stabbed him several times with an American bowie knife (pronounced *boo-ee*, says Murray in the letter B), and, while the police did find a large bowie knife on the assailant, there was no mention in the inquest that it had been used in the killing.

The police caught the attacker. It was Dr Minor. George Merrett was dead. A journalist reported that when the policeman shone his lantern upon the victim covered in blood on the wet cobbles, Minor exclaimed in an American accent, 'Why that is not the man I wanted!' According to another report on what became known as the Lambeth Murder, later on Saturday morning hundreds of locals gathered on Belvedere Road to 'gawk at a bullet hole' in the wall opposite the brewery gates.

The murder happened seven weeks into Minor's sojourn in England. Searching for a motivation for the killing, one local paper suggested that Dr Minor had frequented a local brothel and been robbed. He mistook Merrett for one of the robbers.

At an inquest, Dr Minor was found not guilty of murder on the grounds of insanity, and imprisoned at Broadmoor Criminal Lunatic Asylum in Crowthorne, Berkshire. He was placed in Block 2, known as the lenient 'privilege block'. Although John Dormer was placed in Croydon Mental Hospital thirty-five years after Minor's committal to Broadmoor, and we might have expected conditions to have improved by then, the difference between the two institutions could not have been starker. Broadmoor, despite its designation for criminals, was extremely considerate of the wants and well-being of its inmates.

I wanted to find out more about Minor's time in the asylum, his work on the Dictionary, and his relationship with Murray, so I travelled to the town of Reading to access the Broadmoor archives at the Berkshire Record Office. I learned that the American Embassy had supported Minor during his trial, and I found several letters from the American Vice Consul General in London, who had written to the asylum superintendent as soon as Minor had arrived, asking if it might be possible to send the inmate certain comforts: tobacco, a meerschaum pipe, cigarette paper, a map and guide of London, underclothes, a diary, a frock coat, a watch and chain, photographs, coffee, French plums, prayer book, nineteen drawing books, a paint box (he painted landscapes), his private library and possessions. The superintendent allowed everything and wrote back, 'The regulations of the asylum permit patients to receive from their friends articles which are not likely to cause injury to themselves or to be prejudicial to the discipline of the asylum.'

By all accounts life at Broadmoor was far from gaol-like. Most rooms had extensive views over the Berkshire countryside. A letter from another inmate, Matthew Jackson Hunter, to his sister in 1883, ten years into Dr Minor's stay at Broadmoor and the same year that he started to read for Murray, describes an asylum that sounds more like a health spa: 'Patients spend most of their time . . . exercising in the gardens, reading the daily papers, monthly periodicals etc., there is also a well selected library . . . a cricket club, billiards, cards and other amusements. In the wintertime we have entertainments given by the patients, such as plays, singing, etc . . . a good brass band which gives selections of music every Monday evening during the summer months on the terrace opposite the chapel.' His description of being treated 'with kindness by the officials placed over us' and being allowed to 'have free conversation among other patients' paints the picture of a humane institution. And everything I found in the archives supported this impression.

Minor's military pension continued while he was in Broadmoor, and came to him via his brother; the asylum allowed him to use his money to purchase anything he desired, within reason, whether it be books, clothes, musical instruments (he played the flute), newspapers, or favourite foods. His book collection grew handsomely as a result and had to be housed in its own cell or 'dayroom'.

Dr Minor was well liked and well supported within the asylum. Not only did he have a sleeping cell and a book cell, he was also even allowed to employ another inmate as a servant. We do not know how he originally found out about the Dictionary project but, each morning, he woke up and walked into his book cell to commence on the reading for Murray which consumed every waking hour. His contribution became so comprehensive that Murray told members of the Philological Society in 1887, 'We could easily illustrate the last 4 centuries from his quotations alone.'

Murray received his first bundle of slips from Minor on 26 June 1883. There were sixty words from the diary of an eighteenth-century soldier in Surinam, including *cashew nut, bamboo, banana, barbeque,* and two particularly unusual ones: *blatta,* insects that shun light; and *wanacoe,* a wild llama. Two months later, fifty slips arrived from John Talbot Dillon's *Travels Through Spain* (1780), bringing several completely new words into the English language: *merino,* a type of sheep; *cedrat,* a type of lemon; *orology,* the study of mountains; and *peseta,* a Spanish silver coin. Minor's career as a supercontributor was off to a great start.

Murray noticed that the sender's address was Broadmoor, Crowthorne, Berkshire. He knew that was the site of a large lunatic asylum but simply assumed that Dr Minor was the medical officer there. Their correspondence was confined to Dictionary matters, so Murray never suspected anything unusual. If anything, he felt gratitude for the man's immense help, and some surprise at the rare and expensive old books that he had access to. When the first volume of the Dictionary came out in 1888, Murray listed 'Dr. W. C. Minor, Crowthorne, Berks.' among other volunteers who had sent in between 5,000 to 8,000 slips.

This continued for several years until around 1890 when Murray received a visit from Harvard University's Librarian, Justin Winsor. Chatting over tea in the Scriptorium, Winsor remarked, 'You have given great pleasure to Americans by speaking as you do in your preface of poor Dr Minor. This is a very painful case.'

'In what way is that?' Murray asked with astonishment.

Winsor was equally astonished that Murray had corresponded with Minor for all these years without ever learning or suspecting anything about him. He then, as Murray later recalled, 'thrilled me with his [Minor's] story'.

We can follow the rest through James Murray: not only did their correspondence span two decades, but we also have Murray's side of the story preserved in a letter he wrote to an American librarian in Boston, Dr Francis Brown, in 1902. By that time, Dr Minor was busy in Broadmoor writing out his lists for words beginning with O after the word *other – othergate, otherguess, otherguise, otherism, otherkin, otherliker, otherness, otherself, otherselfish, otherside, othersome, other-times, otherwards, otherways, otherwhat, otherwhence, otherwhere, otherwhile, otherwhither, otherwise, other-world.* He had also recently sent in slips from Edward Hall's *Chronicle* (1548) for the words *traist,* confidence; *upbearing,* support or sustaining; the proverb *if you want peace prepare for war;* and the expression *to open one's budget* meaning 'to speak one's mind'; and from Ihon Daus's translation of Sleidane's *Commentaries* (1560) for *vaivode,* a local ruler in south-eastern Europe (Transylvania); and the verbs *to addict,* to bind oneself to a person or cause, and *to vail*, to lower as a salute or acknowledgement of inferiority.

Murray described to Brown just how he felt when he had learned the truth of Minor's predicament:

> *I was of course deeply affected by the story, but as Dr Minor had never in the least alluded to himself or his position, all I could do was to write to him more respectfully and kindly than before, so as to show no notice of this disclosure, which I feared might make some change in our relations.*

We then learn from the letter how Murray came to meet the inmate in person:

> *A few years ago an American citizen who called on me told me he had been to see Dr Minor and said he found him rather low and out of spirits, and urged me to go see him. I said I shrank from that, because I had no reason to suppose that Dr Minor thought I knew anything about him personally. He said: 'Yes, he does. He has no doubt that you know all about him, and it really would be a kindness if you would go and see him.'*

There are several letters from Murray in the Broadmoor archives showing that he visited Minor and had lunch with the superintendent on three occasions. The first visit was in January 1891, eight years after Minor had begun as a volunteer:

> *I sat with Dr Minor in his room or cell many hours altogether before and after lunch, and found him, as far as I could see, as sane as myself, a much cultivated and scholarly man, with many artistic tastes, and of fine Christian character, quite resigned to his sad lot, and*

grieved only on account of the restriction it imposed on his usefulness.

I learned (from the Governor, I think) that he has always given a large part of his income to support the widow of the man whose death he so sadly caused, and that she regularly visits him.

Dr Nicholson [the superintendent] had a great opinion of him, gave him many privileges and regularly took distinguished visitors up to his room or cell, to see him and his books. But his successor the present Governor has not shown such special sympathy.

Murray often had to 'manage' the Dictionary People. They may have been volunteers but they required just as much attention and cajoling as paid staff. He responded to their problems, shared in their joys, and encouraged them when their spirits were failing. Minor was no exception, as Murray explained:

He has been very slack altogether for many months, and I have scarcely heard anything from him. He always is less helpful in Summer, because he spends so much more time in the open air, in the garden and grounds. But this year it is worse than usual; and I have been feeling for a good while that I shall have to take a day to go and see him again and try to refresh his interest. In his lonely & sad position he requires a great deal of nursing, encouraging, and coaxing, and I have had to go from time to time to see him.

Minor had been suffering for many years from paranoid delusions and visions, especially at night. He constantly complained that the guards entered his book cell while he slept and tampered with the books he was reading for the Dictionary. 'The defacement of my books still goes on', he wrote to the superintendent, 'it is simply certain that someone besides myself has access to them, and abuses it. Last night soon after I awakened – after 3 – I distinctly heard the door of my workroom closed. Twice before in this night after 12 I had thought I heard it, but this time I was absolutely certain.' The asylum kept meticulous records of the issue. On 5 November 1884, 'Dr Minor complaining that someone has been spoiling his books by marking in them. He says he thinks it is done by attendants Annett & Didham.' On 15 March 1885, 'Says someone went to his book case during the night – Says he had 4 cakes locked up in his box in his bedroom and someone took one of them.' On 23 December 1899, 'WC Minor says he has lost another book out of his room & that somebody in the village must be setting up quite a little library with his books.' On 21 February 1901, 'Dr Minor complains about his dayroom having been entered by someone during the night, he says his servant found a drawer open this morning and that he is sure he left it locked last night. This cannot be true because the door is fastened with two locks and Dr Minor keeps one key himself.'

Minor's delusions of book tampering were interspersed with psychotic hallucinations of sexual assault and persecution. He frequently accused the Broadmoor guards of 'using his body' while in bed in the early morning, or of taking him out at night and forcing him to have sex with women.

The situation reached a climax on Wednesday 3 December 1902. Minor took the knife which he usually used to hand-slit unopened leaves of antiquarian books. He subtly put the knife in the pocket of his coat, and walked to a secluded area of the Broadmoor gardens. Opening his trousers, he held his penis and tied a tourniquet around the base of it, and, with all his surgeon's precision, cut it off.

He was in the infirmary for four months, and survived the mutilation. His contributions to the Dictionary never really picked up again, and any hope that removing his penis might also remove his sexual delusions did not work.

Despite all of this, as I was looking through the Broadmoor archives I was struck by how compelling and charming Minor must have been in person. On paper, he clearly suffered from serious mental illness but in person everyone who met him – including Murray – repeatedly praised him as 'sane', 'cultivated', 'sensible', and 'scholarly'. He had an impressive number of supporters and friends advocating for him, visiting him, and writing to the superintendent enquiring after his well-being. I was surprised to see letters from another of the Dictionary People, James Russell Lowell, who was American Ambassador in London in the 1880s and regularly wrote to Broadmoor to check on how the American inmate was doing. Minor was generous with his books, sending many to the Scriptorium in 1902 when his health was failing and he was unable to read them himself (Murray found other Readers for them). He was also generous with his money, and it was due to a gift from Minor that James and Ada were able to visit their son in South Africa in 1905.

In 1910, thanks to a concerted effort by Murray, the superintendent of Broadmoor, members of Minor's family in America, the American Embassy, a number of professors and the Presidents of Yale and Harvard, and Winston Churchill, who was Home Secretary at the time, Minor was transferred to America. His thirty-eight years at Broadmoor were over. Although it had been several years since Minor had sent any slips to the Scriptorium, Murray wrote to the asylum on 7 April 1910 requesting one final visit: 'As there is a likelihood that my old friend Dr W. C. Minor may soon leave your institution, I would rather like to come & say good bye to him on Saturday next, and if the day were fine would perhaps bring Lady Murray with me.' The superintendent granted permission immediately, and added, 'He is much better in health just now than he has been for some time past, & I think that he will be pleased to see you.'

Records in the asylum noted: 'Dr Minor was escorted on Saturday the 16th [April 1910] to Tilbury Deck by an attendant and was handed over to his brother on board the steamer.' Upon landing in America, he was committed to the Government Hospital for the Insane again, and ultimately moved to the Retreat for the Elderly Insane in Hertford, Connecticut, where he died in 1920 at the age of eighty-five. By then, he had gained global notoriety as both a Dictionary contributor and a murderer, and his obituary appeared from Washington to Australia and England.

*

In addition to Dr Minor, I mentioned that I had found two other (unconvicted) murderers among the Dictionary People.

You may remember Sir John Richardson who spent the final years of his life sitting beside his daughter Beatrice at their home in the Lake District, reconnecting with his Scottish childhood by reading Robbie Burns and Sir Walter Scott for the OED. He had been an explorer of Franklin's ill-fated Northwest Passage where he had unwittingly engaged in cannibalism and, to protect himself and others, had killed a suspected rogue member of his exploration team.

The other murderer was an Englishman living in California, and the founding father of motion photography.

Eadweard Muybridge was born in Surrey in 1830, and in his early twenties moved from England to New York where, displaying an entrepreneurial spirit, he developed a prosperous book-importing business and got involved in the emerging field of photography and daguerreotype (silver-covered copper-plate photographs). At the age of twenty-five, in 1855, he seized an opportunity to move to San Francisco, which was thriving financially amid the Gold Rush, and opened a shop selling books and photographs. The latter sold particularly well, so he trained in wet-plate photography and made a name for himself capturing views of Yosemite under the pseudonym of 'Helios', eventually becoming lead photographer on government expeditions exploring the north-west and other parts of the country. On one trip, he nearly died in a stagecoach accident, suffering serious head injury, after which he was reportedly never the same and displayed erratic, eccentric, compulsive, and violent behaviour.

At the age of forty-one, he married a divorcee twenty-one years younger, Flora Shallcross Stone. A year later, his career took off thanks to a commission from the wealthy railroad baron Leland Stanford. Stanford owned racehorses and asked Muybridge to help him with an experiment to see if horses ever ran with all four hooves off the ground (apparently he had a bet of $25,000 riding on the result). Debate about the mechanics of a horse's gallop had captivated casual observers and scientists for several years before Stanford had the bright idea of trying to capture in photography what could not be seen with the human eye. It was a radical suggestion at the time because motion photography did not yet exist. Muybridge was breaking new ground when he rigged up multiple cameras with the equivalent of a high-speed shutter to record, at five-thousandths of a second, the silhouette of Stanford's champion racehorse in motion.

Muybridge's shutter invention took some fine-tuning, but the photographs eventually proved that horses did gallop at times with all four hooves off the ground. Stanford won the bet and hailed Muybridge a hero. He had succeeded in pushing the boundaries of technology, and his work led directly to the development of motion pictures. The photographs of the horse in motion became iconic examples of Leland Stanford's vision of science and entrepreneurship (he and his wife Jane went on to found Stanford University in the heart of what became Silicon Valley). To this day, Muybridge's images are proudly and permanently displayed in the Cantor Arts Center on the Stanford University campus as an example of the intersection of creativity, science, and innovation.

Muybridge and his young bride were enjoying his new-found celebrity when they were befriended by a roguish and good-looking Englishman who had just arrived in San Francisco. The charming Harry Larkyns was single and thirty-five years old. He tried his hand at reporting for the San Francisco *Evening Post*; he helped out at a circus; and he ended up living in the Napa Valley town of Calistoga, mapping mines. Muybridge's fame had spread and he was often away, taking up new photographic commissions around rural California. Arriving home from one particular trip, he had his suspicions that Harry had struck up a relationship with Flora, and warned him never to visit their house again. It was too late; Harry and Flora had fallen in love and the relationship continued. Muybridge confronted Larkyns at the *Evening Post*, they engaged in a struggle, and he punched Larkyns. He then left. For a time, however, the lovers continued to meet secretly at a rented room on Montgomery Street, not far from Muybridge's bookshop.

Muybridge thought things had settled down when, in 1874, Flora gave birth to their first child, a son named after both parents and as such a renewal of ties: Florado Helios Muybridge.

Muybridge proudly took many photographs of his new son, and all seemed happy in the marital home. What he did not know was that Flora was still secretly corresponding with Larkyns who was now mapping mines in Calistoga. She had a nursemaid, Mrs Smith, helping her with the baby.

One autumn day in October 1874, Mrs Smith confronted Muybridge to ask for her wages, which he was late in paying. When he refused to give her the money, she produced a bundle of love letters between Flora and Larkyns. 'Will you pay me now?!' she asked.

Among the letters, Muybridge found an envelope addressed to Harry Larkyns. Inside was one of the photos of baby Florado, on the back of which his wife had written 'Little Harry'.

Muybridge woke early and packed a gun. The morning fog was rolling into San Francisco Bay as he boarded a ferry boat to Vallejo and a train to Napa Valley in pursuit of Larkyns on Saturday 17 October 1874. He asked around Calistoga – everyone knew Larkyns but he had left town for a mapping job at Yellow Jacket mine. Nothing was to dissuade Muybridge who paid a carriage man $5 to take him to Larkyns. En route, he urged the driver to go faster, and asked, 'Any danger of robbers around here? Mind if I try my pistol?' He discharged his gun into the air; it was working.

It was nearly midnight when Muybridge arrived at the door of a cabin where Larkyns was playing cards. He asked for Larkyns, and when he came to the door, Muybridge declared, 'I have brought you a message from my wife.' He shot him at point blank.

Muybridge was immediately arrested.

Stanford came to his aid financially, and at the three-day trial Muybridge had the best lawyer who pleaded insanity and justifiable homicide, testifying that the accused's mental state had been adversely affected by his previous head injury. 'Years ago the prisoner was thrown from a stage, receiving a concussion of the brain, which turned his hair from black to gray in three days, and has never been the same since.' The lawyer painted a picture of a devoted and passionate husband; 'he was wrapped up in her and lived only for her', he told the court.

The judge heard that baby Florado had been born at half past two in the morning. Muybridge was away travelling at the time, so Flora was supported by Mrs Smith and a doctor. Mrs Smith verified that Larkyns was there too, 'bent over her when in bed and in the agonies of child-birth'. Mrs Smith testified that Mrs Muybridge was indeed having an affair with the murder victim. She had been looking after the baby one afternoon when Mrs Muybridge and Larkyns were in bed next door. Mrs Smith was called in, and there lay Flora, 'her bosom bare, and Larkyns with his hand on her shoulder'.

Muybridge's lawyer explained that when Mrs Smith had told Muybridge that the child was not his, 'from that moment he was not himself. Strung up to the pitch with insanity, he made up his mind that he must slay the destroyer of his happiness – the man who had debauched his home. The prisoner went to kill that man. He would have followed him to the ends of the earth for that purpose.'

Muybridge was acquitted.

He hastily divorced his young wife, who died the following year, and Florado was placed in an orphanage. Muybridge took a photographic commission in Central America for some years, after which he returned to his life in San Francisco and to some extent regained his reputation. He always disowned Florado. Stanford continued to be Muybridge's patron, sponsoring him for a few years to do more photographic experiments with the horse in motion at his stud in Palo Alto (the farm which became the site of Stanford University), and this led to several successful photography patents.

That is, until 1882 when relations soured between Muybridge and his generous patron. Muybridge was involved in a legal dispute in which he had fraudulently patented a camera device which had actually been created by a mechanical engineer working for Stanford. In addition, Stanford had commissioned a comprehensive study of horses in motion not from Muybridge but from Dr Jacob Davis Stillman, personal physician to Stanford. The study resulted in a book, generously funded and published by Stanford, called *Horses in Motion* (1882). When Stillman's book came out, it reproduced drawings of the photographs taken by Muybridge, but only mentioned him cursorily in the preface and appendix. Muybridge had no sure claim on the images, and his legal actions against Stanford and Stillman failed.

Nevertheless, Muybridge published his own work and the book that he is best-known for is a massive eleven-volume reference work on animal locomotion, *Animals in Motion* (1899). He created numerous cameras which could photograph an animal from several perspectives, involving 100,000 photographic plates. The book provides the first written example of the word *electrophotographic*, of or pertaining to photography aided by electricity or electric light.

We don't know how Muybridge got involved with the Dictionary, but he was thanked by Henry Bradley in the preface to the section Frank-law to Glass-cloth. There are entries he advised on as a Specialist including that for *gallop* which was published in April 1899 with a quotation from Muybridge's book *Descriptive Zoopraxography*: 'The gallop is the most rapid method of quadrupedal motion; in its action the feet are independently brought to the ground; the spring into the air as in the canter is effected from a fore foot, and the landing upon the diagonal hind-foot.' He also provided quotations for (mostly American) horse-riding terms relating to the gait of a horse such as *rack*, 'an ungraceful gait of the horse, and disagreeable to those who seek comfort in riding'; and *single-foot*, 'the amble has various local names such as the "single foot", the "fox trot", etc'.

Muybridge is credited in the OED for coining two words: *zoopraxiscope* and *zoogyroscope*, devices for projecting photographic images of moving animals. He is mentioned in quite a few OED entries: for *kinematograph*, a device used for recording motion pictures and projecting them onto a screen, 'After Muybridge's experiments, it would take only a few more innovative steps to Thomas Edison's Kinetoscope and the Kinematograph of the Lumiere Brothers'; for *motion studies*, an artistic and photographic study of physical movement, 'Stanford hired Eadweard Muybridge, a photographer interested in motion studies, to train his cameras on one of the governor's horses'; and for *sky shade*, a screen attached to a camera to shade the lens from bright light from the sky, 'designed and patented by English photographer E. Muybridge (1830–1904) in 1869'.

Muybridge never married again and ended up living back in England with a cousin in a small house in Kingston upon Thames in south-west London. Eccentric to the end, he died on 8 May 1904 while building a miniature scale reproduction of the American Great Lakes in his back garden. His son, Florado Muybridge, kept his father's name, and spent his life working as a labourer clearing farmland in California; he lived by himself in rented accommodation, never married, and died in Sacramento in 1944.

N

for NEW ZEALANDERS

Alongside the address-book entry for W. Herbert-Jones, FRGS, of 46 Albany Mansions, Albert Bridge Road, London, Murray had written 'New Zealand Wds'. Who was this person living in London but sending in words from the Antipodes?

Trying to answer this question sent me on one of the wilder research adventures of this whole book. Google 'William Herbert-Jones' and you get an air officer who died in the First World War at the age of thirty-five. That's not our guy.

Our William Herbert-Jones FRGS was a charismatic, yet controversial, character who was described on official documents as 'traveller and lecturer'. He was more of a showman and entertainer than a scholar.

The good-looking and enigmatic Herbert-Jones spent his early thirties touring Britain giving a popular talk to paying audiences on 'New Zealand, Wonderland of the World'. His sold-out lectures in the 1890s were accompanied by the cutting-edge technology of the day – magic lantern slides. Crowds from Dublin to London, and many villages in between, flocked to hear Herbert-Jones's mesmerizing stories and to watch images which very few Britons had ever seen before – of serene fjords, boiling geysers, Māori chiefs, and exotic birds on the other side of the world.

Herbert-Jones's spellbinding lectures were reviewed in local newspapers the day after to high acclaim: 'a powerful speaker and entertainer', 'a brilliant and popular lecturer', 'a born orator' speaking on 'the marvellous wonders of New Zealand'. People from all social classes queued in snow and rain to pay their 2 shillings (adults) and 1 shilling (children) to hear him. They knew nothing about New Zealand, and they believed every word he uttered.

As William Herbert-Jones walked onto the stage of a packed town hall, the lights were dimmed, the magic lantern was lit up behind him with an image of snowy New Zealand alps, and the audience hushed. He was dressed in splendid white tie, waistcoat, a cut-away evening coat with tails, double-braided trousers, white silk braces, and patent-leather dancing pumps. The acrid smell of the limelight lantern hung in the air. As he began to speak, his foppish hair bounced with every dramatic gesture:

'New Zealand is the world's wonderland. There is nothing in Alice's Wonderland so wonderful as what is to be seen in New Zealand. Hot lakes, fiery volcanoes, kauri forests, southern alps, gorges and sounds.'

Reaching his right arm to the ceiling for dramatic effect and projecting his voice directly to those crammed into the back row, Herbert-Jones continued:

'A vast land of 11,000 miles from north to south, New Zealand is one of the brightest gems amongst the jewels which deck the crown of British possessions.

'Animals and plants found nowhere else on earth bemuse the visitor,' he went on. *'There are birds fifteen feet high that lay eggs a foot long. Huge mecca palms grow in natural groves, and ferns abound in variety and splendour. The curay, which is something between a rat and a mouse, goes about in herds. Not to mention large black venomous katipo spiders, small green karariki parakeets, wailing kaka parrots, and large kakapo owls that make a deep booming call and live for 80 years.'*

Herbert-Jones's demonstrative speaking style captured
by an illustrator at *The New Zealand Observer*
(8 December 1894).

Projecting an image of a Māori chief with a long white-tipped feather in his hair, Herbert-Jones was in full stride: '*Huia feathers come from a stunning woodpecker.*' (He made a loud hooting call imitating the bird's peculiar whistle, at which the audience laughed.) '*These black birds, which have bright orange patches on either side of their bills, are a sign of sacred power for the Māoris who are amongst the finest races on earth. They greet each other by rubbing noses which accounts for their flat noses. Māoris live in fortified pah camps. Their war weapons and fortifications are the study and admiration of the soldier. Before going to war they call on their native God of the same name, Pah.*'

Raising his arms in warrior stance, stamping his feet, Herbert-Jones shouted into the air: '*Ake, Ake, Ake is their battle cry – we will fight for ever and ever! The origins of this noble people are still a mystery, their language is one of the most dulcet known, their ancient customs are a strange mixture of barbarism and chivalry, their carvings are a puzzle to the archaeologists. I was one of two Europeans to attend a funeral tangi ceremony, and the echoing notes of the Māori dirges still haunt me.*'

Suddenly the supply of hydrogen gas failed on the magic lantern and the hall fell into darkness, forcing him to finish somewhat abruptly. The consummate entertainer, Herbert-Jones stood alone in the dim light with a straight spine, chest out. He opened his mouth and sang a deep-toned Māori funeral song which sent a shiver down the spines of everyone present. The crowd rose to its feet, full of the wonders of New Zealand, and the two-and-a-half-hour lecture ended in thunderous applause.

Yet Herbert-Jones's reputation suffered a blow in 1892. One of the English newspaper reviews was sent to a journalist in New Zealand who in turn wrote an article exposing Herbert-Jones as a fraud. Under the headline 'A Queer Account of New Zealand', Herbert-Jones was mocked across that country, from Auckland's *Evening Post* in the North Island to Nelson's *Evening Mail* in the South Island.

The newspaper articles exposed fake parts of the 'most fearfully and wonderfully wrong' lecture: the distance from north to south was not 11,000 miles; there was no such thing as a mecca palm; there were no curay rats, let alone herds of curay rats; there were no 15-foot-high birds laying eggs a foot long, not to mention the ludicrous suggestion that Māoris had flat noses because they greeted each other by rubbing noses, or that they called their God Pah. Mr Herbert-Jones's lectures were in essence 'the most deliciously humorous things we have read for many a long day'. 'If many English audiences are treated to such lectures . . . we should not wonder that marvellous misconceptions about the Antipodes are still rife at Home.'

If the lectures were fantastical then what about the words Herbert-Jones (apparently) collected for the Dictionary and the very identity of the man himself?

Many of the plants and animals of New Zealand which featured in Herbert-Jones's lectures made their way into the Dictionary – *huia, katipo,* and *kakapo* – not because of his lecture but because Readers found them in printed sources. His other words such as *curay* and *mecca* (happily) never made it, precisely because there was no evidence for them. Every New Zealand word that did get into the Dictionary – such as *kauri* forests; *huia* birds; *kareao* vines; *poroporo* strawberries; *towai* trees; and *pah* fortified villages – was substantiated by legitimate citations from authoritative sources.

If Herbert-Jones was not a legitimate expert on New Zealand, I wanted to find out why he was listed as such in Murray's address book. It turned out that his life contained a tantalizing mix of truths and fictions. His lectures on New Zealand had not been original. They had been delivered several years earlier by an American for whom Herbert-Jones had been a business manager. I checked if Herbert-Jones had ever actually been to New Zealand. He had, but not until *after* he had given the dubious lectures in England. And when he finally travelled there to tell the New Zealanders about themselves in a lecture called 'Our Country – the World's Wonderland' (and one on 'Australia, the Land of Topsy-Turvydom'!) he received a mixed reception, as summed up by a letter to the editor in the Auckland *Evening Post*:

> *The fact is there are thousands of men in this colony who could tell more in five minutes . . . than Mr Jones can in a week, and who could not only pronounce the musical Māori tongues, but also the Queen's English. The sooner*

*the Government obtains someone to teach Mr Jones his
subject and revise his lectures the better . . . Mr Jones'
statements will be news to those best acquainted with
the localities which he 'describes'. For instance, it will be
news . . . that Heta Te Hara (dead) is the 'last surviving
Ngapuhi chief' and that the missionary-bred Hone Heke
was an atrocious cannibal . . . It will be news to Māori
linguists to know that the words 'Ake Ake Ake' mean 'We
will fight for ever and ever', and so will a great many of
Mr Jones' Māori pronunciations. While as to some of the
splendid views shown, the description given of them will
be decidedly new to those who knew the original.*

He did, however, find a little local support and managed
to charm senior government officials into commissioning
him to write a book on New Zealand for British tourists and
potential settlers, and to pay him to return to England to give
'one thousand lectures' on the country. Neither the book nor
the lectures eventuated, and one suspects the money was not
returned.

His shady practices made me question the validity of
the initials after his name, 'FRGS', which no doubt added
to his profile and lustre as an authoritative public lecturer.
The archivist at the prestigious Royal Geographical Society
helped me find his name in the Society records. He was made
a member but strangely had started to use the initials at least
a year beforehand.

And then Herbert-Jones vanishes. A note in Murray's address book tells us that he last corresponded with him about
a New Zealand word, *huia*, on 5 December 1898. After this
date, Herbert-Jones completely disappears from all public
(and OED) record. His lectures went from being frequently
advertised and reviewed to nothing: from Herbert-Jones
there was now absolute silence. He had not died, or gone to

prison (although in my search of the Old Bailey I discovered that, two decades earlier, a twenty-two-year-old 'William Herbert Edward Jones', with the same birth date as our man, had been imprisoned for six months without hard labour for deception and fraud). He popped up ten years later giving a lecture in Liverpool. He had changed his surname to Garrison and his subject was – you guessed it – 'New Zealand, the Wonderland of the World'. Maybe he changed his name to avoid the brouhaha surrounding his earlier lectures on New Zealand or to escape the consequences of defaulting on his agreement with the New Zealand government, but during the war 'William Herbert Garrison' worked for the War Office giving propaganda talks on the Empire. His career then took a turn towards religion. He joined the British Israelites, a heterodox religious movement that believed that the Lost Tribes of Israel had settled in Britain. He was convinced that Armageddon would be ushered in on 29 May 1928 and, when that did not happen, he believed that the Second Coming would happen in 1936 – an event he never got to see not happen because he died in London the previous July.

If William Herbert-Jones/Garrison was not Murray's man on the ground in New Zealand, who was sending in the authentic New Zealand and Māori words?

Was it the Revd Ernest Hampden Cook? In 1888, when the first volume of the Dictionary came out, Murray credited 'Rev. E. H. Cook, B. A. , New Zealand' for sending in 5,000 slips. Cook was living in a squalid, overcrowded goldfield in New Zealand. Now a missionary, as a boy Cook had been taught by Murray at Mill Hill School. By the time he was in New Zealand, he had been sending his old teacher thousands of slips for nearly a decade: first from Cambridge where he was an undergraduate, then from Lancashire College in Manchester where he trained for the ministry, and then from Upper Clapton in London. He not only sent slips to Murray but also corresponded with him, relating news of other former Mill Hill pupils and using him as a referee when he hoped that the Nonconformist Dr Williams's library might support his preparation for ministry with a scholarship, given his 'pecuniary circumstances' (they didn't). As he was finishing his studies at Lancashire College in 1886, Cook confided in Murray his hopes for his ministry and his search for a pulpit of his own. Finally, he was appointed to a post – but very far from home. He was to be Minister of the Congregationalist Church on Mary Street in the Thames Gold-field, south-east of Auckland.

As soon as Ernest Hampden-Cook arrived by steamer on the muddy shores of the makeshift town of Thames, he would have understood why Captain Cook (no relation) had given it that name a century earlier. The estuary smelled like the muddy shores of the river in London, but not quite as bad as the Great Stink. Here, the mud stretched for half a mile at low tide, and the Hauraki mud flats merged into mangrove and saltmarsh, attracting the most exquisite and noisy birds an Englishman had ever seen. There was only a narrow window each day, at high tide, when the steamer could land, launch-ing passengers to walk a long, dangerous plank between the marsh ribbonwood trees, onto the swampy streets of Thames. 'You can hardly call them streets', wrote a visitor in the North Island *West Coast Times*, 'they are nothing but swamps, up to your knees in mud.' Despite attempts to drain it by build-ing dykes, the *Thames Miners' Guide* warned, 'You cannot walk along the streets without danger of being swamped.'

The seams of gold that attracted people to these smelly mud flats lay behind the town in the densely forested slopes and creeks. Native peach trees and kauri groves were cleared to allow a myriad of mining tunnels to penetrate the scarred landscape at sites evocatively named Poor Man's Friend, Homeward Bound, Shamrock, and Happy Go Lucky. The local rangatira Māori Chief, named Te Hira Te Tuiri, famously remarked on the evil of the mining at Thames, 'What is the use of the land after it is broken?'

Eighteen thousand gold diggers were crammed into a mile radius, and a few hundred others were brought in to support them – publicans, missionaries, police, tobacconists, theatre entertainers, women. Life was crude and raw. Hopeful prospectors, caught by gold fever, flocked here to make their fortunes. They slept wherever they could find space to build a corrugated-iron shack or to pitch a tent made from stitched flour bags. The dirt floors turned to mud all too quickly, attracting mosquitoes and sandflies which crazed the inhabitants of Thames.

Across Kawaranga (now Kauaeranga) Creek from the Church Mission Station, life was completely different for the Māori settlement with its ordered whares (traditional huts) which stretched across the valley, majestically framed by a low mountain range on three sides and the Thames River flowing on the other. Everyone who crossed the creek and climbed a hill to view the Māori settlement was filled with awe at the scene below. The contrast with the diggers' township was stark.

In Thames, the young Revd Cook, still only in his late twenties, ministered to disheartened men who spent their days shovelling gravel, sifting sluice boxes, building crushing batteries, or desperately fossicking in the holes of absent diggers. There were quiet times, when the smell of stewed kiwi (the bird not the fruit) would emerge from the hut of a lonely digger, but those times were rare and short-lived. Soon the noise of the evening revels took over. The white settler diggers spent their nights gambling and drinking at the Lady Bowen and Shortland Hotel, followed by bawdy liaisons with dance girls and prostitutes at Rose's Free and Easy. Chinese diggers – segregated from the whites – had their own camps further up Hape Creek, where they too drank and gambled late into the night.

Being a missionary in this setting was no easy ride. Pastors were not much in favour amongst the gold-digging class. Pickings were slim. Crime was high. Conditions were insanitary. Disease was rife. Mine injuries and deaths were a daily occurrence. It was no coincidence that Cook's Congregational Church on Mary Street was a short walk up the hill from the lock-up, the courthouse, and the burial ground.

The burial ground, on the edge of the mud flats, was a good place to escape the crowds and to seek silence and solitude. It was here, under the shade of the wide-spreading *pohutukawa* trees, flowering like bonfires, that you could take a book and escape the noisy saloons and sly-grog shops. As beautiful as these graceful native trees were with their clusters of blood-red flowers blooming at Christmas time, they were associated with death amongst the local Māori who believed that the flaming red, brush-like flowers with their long stamens were the bloodstains of a young warrior Tāwhaki who had fallen from heaven while trying to avenge the death of his father. The white settlers called them Christmas trees.

Cook replenished his spirits by reading for Murray and writing out slips. But, I discovered, it was not the words of the goldfields or the names of the trees and birds of New Zealand which he collected for Murray. Instead, Cook sought solace in religious texts which he found personally uplifting such as *Lectures in Aid of Self-Improvement Addressed to Young Men and Others* (1853). 'Self-improvement is the improvement of ourself by our own exertions', began the book by the hymn-writer Thomas Toke Lynch. Cook earnestly copied out the next sentence, and it now resides in the Dictionary's entry for *self-improver*: 'The self-improver is both a labourer and a field of labour; a labourer in his own field.'

Perhaps it was a matter of pride for Cook that he worked on the Dictionary, something he talked about with colleagues in the rough setting of their work. In 1884, when the first part of the Dictionary was published, Murray received a fan letter from a government surveyor in the same goldfield. The writer, whose signature is difficult to decipher, praises Murray in a most delightful fashion: 'I have hopes that when the vast material undertaking that you and your assistants are employed at is finished, that placed beside the two national dictionaries of France and Germany, the one may look il-Littreate and the other very Grimm in comparison. Please excuse the attempt at a pun. I put it down to exuberance of spirits at the thought that at last the English language is about to receive due justice.'

The government surveyor's letter illustrates the widespread enthusiasm of so many for the Dictionary. There he was, living on the other side of the world, working in tough conditions, and yet he couldn't wait to get hold of the finished product. 'We look forward to the six vols of 4 parts to each vol of 250 pages with pleasure. Send them along, and every one of us that have these volumes on our bookshelves need not trouble about a library, or joining a circulating library, they will have a library always with them that will take them all their lives to get through, and they can bequeath their research to their children's children as an heirloom.' He ends his letter to Murray with a funny story: 'A Wisconsin farmer returned a dictionary to his neighbour from whom he had borrowed it, with the remark that the thing was pretty good, but "the blarsted book hasn't got an index".'

After New Zealand and a stint in Australia, Cook returned to England and worked as secretary to the Baptist biblical scholar and philologist, Richard F. Weymouth, another OED contributor and former headmaster of Mill Hill School. As a devoted Millhillian, Cook worked as secretary to the school in later life, and kept Murray in touch with Millhillian gossip. But he was not the source of the OED's New Zealand words. I needed to keep searching.

I scoured the address books and found that a vicar, the Revd Thomas Burditt, living in Yorkshire (we will learn more about him in V for Vicars) had sent in fifty words from Lady Barker's *Station Life in New Zealand* (1870). But the true source of New Zealand words came from an Englishman living in Melbourne, Australia: Edward Ellis Morris.

Morris had responded to Dr Murray's appeal by reading as many 'Australasian' (Australian and New Zealand) books as he could obtain. He had been born in India, educated at Rugby and Oxford, and worked as headmaster of Bedford County School before going to Australia in 1875 to be headmaster of Melbourne Grammar School. After seven years he was sacked, or resigned (it was complicated), for strict discipline and financial mismanagement. Luckily for him the British expat boys' club of early colonial Melbourne kicked in, and he ended up at the University of Melbourne as Professor of Modern Languages and Literatures and on the Council of Trinity College, where the previous librarian at the grammar school, Alexander Leeper (also a contributor to the Dictionary), was then Warden.

Morris was one of those volunteers who started to read for the Dictionary and became obsessed. He not only collected words himself but was soon evangelical in reaching out to friends and colleagues in New Zealand and Australia, asking them for help too. Two people in Dunedin helped by gathering quotations and giving advice on Māori words and New Zealand plants and animals: Dr Thomas Hocken was a physician with New Zealand's largest private book collection, and Frederick Revans Chapman was a barrister with a keen interest in botany and Māori culture (he later became a Supreme Court Judge, the first person born in New Zealand to do so). Thanks to their help Morris was able to give detail on plants such as the *ribbonwood* tree, which has several alternative names – *houi* in Māori; *lace-bark* tree because it had inner bark 'like fine lace'; and in the South Island, *thousand-jacket* tree because 'the bark peels, and peels, and peels again'. (All these got into the Dictionary.)

In the New Zealand capital of Wellington, Morris was assisted by a poet, Miss Mary Colborne-Veel, and her sister Gertrude; and Mr Edward Tregear, who had lived in Māori communities, had written a *Māori–Polynesian Comparative Dictionary*, and was able to help with the definition of *kava*, a narcotic and stimulant beverage which is prepared from a plant root and chewed by the natives of Fiji who spit the saliva into a kava bowl. In the town of Oamaru, the writer Mr William H. S. Roberts clarified the meaning of many New Zealandisms such as *futtah*, a corruption of the Māori word *whata* which is a raised storage container with bevelled edges designed to deter rats; *piwakawaka*, a pied fantail bird; *Scotchman*, a type of New Zealand speargrass; and *taipo*, an evil spirit. Morris also consulted Roberts's book *Southland in 1856–57* which provided quotations for all these words.

Morris collected words such as *frost fish*, a delicacy so-called because it is 'found alive on New Zealand sea-beaches on frosty nights', and provided detail on entries such as the *pohutukawa* tree, known to Hampden-Cook and inhabitants of Thames as *Christmas trees* or *fire trees*, the bark of which, Morris said, was used to treat dysentery.

It was through newspapers that Morris reached New Zealanders. In one article in the *Otago Daily Times* on 1 February 1896 (and republished in several newspapers around New Zealand), he asked them to read their local 'books, periodicals, or newspapers' for New Zealand words. 'Each quotation should be written on a separate small slip of paper, with the word at the head, and then sources, together with the date of publication, in every case.' He listed 150 New Zealand words for which he needed more quotations such as *hoot*, New Zealand slang for money; *weta*, described by Morris as 'a huge

Edward Ellis Morris collected so many words from
Australia and New Zealand that he decided to publish
his own dictionary, *Austral English* (1898).

ugly grasshopper' (google and decide for yourself); *kohua*, a
Māori oven; various trees, such as *kauri, koromiko, ngaio, raupo*;
fish, *spotty, hoki, patiki*; and birds, *rifleman, roa, whio*.

The New Zealand volunteers also provided useful comparisons between New Zealand and Australia. The large, venomous *katipo* spider, which is black with a red spot on its back,
is generally found on the beach under old driftwood in New
Zealand, but it is also found widely scattered across Australia
and always frequents dark sheltered spots. He suggested that it
was possibly derived from Māori *kakati*, to sting, and *-po*, night.

Morris asked New Zealanders to send their materials
to him via Dr Hocken in Dunedin. Not only did this arrangement save expensive international postage for the volunteers but it also had benefits for Dr Hocken who had a

vast library of early New Zealand books, including the letters and journals of the famous missionary Samuel Marsden, and was creating a comprehensive bibliography of New Zealand books. The slips sent from members of the public alerted him to anything missing from his bibliography (and his collection). Hocken also wrote his own books and articles on New Zealand history and books. Towards the end of his life, he donated his private library, which had supplied so many words for the OED, to the University of Otago to be free for the public. The Hocken Library was opened in 1910 and has since grown into the renowned 'Hocken Collections' comprising a library, museum, and art gallery in Dunedin.

No OED editors were aware of Dr Hocken's indirect contribution to the Dictionary's coverage of New Zealand words (and, because he sent his work to Morris in Melbourne, his name never appeared in Murray's address books), and he was therefore never acknowledged. However, he appeared in the Dictionary later when subsequent OED editors cited his published articles for three New Zealand words. Hence, Dr Hocken's memory is preserved in the entries for *mihanere*, a Māori convert to Christianity; *nugget*, a rocky outcrop or islet in the sea; and *Tiki*, a large wooden image of Tiki, the creator and first created being of the Māoris.

After a few years of collecting Australasian words, Morris realized that he had far too much material for the scope of Murray's Dictionary. As he put it, 'Dr Murray several years ago invited assistance from this end of the world for words and uses of words peculiar to Australasia, or to parts of it. In answer to his call I began to collect . . . The work took time, and when my parcel of quotations had grown into a considerable heap, it occurred to me that the collection, if a little further trouble were expended upon it, might first enjoy an independent existence.'

Collecting for the OED had made Morris realize that Australia and New Zealand lacked a local literature that reflected the spoken tongue. Morris made a plea at a conference of librarians in 1900 that 'books dealing with Australian subjects and with local colour should be received more readily here, and that Australian libraries should buy them'. After all, it was availability of written evidence that got a word in the OED, not whether it was spoken. Regional varieties of English which were spoken in young British colonies lacked published sources.

Morris decided to use all the material he had collected for the OED for his own Australasian dictionary. *Austral English: A Dictionary of Australasian Words, Phrases and Usages* was published in 1898. Modelled on the OED, each entry had dated citations showing the word's usage across time. Morris had created a superb record of Australian and New Zealand English in the nineteenth century. Although he was awarded a Doctor of Letters from Melbourne University the year after the dictionary was published, he deserves more credit for his extraordinary accomplishment and, even today, his dictionary deserves to be better known than it is.

Murray credited Morris's dictionary in the body of the OED (in various entries for New Zealand and Australian words) but, strangely, never acknowledged him personally in the Dictionary prefaces or in his lectures at the Philological Society. Morris had been extremely generous with his content. He copied duplicates of each slip for Murray and shared proofs of his dictionary which resulted in the OED citing Morris's dictionary before it was even published in 1898. A year earlier, Murray quoted from Morris's (yet unpublished dictionary) in the Australian sense of the verb *dump*, to compress wool bales; and Henry Bradley put '(Morris)' beside the first quotation for the verb to *fossick* – a word well-known to Hampden-Cook at Thames which meant 'to pick out gold'.

It worked both ways. Morris gained feedback from Murray as sections were completed, and he included some of Murray's comments verbatim in his dictionary, as can be seen in his entry for *creek*, a brook: 'Dr J. A. H. Murray kindly sends the following note:- "Creek goes back to the early days of exploration. Men sailing up the Mississippi or other navigable river saw the mouths of tributary streams, but could not tell with out investigation whether they were confluences or mere inlets, creeks. They called them creeks, but many of them turned out to be running streams, many miles long – tributary rivers or rivulets. The name creek stuck to them, however, and thus became synonymous with tributary stream, brook." 'Murray included a version of this same note in his 'U. S. and British Colonies' sense of the word. Murray was a mentor to Morris, advising him to acknowledge every source for every word, a practice which Morris followed scrupulously despite difficulties; 'but it is not always easy to trace the source whence information has been derived', he admitted in the preface of *Austral English*.

It takes a village to create a good dictionary, and Morris was not alone in his task of documenting the language of Australasia. In addition to his faithful helpers in New Zealand, he was supported by over two hundred volunteers in Australia. His key collaborators were four scholars at the University of Melbourne: Edward Sugden (Master of Queen's College), Edward Hippius Bromby (University Librarian), Alexander Leeper (Warden of Trinity College), and Richard Thomas Elliott (Classical Lecturer at Trinity College). The Melbourne Dictionary People, as I refer to them, are a classic example of how elite British expats negotiated and maintained their power in a new colony. All of these men had been born and educated in Britain (most attended Oxford), and moved to Australia to work at the Melbourne Grammar School where Bromby's father was the first headmaster, before all moving on (at slightly different times, but thanks to the support of the others) to work at the University of Melbourne. Sugden had been volunteering for Murray for many years before leaving England. Elliott, who had studied and lived in Oxford, was known to Murray too.

Morris provided Murray with everything he needed for New Zealand entries in the OED – etymologies, definitions, and quotations. Murray's detailed entry for *pah* or *pa*, a native fort or fortified camp in New Zealand, benefited from Morris's knowledge that the word came from the Māori verb *pa*, to block up (a collection of houses to which access is blocked by means of stockades and ditches). Morris pointed out that it is sometimes written as *hippah* from taking the definite article *he-* in Māori as part of the word. Morris had collected three *pa* quotations from various travellers' tales, including the first time it was used in a written source by Captain James Cook (in his diary). Murray included all these, plus a couple of quotations which he found himself. Similarly, Murray supplemented parts of the entry for *kea*, a green, flesh-eating parrot that kills sheep by perching on their backs and pecking its way to the fat around the kidneys, with a note explaining that the parrot 'was originally frugivorous [eating fruit only] but had become before 1881 a pest to sheep-farmers in the Southern Alps of N. Z.'. Murray added an additional note to *stitch-bird*, *Pogonornis cincta* of New Zealand, 'the clicking note of which has a fancied resemblance to the word "stitch" '.

Sometimes Morris's details were a little too specific and 'local' for the OED. Murray put in *kie-kie*, a New Zealand climbing plant, but not Morris's details about how New Zealanders pronounced the word: 'frequently pronounced "ghi-ghi" in the North Island of New Zealand, and "gay-gie" in the South Island'. Neither did Murray include a particular Dunedin term, *Old Identity*, which Morris explained was someone well-known in a place, that is, a former resident of

Dunedin as distinguished from the *New Iniquity*, an unwanted immigrant or someone who came to New Zealand from Australia. Both expressions were added to the OED later in the twentieth century.

Often every single part of Murray's entry for a New Zealand word was supplied by Morris, from the etymology to the definition and every quotation, such as *pakeha*, someone who does not identify as Māori. Likewise for a whole series of New Zealand parrots which Murray included: *kaka*, a brown parrot; *kakapo*, an owl-parrot; *kakariki*, a green parakeet. Without Morris collecting hundreds of quotations from over sixty New Zealand sources, Murray's coverage of New Zealand words would not have been as rich as it was. And if Murray had relied solely on contributors such as Herbert-Jones or Hampden-Cook, there would have been very few New Zealand words indeed.

O

for OUTSIDERS

Jane Austen was the first person to write the word *outsider*. It did not appear in one of her novels, but rather in a hilarious and gossipy letter to her sister, written on Thursday 20 November 1800:

> *I beleive [sic] I drank too much wine last night at Hurstbourne; I know not how else to account for the shaking of my hand today. We had a very pleasant day on monday at Ashe; we sat down 14 to dinner in the study, the dining room being not habitable from the Storms having blown down its chimney. – Mrs Bramston talked a good deal of nonsense, which Mr Bramston & Mr Clark seemed almost equally to enjoy. – There was a whist & a casino table, & six outsiders. – Rice and Lucy [the Revd Henry Rice and Lucy Lefroy] made love, Mat. Robinson fell asleep, James & Mrs Augusta alternately read Dr Jenner's pamphlet on the cow pox, & I bestowed my company by turns on all.*

A small group of Dictionary women were responsible for reading Austen – Mrs Effie Laura Browne of London, Miss Leonard of Clifton, Misses Isabel Wilkinson and Catherine

Gunning of Dorking (later Cambridge and London), and Miss Beatrice Richardson of Grasmere whom we met in C for Cannibal. Austen's letters and her novels were a great source of first quotations: she was the first person to write the words *sponge cake, spoilt* (as in a 'spoilt child'), *sprawly, chaperone, fragmented, irrepressible, doorbell,* and *noonshine* (her own name for an afternoon snack – yes, it is in the OED).

In constructing the entry for *outsider*, Murray simply extracted Austen's phrase, 'There was a whist & a casino table, & six outsiders.' This was the dilemma of the lexicographer before the digital age, when space on the dictionary page was restricted and quotations were cut to a bare minimum. He defined *outsider* as: 'One who is outside of or does not belong to a specified company, set, or party, a non-member; hence, one unconnected or unacquainted with a matter, uninitiated into a profession or body having special knowledge.'

Most of the Dictionary People, including Murray himself, were outsiders. They were not the establishment or the intellectual elites. They were not the writers, the journalists, and literary set, but rather those who did not belong to a particular circle, community, or profession; those who were self-educated, the hard-working ones born to the wrong people at the wrong time in the wrong place. When it came to the Dictionary project all these wrongs were exactly right. Their hunger to be part of a big prestigious project meant that this was a crowdsourced project that worked.

There were two volunteers among the Dictionary People who personified the range and value of the outsider. First among them was Joseph Wright, who was born in a poor Yorkshire village and by the age of fifteen could neither read nor write, yet rose to become a respected Oxford professor through the most extraordinary of circumstances. The other was an American named Fitzedward Hall, who started out as a cosmopolitan Harvard-educated insider and army officer but whose life appeared to do a swap with Wright's: he ended up living in poverty in a small Suffolk village. While Wright went from outsider to insider, Hall was the insider who became an outsider.

Joseph Wright does not have an entry in the address books, perhaps because he was one of Murray's closest friends and they spoke rather than wrote to each other. He is thanked in the prefaces for helping with etymologies, especially those of words from regional British dialects, on the letters H, I, J, K, and M. Wright's help was limited because he was busy writing his own dictionary, a splendid six-volume work on the dialects of England called *The English Dialect Dictionary* which was published between 1898 and 1905. It is a treasure trove of regional English terms such as *aquabob*, a word in Kent for an icicle, and *zwodder*, a Somerset term for feeling drowsy.

Wright's dialect dictionary followed the same structure as the OED and it was also a crowdsourced project with many of the same volunteers, especially women who lived in rural areas of England and sent in their local words – Miss Eleanor Lloyd of Ripley, Yorkshire; Miss Isabel Wilkinson of Dorking, Surrey; Miss Yates of Worthing, West Sussex; Miss Williams of Salisbury, Wiltshire; Miss Prudence Walter of Wellington, Somerset; and Miss Eliza Burton of Carlisle, Cumbria.

Professor Wright was a Fellow of Corpus Christi College, Oxford, and had one of the most prestigious academic titles in the world: Professor of Comparative Philology in the University of Oxford. He lived on Keble Road, a tree-lined street near the Museum of Natural History and close to the beautiful University Parks. He regularly walked through the Parks and up to the Scriptorium at 78 Banbury Road to lure Murray away from his desk and to sit in the garden together. Sometimes they were joined by another etymologist and friend of the Dictionary, Walter Skeat, who often stayed with Murray when he visited from Cambridge – and not just for the challenging tandem rides. Skeat was an Anglo-Saxonist who had written his own dictionary, *An Etymological Dictionary of the English Language* (1879–82), an impressive four-volume work tracing the origins of English words. He was a mentor to both men, because he had actually founded Wright's dictionary and the English Dialect Society which supported it, and he had helped secure Oxford University Press as the publisher of the Dictionary.

On one happy Saturday afternoon in early summer 1893, the three lexicographers sat in the garden of Sunnyside, the Murray family home in north Oxford, sharing philological gossip. As Ada brought out tea and several of the children gathered on the grass, Skeat entertained them with a silly ditty he had written in celebration of Murray's recent completion of the letter C: 'Wherever the English speech has spread, / And the Union Jack flies free, / The news will be gratefully proudly read, / That you've conquered your ABC!'

Wright regaled them with stories from his humble Yorkshire childhood and a recent visit from his brother and mother to 'Ahr Jooee'. 'I took them on a tour of the colleges', he explained. 'We stopped at the grand gates of All Souls, and I told them that it was the only college with no undergraduates. My mother exclaimed, "Eh! but it wod mak a grand Co-op!"' He saw the humour in every situation, and told them how his brother, Dufton, specialized in stonework, and was distressed to see that some Oxford colleges were built of stone cut the wrong way of the grain, exposing it to weather peeling and crumbling. 'Duff was feeling the surface of an ancient wall when a policeman came up behind him and thought he was defacing college property.'

Joseph Wright was born in 1855 into a poor family in the coal and quarrying township of Idle, Yorkshire. He had a feckless father but a hard-working mother who raised her four sons by working at washing and charring. Later in life, he delighted in joking, 'I have been an Idle man all my life,

Joseph Wright (left) and Walter Skeat (right) often
joined Murray (centre) for tea in the garden of his
Oxford house, Sunnyside.

and shall remain an Idle man till I die.' Anyone who knew
him and his unmatched work ethic got the joke.

At the age of six, his mother had put him to work as a
donkey boy in the local mine. He drove a donkey-cart from
7 a.m. until 5 p.m., carrying tools for the quarrymen. He got
paid 1 penny a week by each quarryman and 18 pence by the
blacksmith. When he turned fifty-six, he had a birthday party
in Oxford at which he announced proudly, 'I have earned
my living for half a century.' At the age of seven, his mother
moved him from donkey boy in the quarry to doffer in the
spinning department of the local mill, replacing the bobbins
on the spindles. The mill was an hour's walk from home,
which he took by himself at 5 a.m. He worked as a 'half-timer'
from 6 a.m. to 12.30, with half an hour for breakfast at 8 a.m.
'I remember how my legs used to ache on a Monday morning, when I started work again after some rest on a Sunday,

but they got right again in the course of the week.' He reminisced towards the end of his life, 'I went through many hardships as a lad but I didn't feel they were hardships at the time, I always felt I was getting on.'

In the afternoons Wright went to a special school for half-timers. It was the only schooling he ever had, and while most half-timers stayed until the age of thirteen, Wright was in full-time work long before then. 'When I left school I knew very little more than when I first went. I knew the alphabet, and had a smattering of elementary arithmetic, and I could recite parrot-like various Scriptural passages, and a few highly moral bits of verse; that was almost precisely the extent of my educational equipment after three or four years of schooling. Reading and writing for me were as remote as any of the sciences.' He also knew nothing of Standard English as all he spoke was a strong Bradford dialect.

At the age of nine, little Joey moved on to wool sorting, working from 6 a.m. to 5.30 p.m. His life changed one lunchtime, six years later, when one of his fellow sorters was reading aloud from a newspaper about the Franco-Prussian war. Wright was mesmerized by the vivid tales of battle, and got a sudden desire to want to read. He began to teach himself using two books: the Bible and Bunyan's *The Pilgrim's Progress*.

Wright practised writing during his lunch hour. An older man, Alfred Brooks, who was educated, took an interest in the fifteen-year-old and encouraged him to use his right hand but Wright ended up being ambidextrous and was famous at Oxford for writing on a chalk board simultaneously with two hands. He soon attended night school for 'the working lads' for three nights a week. He taught himself from Cassell's *Popular Educator*, which, published fortnightly, contained lessons on subjects as varied as geology, bookkeeping, chemistry, Italian, French, and Greek. Undeterred by outside noise, every spare minute that he had, he studied – every lunchtime, every night until 2 a.m., and all day on Sunday after chapel. Fellow workers recalled looking across at Joey and seeing him with several books propped up in front of him while he sorted the wool. He loved languages and went to night school to learn French and German. He slept very little, but still reliably turned up for work at the wool mill at 6 a.m. each day.

Many years later, his wife Lizzie remarked to him, 'I can't think how you managed to learn all that when you were working at the mill from six in the morning till six at night.' 'Oh! It wasn't as bad as that', he replied. 'I stopped at half past five.'

He attended night classes at the Mechanics Institute in Bradford twice a week to learn arithmetic, Euclid, algebra, and shorthand, walking 3 miles each way. At the age of eighteen, while still working as a wool sorter during the day, he needed money to buy books so he began his own night school. Up to a dozen young men would crowd into his mother's small house – some stood, some sat on the floor, some on the bed.

At the age of twenty-one, while the mill was temporarily closed, he used his savings to travel to Germany to study German and mathematics in Heidelberg, walking all the way from Antwerp. On his return he left the mill and got a job as a schoolteacher in Bradford, studying part-time at the Yorkshire College of Science (later Leeds University). At twenty-seven, he passed exams for a London BA degree, and returned to Heidelberg where he got his PhD in Greek and became a leading figure in historical linguistics and Continental philology. He worked at the University of Leipzig until the age of thirty-three when he moved to Oxford as lecturer in Gothic, Anglo-Saxon, and Old German to the

Association for the Higher Education of Women. Wright's publications included a grammar of the dialect of his home town in Yorkshire.

Meanwhile, Professor Walter Skeat had begun to compile a comprehensive *English Dialect Dictionary*, which he handed over to Wright in 1891 when the latter was appointed Deputy Professor of Comparative Philology at Oxford.

Wright fell in love with one of his most able students, Elizabeth Mary Lea. Their love letters are some of the most charming ever written.

Lea specialized in Old English and, as a student, had written an excellent article on 'The Language of the Northumbrian Gloss to the Gospel of Mark' which she shared with several scholars for advice, one of whom was James Murray. Murray's correspondence with Lea was on these matters of intellect – though perhaps we can detect a hint of flirtation in Murray's reply to the brilliant young woman?

> *Dear Miss Lea,*
>
> *I am a naughty person not to have ere this acknowledged the present of the portion of your article, especially when you so generously & so gratuitously named me in it, who did nothing but give you a little pay & say 'go on like a brave lass'. I only wish it had been presented so as to be rewarded with a PhD like Miss Wardale's. The PhD is of course coming; still I grudge to see this come out without that crown. I welcome you to Oxford. May you have much success. Come and see us soon. Miss Leighton goes Monday afternoon, and will be greatly disappointed if she does not see you first.*
> *Yours very truly, J. A. H. Murray*

Lea never did get her PhD. She married Wright and devoted herself to his dialect dictionary and his scholarship, eventually writing an affectionate biography of him.

While Joseph Wright was learning his way out of rural poverty, another of the Dictionary volunteers was – at least at first – on his way to a far more conventional academic career had it not been for his bad temper and unlikeable nature. It was Fitzedward Hall's own behaviour that turned him into an outsider. Born in New York State, he studied civil engineering at Troy Rensselaer Polytechnic and was enrolled at Harvard in 1846, when his parents asked him to track down one of his younger brothers whom they believed had absconded to India. Hall dutifully boarded a boat from Boston to Calcutta. The ship capsized in the Bay of Bengal, and the young Hall was rescued. Recovering in Calcutta, he was captivated by the languages which surrounded him and became proficient in Bengali, Hindi, Sanskrit, and Persian. He ended up becoming the Anglo-Sanskrit Professor at the government college in Benares (now Varanasi) and discovered many unknown Sanskrit manuscripts, which he edited, translated, and published. He became the first American to edit a Sanskrit text, and many of his meticulously edited works found international recognition and praise, resulting in 1860 in an honorary degree of Doctor of Civil Law from the University of Oxford.

In 1854 he married Amelia Ward, the daughter of an East Indian Company official, in Delhi, and they had five children, three of whom died young. He served as a rifleman for nine months during the Sepoy Mutiny. They moved to England in 1862 where he was appointed Professor of Sanskrit Language and Literature at King's College, London, and Librarian at the India Office. Furnivall had brought him into the Dictionary project early on, and in 1860 Hall had begun collecting slips.

From the 1860s onwards, Hall's own behaviour turned him into an outsider. He became increasingly bitter, argumentative, cantankerous, and paranoid. Based on his belief that British people disliked Americans, he became convinced that he was discriminated against in Britain. The year 1869 marked a turning point. At a meeting of the Philological Society, he became embroiled in a heated argument with another of the Dictionary volunteers, Dr Theodor Goldstocker. Goldstocker was the Professor of Sanskrit at University College London, and a neighbour of Furnivall on St George's Square, who had been struggling to publish a revision of H. H. Wilson's Sanskrit dictionary but the project had become so huge he had had to abandon it. We do not know the details of the argument between Hall and Goldstocker but Hall clearly lost the fight – he was banned from the Philological Society and lost his job as Librarian of the India Office.

In the aftermath of that bitter public disagreement and amidst new accusations by colleagues that he was a foreign spy and a drunkard, Hall retired to Suffolk in 1869 where he spent the rest of his life working on his edition of the *Visnu-purana*, writing books on the English language, and gathering quotations for the OED under Furnivall's watch. Once in Suffolk, his marriage broke up (his wife reportedly left him for a local vicar) and he became something of a hermit, rarely leaving his cottage.

Hall grew increasingly frustrated by Furnivall's lack of organization and loose leadership of the Dictionary project and complained publicly in a letter to the *New York Times* in 1874 that 'between 1860 and 1871 I furnished for the projected dictionary of the Philological Society something like 200,000 extracts. Each of these was on a half sheet of notepaper, and consisted of at least a complete sentence, with a heading and specification of the author quoted, the title of his work, its date, the edition, the number of the volume, the page, etc. I was also offered a subeditorship of the dictionary. This mighty undertaking is now, I fear, at a standstill.' There is no proof that he did send in so many slips to Furnivall. Furnivall may have lost them, of course, but Hall may also have exaggerated his contribution.

Once Murray took up the Editorship in 1879, Hall re-joined the efforts with full attention, devoting up to six hours each day to the OED. Murray was spared from any of his vitriolic outbursts. The two men never met, but wrote to each other most days. Hall was Murray's main proofreader and supported him on several occasions by writing letters to the Delegates of Oxford University Press advocating for Murray's lexicographic decisions which favoured quality over speed. He also managed to help that outsider who had become an insider, Joseph Wright, with over 2,000 Suffolk words for the *English Dialect Dictionary*.

The reclusive Hall rarely left his cottage in Suffolk for anything, not even to collect an honorary doctorate from Harvard in 1895 nor to attend a special dinner in Murray's honour which was held at the Queen's College, Oxford, on 12 October 1897 to celebrate the completion of the third volume of the Dictionary. Henry Bradley wrote to Hall afterwards, telling him about the evening and reporting that when the Vice Chancellor mentioned Hall's name in a speech there was 'a unanimous and hearty outburst of applause as was not evoked by any other name'. The Dictionary had given Fitzedward Hall purpose and work when he had lost his job and his wife. And the Dictionary had gained an expert who would not, in usual circumstances, have had the time to do so much Dictionary work.

At Christmas 1900, Hall became ill with pneumonia and died on 1 February 1901. He left partially referenced slips for letters not yet published, which Murray needed urgent help completing. An appeal resulted in 100 volunteers coming to Murray's aid with the equivalent of 12,000 person hours. It was just another reminder of the massive contribution that Hall had made during his lifetime. As expressed by Bradley, 'the loss of so laborious and so profoundly skilled a worker is a misfortune the magnitude of which it is hardly possible to estimate'.

P

for PORNOGRAPHER

Every once in a while, a bundle of slips arrived at the Scriptorium which would have made Murray and his assistants blush: they contained words like *infibulation*, fastening the sexual organs with a clasp; *procision*, shortening the foreskin by removing the foremost part; *use*, to have sexual intercourse with; *revinct*, bound up, girded with something; *imperforated*, lacking a normal or functional orifice; and *devirgination*, deflowering of a virgin.

These slips also demonstrated a penchant for bodily functions: *courses*, menstrual discharge; *subrepent*, seeping, oozing; *exspuition*, spitting out from the mouth; *erumpent*, that bursts forth; *flux*, flowing out, issuing, discharge. Freakish body parts were an interest too, such as *labion*, a person who has large lips. They were words to do with pornography, genitals, bondage, and hapax legomena – the dictionary equivalent of a 'Google whack', words that only occur once in any written source.

The most likely sender of those slips was the Reader Henry Spencer Ashbee. He had those words literally at his fingertips because he owned the world's largest collection of pornography and erotica.

Whoever sent in these words – and we shall see why Ashbee is the best candidate – had a mischievous nature and an obsession with sex, as demonstrated not only in their choice of words but also in their selection of illustrative quotations. If they spotted a word being used in what the Victorians would have thought a scurrilous or depraved manner, and especially if it involved violence or flagellation, then they chose that sentence to send in to the OED. Between 1840 and 1880, half of the pornography produced contained flagellation and beating, so it shouldn't surprise us that this was the 'bent' of so many of the selected quotations. For the word *putrefactory*, causing something to rot, the Reader chose, 'Their way is to cut a man in pieces, and then put him into a Putrifactory Vessel'; and the word *glans* (for the penis glans) is supported by 'Buttoning up the Prepuce with a Brasse or Silver-button on both sides of the Glans'.

Even for common words, which usually bore no sexual connotation whatsoever, this Reader managed to find sexualized or body-related examples. These are now embedded within otherwise bland quotation paragraphs in the Dictionary: for *transversely*, across, crosswise, 'Another membrane, which transversely . . . doth cover the chink of the Hymen'; for *depopulate*, to destroy, cut off, 'The Depilatories burn up and depopulate the Genital matter thereof'; and for *wall*, something that confines or encloses like the wall of a house, 'The walls of the Breasts [of infants] are . . . depraved by Nurses, while they do over-strictly bind them.'

These slips about sex and bodies created a dilemma for the diligent Editor and respectable family man, Murray, who wanted to adhere strictly to the scientific policies he had devised. These rules stipulated that every word used in an English context had a valid place in the Dictionary, and that the earliest quotation for every word must be found in order to demonstrate its first use. But Murray, a man shaped by his Presbyterian and teetotal upbringing, who had to answer to the rather strict Delegates of Oxford University Press, also felt responsible for guarding the tone of his work. Not to mention trying not to get into trouble with the Obscene Publications Act as John Stephen Farmer had (see D for Dictionary Word Nerds).

We can only imagine how he may have reacted when he received the packets of slips with their risqué words. Caught between respecting his own lexicographic policies and keeping the Dictionary within the bounds of Victorian respectability, what was he to do? Scientific rigour won out.

One book in particular, *Anthropometamorphosis: Man Transform'd, or, the Artificiall Changling* (1650), a comparison of how different cultures alter their bodies, by physician John Bulwer, was a key source for these words. It is an important text because it contains many first quotations and new words – especially about sex and bodily mutilation. In Murray's address books, he had noted that three people had read the book and sent in over 1,000 slips between them. They were: Ashbee; a woman in London; and a man in New Jersey, USA. I wondered what words each person sent in. If I wanted to know the identity of the main Reader of words about sex, I was going to have to do some detective work, looking at the handwriting on the slips.

A part of me was hoping that the woman, a prim spinster called Miss Jennett Humphreys (see W for Women), had sent in the smutty words. I already knew her handwriting. I checked the slips – but there were no sex words among them. I then set about looking for Ashbee's handwriting, which I found in his diaries stored in the British Library. It was remarkably similar to that on the slips with the salacious words, if not always exactly identical; different paper, different ink, different period of his life may all have been factors in the slight variations.

Case closed? Maybe not. Aside from Ashbee, the other Reader of Bulwer's book was Halkett Lord, an Englishman living in America where he edited a literary magazine. He had previously worked on *Punch* and, at the time, had been labelled 'the wittiest man in London'. I could just imagine him seeing the humour in sending Murray hundreds of words that the Editor would find embarrassing. But when I checked the slips, I could not find any in his hand: they all seemed to be in Ashbee's.

Further detective work was still needed. I checked other books Lord had read, and the handwriting on those slips also looked quite similar to Ashbee's, so I could not be sure. I brought in a handwriting expert from the Bodleian Library, and he agreed that nothing was definitive or conclusive. He explained that both Ashbee and Lord had typical hands of the period, and many people had very similar styles. But the evidence weighed on the side of Ashbee. So: P for Pornographer it was.

Ashbee had seen the value of language and words that many Victorians would have judged inappropriate or unsuitable for a respectable tome such as the OED. Without his contributions, and Murray's willingness to put the words in, the Dictionary would be a diminished text, a sanitized version of the English language, and far, far less entertaining.

*

Who was Henry Spencer Ashbee and what drove his lascivious obsessions? To the outside world, he was husband to Elizabeth, father of three daughters and a son, and manager of a family trading business, living in a beautiful house in Bloomsbury, London. He was the respectable paterfamilias who collected books and travelled widely across Europe for his business, speaking several languages fluently. In the City, he commanded respect for his commercial acumen and success, and became Warden of the Curriers' Company (specialists in leather) in 1897–8. In literary circles, his expertise as a bibliophile was acknowledged by election as a Fellow of the Society of Antiquaries (1877), the Société des Amis des Livres, Paris (1879), and the Royal Geographical Society (1881). He was a founder member of Les Bibliophiles Contemporains (1889) and of the Bibliographical Society, London (1892), and a corresponding member of the Royal Academy of Madrid (1896). Aside from his pornography collection, he collected other books; he was an expert on the sixteenth-century Spanish writer Cervantes and collector of illustrated editions of Cervantes's great work, *Don Quixote.*

In many ways, he was a self-made man, who left school at the age of sixteen and never went to university. He was an autodidact like so many others who contributed to the Dictionary – though, unlike the others, it was in the niche area of sexual words and erotica that he was self-taught. It is fitting that the word 'pornography' first appeared in his lifetime – in 1842 when he was eight. Just a very few years later, he started collecting clandestine erotica as a teenager living near London's Blackfriars Bridge and accompanying his father to work at a gunpowder mill. After leaving school, he worked in an import–export warehouse, which involved travel throughout Europe. These European trips allowed him to build up his pornography collection.

Henry received a mighty leg-up in his career from his father-in-law. His wife Elizabeth Lavy, whom he met in Hamburg and married in 1862, was the daughter of a wealthy German-Jewish merchant, Edward Lavy (and his English wife Marian). Lavy bankrolled a London branch of the family company for Henry to manage and provided the couple's home around the corner from the British Museum. The company exported British machinery and textiles to Europe with great success, and Ashbee was able to open a branch in Paris only five years later, in 1867.

Ashbee instantly took to the Bloomsbury lifestyle of book

collecting and hanging out in the bohemian milieu of publishers with similar interests in erotica. His continued travels
for business across Europe allowed him to expand both the
quantity and variety of his pornography collection and by
the 1870s there was so much of it that he needed to store
it elsewhere – in a purpose-built bachelor pad at 'the Inn'
(Gray's Inn). Each Saturday, he invited fellow pornophile
friends to gather at the Inn to muse over items in the collection. These included the explorer Richard Burton; Foster
Fitzgerald Arbuthnot who, as a civil servant in India, had developed a taste for Sanskrit erotic texts and a niche interest
in the phallic origins of religious symbols; and the aristocrat
Richard Monckton Milnes, who wrote a pornographic poem
on the subject of flagellation, 'The Rodiad' (1871).

By 1879, when Ashbee's pornography collection had
reached a very considerable size, he began to contribute to the
Dictionary, reading books in his own library to send in slips to
the OED. Just two years earlier, Ashbee had published a bibliography of obscene literature, which is now acknowledged
as his masterwork, the *Index Librorum Prohibitorum*, or *Index
of Books Worthy of Being Prohibited* (1877), under the pseudonym Pisanus Fraxi, an anagram of the Latin for ash, *fraxinus*,
and bee, *apis*. He explains in the book's preface that 'I am
not an author by profession; but being actively engaged in
pursuits of an entirely different nature, have sought recreation in compiling this work during my few leisure hours . . .
The pleasure I have experienced in making it has already
rewarded me for my labour. "The struggling for knowledge"
(aptly observes the Marquis of Halifax) "hath a pleasure in
it like that of wrestling with a fine woman." '

Ashbee was also quite possibly the anonymous author of
an infamous publication, *My Secret Life*, a narrative (likely ficti-
tious, albeit based on the author's experiences) of the 1,500
sexual exploits of a man called 'Walter' who frequented the

bars and brothels of London in the 1880s. The memoir was in excess of a million words, coming in at 4,000 pages, over eleven volumes. Only six copies exist today of the original print run of 475, self-published for private subscribers, but it was reprinted in the 1960s and has since grown in reputation and fame. Its author is still unidentified, but Ashbee is the front-runner. Given the words sent in to the Dictionary by Ashbee, it would not be surprising if he authored a book with chapter

Henry Spencer Ashbee, who had an eye for words
and books related to sex, pornography,
genitals, and flagellation.

headings such as 'My Cock', 'A Frisky Governess', and 'My Cousin's Cunts' (the plural is mind-boggling!). It was only very recently, in the twenty-first century, that *My Secret Life* was read for the OED and the editors discovered that it contained the first written evidence for the words *cocksucking, cunty, fist-fuck* (originally meaning masturbation), *frig, fuckee,* and *randiness.*

Ashbee was a man of many facets, and he was described as such by one contemporary: 'Mr H. S. Ashbee who lived at 53 (the big corner house) Bedford Square, was a curious matter-of-fact, stoutish, stolid, affable man, with a Maupassantian taste for low life, its humours, and its laxities. Of art and literature he had absolutely no idea; but he was an enthusiastic bibliophile, and his library, which included a unique collection of rare and curious books, had been built up at enormous expense.' Another described him as 'not a bad old chappie, and he has a favourite cat, which says something for him'.

But in 1891, his artfully compartmentalized life split apart when his marriage broke down. His wife, Elizabeth, left him, taking their daughters Agnes and Elsa with her. Their eldest, Frances, had already married, and their son, Charles, a recent graduate, now lived independently. Henry and Elizabeth had been quarrelling for some years after Elizabeth made two alarming discoveries: not only did her husband have a massive collection of pornography in multiple languages, but he also had a secret lover, Ellen Mary Jane Montauban, by whom (it is thought) he had a daughter, Irene.

Ashbee expected toleration of his own sexual predilections, but it turns out he had his limits towards others and was intolerant of his son's homosexuality. This too may have led to differences with his wife, who was profoundly attached to Charles. As an undergraduate at King's College, Cambridge (1883–6), Charles was part of a homosexual network of male students and came to accept his sexuality, though he later married a woman and had four daughters. While he was still a teenage schoolboy boarding at Wellington College, Charles had begun contributing words to the OED. His words were very different from those of his father – who began contributing in the same year, 1879 – and he sent in 500 slips from poetry and travellers' tales. This continued until he went up to Cambridge four years later. Whether he was encouraged to contribute to the OED by his father or by a schoolmaster, the Revd Charles Penny, who was also a contributor, or by a schoolfriend Paget Lambart Bayly (who read contemporary writers Thackeray and Gladstone, and sent in 600 slips), or whether he was the one who first answered the call to read for the OED, we don't know. This small circle of interconnected people, who all began contributing to the Dictionary at the same time – the late 1870s – reminds us how important word of mouth and networks were, in getting people to read for the Dictionary.

After graduating from Cambridge, influenced by the ideals of craftsmanship espoused by the writer John Ruskin and artist William Morris, and the utopian politics of the writer (and homosexual) Edward Carpenter, Charles became an Arts and Crafts designer and architect of note, and socialist in his ideals. He moved back to London – but to the East End – and set up the Guild and School of Handicraft, where men learned the crafts of furniture-making and metalwork, received decent wages and profits from sales, and shared in the decision-making. Charles's cooperative workshop was designed to be the very opposite of the sweatshops that were all around them in that poorest part of the city. In the 1890s the Guild became both successful and profitable, and branched into other areas, from blacksmithing to artisan printing. Silver pieces designed by Charles and made by Guild members now sell for many thousands of pounds.

In the rift between his parents, Charles and his two unmarried sisters sided with their mother. Charles designed a house on Cheyne Walk (number 37) where the four of them lived once their mother was formally separated from Henry in 1893. Living in Chelsea, and enjoying the artistic atmosphere of the area, he cycled every day to the workshop in the East End, while also designing six other houses on Cheyne Walk (two of these survive today: numbers 38 and 39). He only moved out of number 37 in 1898, when he married.

Henry Ashbee now had little to do with his family. In the mid-1890s he moved to Kent, where, now ailing, he – strangely – turned to a fifteen-year-old first cousin, Louisa Maud Ashbee, to care for him. He died in 1900 of congestion of the lungs, heart trouble, liver and kidney complaints, and dropsy. He died wealthy but disinherited his estranged wife, son and daughters, leaving his estate of over £63,000 to his grandchildren (the children of daughter Frances), Cousin Louisa who had cared for him, the Montaubans (his unconventional family), and his business partner.

He also left the largest collection of erotica in the world. He bequeathed his whole library – not only the erotica (1,600 volumes) but also his extensive collection of Cervantes, including 384 editions of *Don Quixote* – to the British Museum (later the British Library). The institution was faced with a dilemma: they wanted the Cervantes but were horrified by the pornography. Could they take one and reject the other? In the end, they accepted the lot, burning some of the pornography and locking away most of the remaining 900 works of erotica in a secret cabinet labelled 'the Private Case', where it lay untouched and inaccessible until the 1960s when it was finally added to the public catalogue. A full record of all of it was only completed in the 1980s. In the story of Ashbee's pornography, the OED turns out to have been far more liberal in its outlook than the British Library.

Q

for QUEERS

The three women listed in the address book at Stoke Green in Stoke Bishop, a leafy neighbourhood of Bristol, were passionate about reading, the arts, and the world of letters, so it is no surprise that they were enthusiastic contributors to the Dictionary. Between them, the two sisters, Amy and Edith, and their aunt (their mother's sister), Katharine, sent in 7,900 slips over a decade, from 1879 to 1889. They were listed separately in the address books, but in small writing against the name of Amy, Murray had made the connection by writing, 'Misses A, K, & E'. All three were thanked by him in the 1888 preface. They were, in that sense, no different from other family contributors, though the sisters' parents, who also lived in the household, did not participate. Their father, James, was uninterested or too busy, and their mother, Emma (also known as Lissie), who was frail and in poor health after the birth of Amy, needed a full-time carer. It was Emma's younger sister, Katharine, who cared for her and acted as guardian and teacher of Edith, sixteen years her junior.

What is surprising is that Katharine and her niece Edith became lovers during that period, and remained together as a couple for the rest of their lives until their deaths ten months apart from each other in 1913 and 1914.

For many years Katharine Bradley and Edith Cooper lived in the family home in Bristol and then Reigate; later, after the death of Edith's parents, they set up home together. Their incestuous intimacy seems to have been accepted in the family: each had her own bedroom, but they usually spent the night together. No one minded when they started to call each other 'My love' and 'My beloved', though their language with and for each other in their private letters and diaries was far more passionate. They forged their union at a moment when romantic friendships between women could just about still be regarded with innocence but also just as homosexuality was emerging as an identity; the 'science' of sexology was being formed, medicalizing homosexuality; and the notion of the invert (as one whose sexual instincts were reversed or 'inverted') began to circulate. This was never language they used of themselves, though it was their friend Havelock Ellis whose use of the term especially brought it into English circulation, via his book *Sexual Inversion* (1897). They regarded their union as lifelong: a queer Victorian marriage.

The word *queer* in this sense of 'homosexual' may have been used in speech in the 1870s and 1880s, but it certainly was not used in writing (nor was the word *homosexual*). *Queer* did not get into the Dictionary until 1982, when it appeared as a noun, slang for a male homosexual, with a first quotation from the poet W. H. Auden from 1932, though its use as an adjective dated back to 1922. Recent editors at the OED have found that the first time it appeared in writing was in a letter written by the homophobic and inflammatory Marquess of Queensberry (the man who triggered the trial of Oscar Wilde) in 1894: 'I write to tell you that it is a *judgement* on the whole *lot of you*. Montgomerys, The Snob Queers like Roseberry & certainly Christian hypocrite Gladstone.' And in the most recent OED entry for *queer*, it is noted that from the late 1980s the term was reclaimed and used in a neutral or positive sense.

Katharine and Edith would not have called themselves *lesbian* either, as the word was not yet in use – although recently editors at the OED found an isolated instance of the word dating back to 1732. When the letter L was published in 1903 it only carried the sense 'of or pertaining to the island of Lesbos'. By the time the 1933 OED Supplement appeared thirty years later, there was plenty of evidence for the homosexual sense of the word, but the editor responsible for L, William Craigie, did not put it in. A letter in the Dictionary's archives shows that his co-Editor Charles Onions complained about the exclusion of *lesbian* and *lesbianism* to Robert Chapman, the Secretary of the Delegates of Oxford University Press, who cheerfully agreed it should go in and wrote back, 'C[raigie] is capable of not knowing what it is!' The word was not included in the OED until 1976.

The words *homosexual* and *homosexuality* were introduced in the 1890s: they had appeared – in German – in the German sexologist Richard von Krafft-Ebing's work in 1892, but not in English until 1897, in Havelock Ellis's *Sexual Inversion*. The words were not included when Murray published the letter H in 1899 – perhaps because Ellis's book had been banned for obscenity that very year, two years after it had been published. Nor did Murray include the sexual sense of *inversion* in his 1900 publication of the letter I, possibly for the same reason. It was Charles Onions who put these words into the 1933 OED Supplement: he dated the earliest use in English of *homosexual* to Ellis's 1897 book, and of *inversion* to John Addington Symonds, the poet and critic who was initially Ellis's co-author of *Sexual Inversion*, in his 1896 pamphlet *A Problem in Modern Ethics, being an Inquiry into the Phenomenon of Sexual Inversion* (a critique of Krafft-Ebing's negative stance on the subject).

If late-Victorian society was largely still oblivious to the romantic dimension of Katharine and Edith's relationship, it was shocked by another aspect of their union: the two women wrote poetry and plays together under the male pseudonym of Michael Field. Katharine described this writing union in language borrowed from the Book of Common Prayer marriage service when writing of it to Havelock Ellis: 'The work is a mosaic. We cross and interlace like a couple of dancing summer flies; . . . Let no man think he can put asunder what God has joined.'

Katharine Bradley and Edith Cooper, two Readers who were aunt and niece and also lesbian lovers.

Katharine and Edith first published together in 1881 under the names Arran and Isla Leigh: a volume of poems on classical themes, including a four-act verse drama, which garnered little attention. Michael Field was born three years later in 1884, two female writers (and lovers, what's more) masquerading as one male writer. Michael Field published two verse dramas that year, *Callirrhoë* and *Fair Rosamund*, and was a great success. Field was likened to Shakespeare and Swinburne, and the *Spectator* described 'his' arrival on the literary scene as 'the ring of a new voice, which is likely to be heard far and wide among the English-speaking peoples'. Michael Field was prolific, publishing plays and poetry for the rest of 'his' life. Katharine and Edith drew on classical myth and medieval romance for inspiration, tapping into ongoing currents that revived the Classics and the medieval Gothic for their own times. In 1880, Katharine had written to Edith, 'Let us be true to the two great tracks of Greek Thought and Medieval Romance; the times when the head of man was at its soundest, and the heart of man at its tenderest; and to this 19th century a goodly song shall yet be sung.' One of their poems, 'It was Deep April', captured their love for each other: 'My love & I took hands and swore, / Against the world, to be / Poets and lovers evermore.'

It was in the 1880s, the decade of Michael Field's birth and the blossoming of their romance, that Edith and Katharine were contributing words to the Dictionary. When they first sent in slips, Edith was seventeen years old and Katharine thirty-three. Katharine gave it up in 1882 to concentrate on writing but the sisters Edith and Amy continued to contribute until 1889. Katharine and Edith had been drawn together in part by their shared love of literature. The early days of their relationship were marked by walks across the Downs near their home to attend classes at University College Bristol – recently founded in 1876. There they studied classics and philosophy, and attended extension lectures on literature given by James Rowley, one of the first professors appointed at the new college. Katharine had already attended classes in Birmingham, Cambridge, and at the Collège de France.

Katharine and Edith read together for pleasure and for the Dictionary, and their literary networks as well as their literary passions determined the books they selected. Robert Browning was a great favourite and also a great friend. Katharine sent in 500 slips from his *Dramatic Idyls* of 1879, and Amy produced 300 slips from the same book. But Browning's creative use of words was a headache for Murray. When Murray's son Oswyn spoke of his admiration for the poet, Murray replied, 'Browning constantly used words without regard to their proper meaning. He has added greatly to the difficulties of the Dictionary.' From a lexicographical point of view, Murray had a general suspicion of words used by poets, as expressed in a letter written in 1901 discussing the use of *voidee-cup*, a cup of wine with spices taken before retiring to rest or at the departure of guests, in a poem by Dante Gabriel Rossetti. Murray did not know the meaning of the word:

> *One cannot now ask Rossetti where he got it or how he coined it; but if I may infer from the results of appealing to other poets for explanation of their cruces, he would probably say 'I have really forgotten; I was under the impression that I had seen or heard it somewhere; can I have been under a misapprehension? What terrible people you dictionary fellows are, hunting us up about every word; you make life a burden.' That is the general sort of answer one gets which means 'we write for amusement, & not to be studied as texts; if you make school-texts of us, yours be the responsibility!' I believe Browning once answered a request for explanation of a passage, with 'I really do not know; ask the Browning Society.' I know he once confessed ignorance to me of the meaning of one of Mrs B's lines.*

Katharine also read her friend John Ruskin's book *The Eagle's Nest* (1872), lectures on the relationship between natural science and art, for the Dictionary, writing out 1,000 slips. That was in 1879 when she and Ruskin were still friends: soon after that they fell out, apparently over Katharine's literary ambitions and her professed atheism, and he expelled her from his Guild of St George. Three years later, in 1882, when she was in the Lake District, she visited Ruskin's house in Coniston, but as a tourist rather than a friend. She wrote to Edith describing it all and noting that, on his bookshelf, Ruskin had Chapman's edition of Homer's *Iliad*, which she had just read for the OED (750 slips, over two years) and, to her surprise, the Unitarian Harriet Martineau's three-volume autobiography which Ruskin had forbidden 'not because she is an infidel, but because she is a vulgar foolish one'.

The end of the 1880s saw change in the lives of all the Bradley–Cooper household. They moved from Bristol to Reigate in Surrey (conveniently 30 miles south of London) in 1888. Here, Katharine and Edith may have known the Revd William Lees, a vicar in the Reigate area, as they were still nominal Anglicans at this time. Lees was not only a contributor to the Dictionary but also a networker who encouraged others to do their bit, thereby making Reigate something of a hub. But, ironically, it was just after this move that Edith and Amy gave up reading for the Dictionary. Change, busyness, and bereavement all played a part in their having to give up the Dictionary work. In August 1889, Edith and Amy's mother died, and this was followed by the death of Katharine and Edith's great friend Robert Browning at the end of the year. Edith wrote in her diary, 'Is this year going to bereave us again – yet again, O God?' She continued, 'We never wrote a song, without thinking how he would react to it', and she feared this would 'half-kill our poetry'. They attended Browning's funeral in Westminster Abbey on the last day of the year. It was also in

1889 that they began to keep a joint diary, which they titled 'Works and Days'. Whatever happened emotionally to them, they kept on working and writing, albeit not for the OED.

Their devotion to Browning had remained constant to the end of his life, despite the fact that he was the one who leaked the identity of Michael Field. In 1884, Katharine had told him about their pseudonym in strictest confidence. After the secret was out, Katharine reproached him and explained that they needed that male authorial identity so they could write freely and be taken seriously for it. Gradually, others found out. One critic, Marc-André Raffalovich (a Frenchman living in Britain), who had been so laudatory of Michael Field, now wrote to Katharine and Edith quite upset, saying, 'I thought I was writing to a boy.' He might have wished they were a man, as that is where his desire lay. Later, in 1896, he published in French *Uranisme et unisexualité*, in which he described 'unisexuality' as attraction to the same sex.

When Violet Paget, the Florence-based art critic and writer (and lesbian) who used the pseudonym Vernon Lee for her published work, gossiped about the true identity of Michael Field, Katharine chastised her. She wrote to Paget in January 1890, 'It cannot be too frequently repeated, that belief in the unity of M.F. is absolutely necessary, alike for the advance of his glory & his attaining his favour. He is in literature *one* . . . even public reference to him should be masculine.' Katharine felt that Paget, of all people, should have understood that: 'But need scarcely warn Vernon Lee on this point?' A visit by Katharine and Edith to Paget and her companion Clementina 'Kit' Anstruther-Thomson in Florence in 1895 did not go well. On the surface, the two lesbian couples, female writers in the largely male world of late-nineteenth-century aestheticism, might have become great allies and friends, but that was not to be. Edith and Katharine were put off by the other couple's mannish clothes, disapproved of Paget's disregard for the aesthetics of her home and food – 'lunch was as tasteless a meal as one would expect in so unhomely a home' – and were scared when they were chased by some dogs on a walk.

Michael Field continued to publish – dramas and poetry – until not long before the end of Katharine and Edith's lives: writing was at the heart of everything they did together. 'His' identity became an open secret in certain literary circles (though not more widely known until the end of the 1890s) and their friends often referred to them as 'the Michaels'. Sometimes acquaintances and friends liked to show off that they knew the identity of Michael Field and this made Katharine, especially, annoyed. When the American writer and hostess Louise Chandler Moulton (who always summered in Europe) introduced them at her party as the poet, Katharine wrote, 'We stood, our wings vibrating in revolt while hollow fashionable women lisped their enchantment at meeting with us.' And yet they themselves were sometimes tempted to show off their literary identity; when they met Oscar Wilde, they dropped many hints that they were Michael Field but he was too busy regaling them with a discourse on the English language's lack of words for colours to pick up the clues; when they next met him, he barely acknowledged them and they felt snubbed.

Katharine, as the older of the two, had brought her commitments and affiliations to the relationship: support of the anti-vivisection movement, female suffrage activities, and commitment to higher education for women, three 'causes' that often went together and are found amongst many of the Dictionary People. Katharine also brought her friendships and all that they signified: Robert Browning and a love of poetry; John Ruskin and a passion for the arts. Edith adopted these causes, and she joined Katharine in learning as much as she could about literature.

Gradually, as the Michaels' relationship developed and matured, they found themselves less involved in the life of their larger household, made new friends, and shaped and espoused their ideals together. Their study at the house in Reigate was testimony to their aesthetic sensibility, with its William Morris wallpaper, reproductions of Renaissance paintings, and cream-painted bookcase; they vowed to eschew all dark wood, beloved of so many of their Victorian contemporaries. They were devotees of Walter Pater's notion of art for art's sake and always ensured that their books were beautifully designed objects. They loved clothes and hats and shoes, discussed them endlessly and often wrote in their diary what they had worn to a particular event, preferring the loose-flowing dresses (no corsets) of the artistic, liberal crowd in which they increasingly ran.

They now spent more time in London, travelling up on the train together with their matching leather cases, each monogrammed MF, and staying at the University Club for Ladies – 'our little Bond Street home'. In London, they were free to go to art galleries and museums and work in the British Library, and they made new friends – more male than female, usually queer or at least bending society's conventions in some way or another. They travelled to Europe together and in Paris met the budding art critic Bernard Berenson, then just twenty-five years old. Through 'BB' they became friends with his American companion, the married Mary Costelloe (she later divorced her husband and married Berenson), and her brother Logan Pearsall Smith, who had settled in London and was another of the Dictionary People (helping as a Subeditor). They befriended the critic and poet Lionel Johnson; Edith's comment in their diary, after they had met him, was typical of their searing observation and their fascination with others' dress: 'We looked down at Lionel's feet – they were fabulous, tiny, in girlish shoes, and blue silk stockings.' Other new friends were artists: Charles de Sousy Ricketts and Charles Haslewood Shannon, a couple whom they nicknamed 'the Painters', and Thomas Sturge Moore.

In 1897, Edith's father, James – aged seventy-nine – and Amy went hiking in the Alps. One day, James went ahead of the party and never returned. It was a hard time for Katharine, Edith, and Amy back in Reigate. Comfort arrived in the form of a Chinese chow puppy, whom Katharine and Edith named Whym Chow (after Edward Whymper, the mountaineer, who kept James's case open and offered the family support). Whym Chow now became the centre of Katharine and Edith's lives, the subject of many poems. In 1898, Katharine and Edith decided it was finally time to leave Reigate for, as Edith put it, 'the wedded life with my Love in our own home'. They moved to a Georgian house with a garden going down to the river and a view of Richmond Bridge, and now had the joy of decorating their own house; surrounded by fabric swatches and wallpaper patterns, they were given plenty of advice by the Painters. They still kept separate bedrooms but slept together in a curtained bed designed by William Morris – Whym would wake them every morning by jumping onto the bed.

In 1906, their beloved Whym, just eight years old, died, and they buried him under the altar of Dionysus in their garden. They were beside themselves with grief, and having always created their own rituals around beloved human beings who had died, reading their poems to them, creating shrines with flowers around their portraits and holding private ceremonies on the anniversaries of their deaths, now they put their dog at the centre of their devotions to the dead. They began to think of him as their spirit guide and understood his death as a divine sacrifice – which made them think of Jesus. They converted to Roman Catholicism. Whym Chow had been 'God's minister' in bringing them to the 'true church'. A recently acquired (human) friend played a role too: the poet John Gray, companion of their old acquaintance Marc-André Raffalovich. Gray, a friend of Charles Ricketts and formerly part of Oscar Wilde's circle, was now a

Roman Catholic priest in Scotland and gently guided them to faith. The younger Katharine had rejected her parents' conventional Christianity and turned to the Greek and Roman gods of literature she loved so much. Now, she had come full circle, from John Ruskin ejecting her from the Guild of St George for atheism to her wholehearted embrace of Roman Catholicism. Now she discussed doctrine with Edith over breakfast, and whether Edith would have to fast from meat on Fridays as she had difficulty swallowing fish. And they both loved the drama of Roman Catholic liturgy.

In 1911, Edith was diagnosed with terminal cancer and refused surgery, preferring a mixture of violet leaves and water from Lourdes with a great deal of prayer – though she did take a new drug, which meant that she lived for another three years. She carried on writing, as did Katharine, who was herself diagnosed with breast cancer in June 1913. She too refused an operation. She also chose not to tell Edith – the woman with whom she had shared everything for most of her life – who thought that Katharine was merely suffering from a bit of heart trouble. Edith died six months later in December 1913, aged fifty-two, at their home in Richmond. Katharine carried on writing and published their poems about their most beloved dog: *Whym Chow: Flame of Love.* As she grew weak, the stairs of the five-storey house in Richmond became too much, and in the summer of 1914 she moved to a cottage near Hawkesyard Priory in Staffordshire to be near Edith's confessor, Father Vincent McNabb. Ten months after Edith's death, on 26 September 1914, Katharine collapsed and died as she was dressing for church. She was sixty-seven.

Thomas Sturge Moore was their literary executor and proved to be the right man for the job, tirelessly preserving, publishing and promoting Michael Field's papers with great devotion. Twenty-nine volumes of their diaries, from 1888 to 1914, were deposited in the British Library, though the strict instruction was that they could not be opened for fifteen years. Excerpts of them were published as *Works and Days* in 1933.

In 1888, the names of Katharine Bradley, Edith Cooper, and Amy Cooper had appeared in Murray's preface. The pseudonym Michael Field had never appeared in his address book, but in 1896, as soon as Field's play *Attila, My Attila* had been published, it was read by Edith Thompson who by then had moved from Bath to Reigate, and sent in 100 slips. More of Field's poetry and plays were read in the twentieth century, ensuring that the queer poet is quoted over two hundred times in the Dictionary. Even Whym Chow is there in the entry to *re-embody*, to restore a soul or spirit to bodily form; to reincarnate, with a most appropriate quotation from *Whym Chow: Flame of Love*: 'Let me hold again / The ruddy form my arms would close on tight / . . .; Oh, re-embody! Be thy Spirit proved.'

A personal card of Whym Chow, which Michael Field
(M. F.) sent out to friends in 1898.

R

for RAIN COLLECTORS

Mrs Mary Pringle collected rain and words. This was not a common pastime in the mid-nineteenth century, just as it is not today, but it occupied Mary on a daily basis. She felt a certain satisfaction knowing that her daily rainfall measurements for the British Rainfall Organisation and the hundreds of words which she sent to the fledgling Oxford English Dictionary were helping to build something greater than herself, for the good of science and knowledge (worlds from which she was otherwise excluded), and to be part of something that carried prestige and a sense of grandeur. Besides, she enjoyed the daily connection with nature and the reading of religious books.

Mary Vernon was a Quaker and twenty-five years old when, in 1870, she married Charles and became Mrs Pringle. To outsiders, her life in the emerging London commuter belt of Beckenham, Kent, appeared no different from that of any other middle-class housewife and mother, with a child, a housemaid, and a cook. Except for one thing. Every day after Charles left for work at the War Office, she bundled up her baby son and went out to measure what had gathered overnight in the copper gauges and long glass tubes lined up on her garden wall and lawn. She noted when intense frost had burst the elevation gauges, when they were buried in snow, or when the level was affected by troublesome leaves. Although it was a solitary pursuit, Mary took comfort in knowing that Percy Bicknell down the road was also measuring his gauges at precisely nine o'clock, as were hundreds of other volunteers across the nation, Charles helping her on Sundays.

The rest of her day was spent indoors reading books on religion, and collecting quotations and words for the Dictionary. It was a slow process. She spent eight months trawling through one book, Burkitt's seventeenth-century biblical commentary on the New Testament. The 535 words she selected and, more significantly, the quotations she chose to illustrate them, tell us something about what she considered noteworthy, and her prudent yet practical nature.

Extracting the word *alone*, she chose the quotation, 'Man, and man alone, is the cause of his own destruction'; and for *ravishing*, 'Oh what a ravishing comfort is the fellowship of the saints.' She showed her no-nonsense practical bent by choosing *feculent*, containing faeces or dregs, 'A river; not of muddy or feculent water, but clear as crystal'; and her appreciation for the archaic with *antiperistasis*, opposition or contrast, 'The cold blasts of persecution did by a spiritual antiparistasis, increase the heat of grace within'; and *make-bait*, someone who creates discord, 'Lust within is the make-bait in all societies and communities without.'

Once a month, Mary placed the stack of quotations in one envelope and the rainfall measurements in another. She put one-penny stamps on the envelopes, and posted them off to the Dictionary in Oxford and the British Rainfall Organisation in London.

Perhaps surprisingly, Mary never sent in rain-related words, even though it was a prolific time for neologisms relating to the weather. Rain, for example, is one of the oldest words in the English language (from Old English, related to

Old Frisian, *rein*), but it may come as a surprise to know that *rainfall* and words relating to its measurement are phenomena from the nineteenth century, which saw the invention of new devices and instruments. Some were rain gauges for manual collection (the *udometer* in 1825), others were automatic instruments for registering rainfall over time (the *hyetometrograph* in 1886 and the *ombrograph* in 1895). New instruments were invented for measuring radiation from the sun (the *pyrheliometer* in 1841, from the Ancient Greek *pyro*, fire + *helios*, sun); determining the direction and velocity of moving clouds (the *nephoscope* in 1880, from the Ancient Greek *nephos*, cloud); and for measuring cloud cover (the *nephelometer* in 1884). These were all relatively new words at the time that Murray was editing the Dictionary, and he put them all in.

Seeing the weather in a scientific way had begun slowly in the seventeenth and eighteenth centuries – Thomas Jefferson in eighteenth-century America had famously kept daily logs of the weather for fifty years. But it took until the nineteenth century for weather observation, and rain observation in particular, to take on a systematic approach. The middle of the century had seen the creation of new branches of meteorology that specialized especially in rain (*ombrology*, from the Ancient Greek *ombros*, rainstorm) and the distribution and mapping of rainfall (*hyetography*, from the Ancient Greek *huetos*, heavy rain). The word *rainfall* itself was thought to have been coined in 1854 and found in Hugh Miller's *Schools and Schoolmasters* by the volunteer Miss Percival of Portman Square, London (it was recently antedated by four years).

A new understanding of atmospheric pressure spawned words which we hear on most weather reports today: *ridge* (1847), *isobar* (1864), *heatwave* (1878), *high* (1878), *low* (1878), *depression* (1881), and *trough* (1882). The creation of the Beaufort Scale (1858) for measuring the force of wind brought new ways of measuring age-old phenomena: *gentle breeze* (force 3 on the scale), *moderate breeze* (force 4), *fresh breeze* (force 5), *strong breeze* (force 6), *moderate gale* (force 7), *violent storm* (force 11). The term *weather system* appeared in 1862.

Certain weather phenomena were named for the first time such as *cyclone* (1848), a general term for all storms in which the wind has a circular or whirling course (from the Ancient Greek for *circle*). Clouds were classified with the naming of *cumulus, cirrus, nimbus,* and *stratus* at the start of the century (1803), being fine-tuned, by the end of the century, to variants such as *altocumulus* (1881), a cloud forming a layer of rounded masses with a level base occurring at medium altitude; *nimbostratus* (1887), a rain cloud forming a horizontal layer; and *altostratus* (1890), a stratus cloud that occurs at medium altitude.

Around the same time, new weather-related phobias appeared: *astraphobia*, a fear of lightning; and *brontophobia*, a fear of thunder and thunderstorms. *Lightning strike* appears in 1876. Even *raincoat* and *rained on* did not exist before 1830 and 1857 respectively. Knowing the British penchant for talking about the weather, it makes you wonder what words were used before these new coinages in the nineteenth century!

It was in this weather-mad context that a young boy called George Symons, born in London in 1838, began making rainfall observations in his back garden with his own home-made instruments. At the age of seventeen, he joined the British Meteorological Society, and by nineteen he had become a meteorological observer for the Registrar General. In his early twenties, he had a job in the meteorological department of the Board of Trade, and in 1860, he established a network of devoted rainfall observers. He and his wife, Elizabeth, set up a collection of instruments in their back garden in Camden Square, London, where they took daily observations for forty years. At its height in the late 1890s, Symons's network had over 3,000 observers, including the OED's Mrs Mary Pringle. It was so popular, he gave up his day job and devoted himself entirely to coordinating the British Rainfall Organisation, a crowdsourced project which, like the OED, was definitely a full-time job.

Mary was not the only person who collected both rain and words. Other Dictionary People who were also rain collectors included surgeon Mr William Kesteven of Little Park, Enfield; Miss Elizabeth Brown, an astronomer who lived with her sister in Further Barton, Cirencester, and one of Murray's top female volunteers; and the Revd George Bousfield and his two daughters Beatrice and Lillian of Maida Vale, London.

How did Mary first get involved in collecting rain and words? It was probably through word of mouth. Even though Murray and Symons had distributed leaflets and had advertised their projects in newspapers and journals, most people who joined in the crowdsourced projects did so through the recommendation of another volunteer. In Mary's case, others in her village also volunteered in one or other of the projects: Richard Porter, a local factory owner, had been reading Darwin and sending words from anatomy books to Murray for a year before Mary; and Percy Bicknell was well-known in rain circles and had been sending measurements to Symons for a decade before she began.

George Symons reported something similar to Murray's experience of hopeless contributors: 'Some people have the terrible habit of procrastinating, and the tardiness of some observers in forwarding their records gives my assistants weeks of work, costs many pounds for postages alone, and worst of all, seriously retards the date of publication.'

If Mary Pringle's excellent contribution to the OED is any indication, we can presume that she was not one of Symons's procrastinators. However, her contributions to both projects stopped suddenly in 1884 after the death of her son. She and Charles moved to the seaside town of Weston-super-Mare in Somerset, where she lived out her days. In her final years, her allegiances shifted away from dictionaries and the weather: she left money in her will to Dr Barnardo's Homes for Orphans and to the Metropolitan Drinking Fountain and Cattle Trough Association. (A charity dedicated to providing free and uncontaminated drinking fountains, in case you're wondering.)

S

for SUFFRAGISTS

The lifespan of the making of the OED runs in parallel with the fight for votes for women. The Dictionary was started just as the first female suffragist societies formed in Britain. It ended with the Prime Minister giving a toast at a celebratory Dictionary Dinner in London on 6 June 1928, on the publication of A–Z in twelve volumes. A month later the Equal Franchise Act was passed which allowed all British women over the age of twenty-one to vote. It had been a long struggle across seventy years, and that's saying nothing of the fight for women's suffrage.

When Charles Onions put *suffragette* and *suffragist* in the Dictionary in 1915, he defined them thus: *suffragette*, 'a female supporter of the cause of women's political enfranchisement, esp. one of a violent or militant type'; and *suffragist*, 'an advocate of the extension of the political franchise, esp. (since about 1885) to women'.

There were many suffragists among the Dictionary People. Looking through Murray's address book, I was struck by the number of feminist pioneers, among them Clara Dorothea Rackham, a factory inspector who served as President of the Eastern Federation of Suffrage Societies and became a politician once women got the vote; and Miss Emily Davies,

Secretary of the National Society for Women's Suffrage and Mistress of Girton College, Cambridge, who had fought for women's admission to higher education. Davies had been assigned John Stuart Mill's *Logic*, but the address book records that she did not have time to read it, and the title of the book is crossed out. Digging a little deeper, I discovered more suffragists: the archaeologist Margaret Murray; the novelist Beatrice Harraden; Murray's own daughter, Gwyneth; the political activist Miss Charlotte Ellis; as well as the Royal physician Dr John Lowe; the eccentric Cambridge classicist the Revd John Eyton Bickersteth Mayor; and the antiquarian Edward Peacock, who had multiple roles on the Dictionary as a Subeditor, Reader, and adviser.

But one name, Catherine Courtauld Osler of Birmingham, stood out from the others. Osler was Secretary of the Birmingham Women's Suffrage Society (BWSS) and author of the influential pamphlet *Why Women Need the Vote*. Her entire family (parents, aunt, uncle, husband, children) were suffragists, and she was involved in the movement from the age of fourteen in 1868 to her death in 1924. She lived to witness the 1918 legislation which gave the vote to women over the age of thirty but she died before women were granted the vote on equal terms with men in 1928. Her reading for Murray was similar to that of the other Dictionary suffragists in one respect: they did not send in slips from suffrage materials or their activist lives, but rather from their own personal interests. For Osler, this was mainly philosophy and religion.

The suffrage-related words still found their way to the Scriptorium. The story of the struggle for female suffrage can be plotted according to the creation and evolution of a plethora of new words related to the movement: *the woman question* (1833), *womanism* (1850), *women's movement* (1851), *feminist* (1852), *unfeminineness* (1856), *the New Woman* (1865), *women's suffrage* (1868), *women's righter* (1870), *woman suffragist* (1871), *liberationist* (1879), *emancipatress* (1882), *anti-suffragism* (1895), *feminism* (1895), *freewoman* (1895), *equal righter* (1896), *sex warfare* (1896), *women's liberation* (1898), *womanist* (1902), *sex war* (1905), *suffragette* (1906), *masculinist* (1912), *sisterhood* (1914), *hungerstruck* (1914), *hunger striking* (1916). Of course, not all these words had been coined before the corresponding letter of the alphabet was published, and others were missed out (not many suffragist materials were read for the Dictionary), but they have all been put in since.

All these words come from a period in history when notions of equality and sexual difference were changing radically. Catherine Osler – or Catherine Taylor as she was born in 1854 – was at the heart of these changes. In 1866, when she was twelve, her aunt Clementia Taylor and uncle Peter Taylor MP, working with John Stuart Mill, had gathered signatures in their home in London for the first mass petition on women's suffrage, and sent it to Parliament. This effectively marked the launch of the nineteenth-century suffragist movement, and Clementia became Secretary to the newly formed London Suffrage Society. When, two years later in 1868, Catherine's parents founded the BWSS, Catherine was an early subscriber at the age of fourteen, and might have a claim even to being the youngest.

The Unitarian family – and the broader milieu – in which Osler grew up was dedicated to radical causes. As a teenager, she met all the key players in the women's rights movement in her aunt and uncle's London home, including the leading suffragist Millicent Garrett Fawcett and her husband, Henry; the activist and translator Emilie Ashurst Venturi; and the Italian political reformer Giuseppe Mazzini whom she later described as her childhood idol and whose image she always wore around her neck on a gold chain – 'one of my cherished possessions', she told a journalist.

When she married the wealthy glass manufacturer and fellow Unitarian Thomas Osler, in 1873, the minister who performed the marriage ceremony at Church of the Messiah in Birmingham was the prominent preacher Henry Crosskey, who was for ten years President of the BWSS, and campaigned for numerous progressive causes, such as free state education and old-age pensions. Thomas Osler shared his wife's political views and served as President of the Birmingham Liberal Association while Catherine was President of the Birmingham Women's Liberal Association. Suffrage meetings were held in their home in Edgbaston, Birmingham, and this is the main address listed in Murray's address book, but she also sent in slips from Bridgwater, Somerset (where she was born), and from Leicester where her uncle was MP and where she met the Revd John Page Hopps whose work she read for the OED.

In 1879, when she was twenty-five years old, a mother of two small children (she would have three more), and busy organizing and speaking at suffrage demonstrations, Catherine also found time to read several books for the Dictionary and to send in 550 slips. Two were from her religious environment, books written by the Unitarian minister John Page Hopps, who was also a Reader for the Dictionary. She sent in 150 slips from his *First Principles of Religion and Morality* and 75 slips from his *Life of Jesus*, both books written for younger readers. She also sent in 275 slips from Sir John Lubbock's *Scientific Lectures*, a recently published series of lectures on plants, insects, and archaeology. Reading for the Dictionary was quite an art and, looking at the quotations which Osler selected, it is clear that she was an excellent Reader who chose quotations that were in a natural voice and yet also explained the word by the context. Murray put most of them in the Dictionary, such as *ant rice*, 'A Texan ant . . . is also a harvesting species storing up especially the grains of *Aristida oligantha*, the so-called "ant rice"'; and *eel-trap*, 'The bladders are on the principle of an eel-trap, having a closed entrance with a flap which permits an easy entrance, but effectually prevents the unfortunate victim from getting out again.'

Although Osler read no further books for the Dictionary after that, her son Julian – a member of the Men's League for Women's Suffrage – advised the Dictionary on glass terminology in 1909. His older brother John, who ran the Osler glassware shop in London, shared the family's passion for female suffrage, and always ensured that the shop advertised regularly in *The Common Cause*, the magazine of the National Union of Women's Suffrage Societies (NUWSS).

From 1885, Catherine Osler was secretary of the BWSS, dedicated to the suffragist mission of peaceful campaigning for constitutional reform, which she expounded in her 1910 pamphlet, *Why Women Need the Vote*. As a friend and follower of Millicent Fawcett, she believed in peaceful protest and campaigned for votes for middle-class, property-owning women. Osler exemplified the approach of Fawcett's followers by her law-abiding activism. She remained a 'suffragist' and was never a 'suffragette' once the movement split in 1903. Emmeline Pankhurst and others had grown frustrated by the lack of progress using peaceful methods, and they moved towards increasingly violent campaigns with 'deeds not words'. Members of Pankhurst's newly formed Women's Social and Political Union (WSPU) were labelled *suffragettes*, women who advocate for women's right to vote through direct action and civil disobedience. Originally a pejorative term, *suffragette* was first written in 1906 in the London *Daily Mail*, and was soon proudly reclaimed by the suffragettes themselves as a self-descriptor, a badge of honour even, and as the title of their own newspaper. The etymology of *suffrage* + *-ette* seems to have bemused the editor Charles Onions who commented in the preface to S that the word was an 'etymological anomaly' and, writing in an article in the *Observer* in 1925, 'we included the word suffragette though it is not a proper formation'.

Osler did not agree with the violent practices of Pankhurst's followers who fought for the cause by smashing windows, planting bombs, damaging public art, handcuffing themselves to railings, and going on hunger strikes when jailed. But when she learned that suffragettes in the local prison were being force-fed, a policy of the Liberal Government, she resigned her position as President of the Birmingham Women's Liberal Association.

Nor was Osler a *New Woman*, a woman considered different from previous generations, especially one who challenged the traditional roles of wife, mother, and homemaker. The New Woman was considered detrimental to 'femininity', a sense of the word created in the nineteenth century in opposition to the woman's suffrage movement meaning 'the quality or condition of displaying characteristics associated with a woman; feminine style, design, etc'. The words *defeminization* and *defeminized* were created at the same time.

An interview with Osler, published in 1895 in the magazine *The Woman at Home*, contrasts her with the New Woman and paints a picture of an articulate and effective public speaker who also displayed conventional 'femininity . . . her power lying in a clear, quiet, well-balanced style'. She is presented as a woman who, having five young children, 'formed a very attractive picture of womanly grace and refinement as she sat by the drawing-room fire gowned in pale green silk trimmed with black lace, relieved here and there by cunningly devised touches of pink velvet. Her hair was brushed up high from the forehead, giving her face a bright, open look.' Osler told the interviewer, 'We are a merry, noisy household here. It is such a pleasure to be young along with one's children, to go about with them and enter into their sports.'

Some of the Dictionary People were anti-suffrage – most notably the pornographer Henry Spencer Ashbee and the Headmistress of the Queen's School in Chester, Mrs Margaret Elizabeth Sandford. An American Congregational minister in West Battleboro, Vermont, the Revd Charles H. Merrill, read an anti-suffrage book for Murray called *Women's Suffrage: Reform Against Nature* by Horace Bushnell (1869), and sent in 25 slips, including the sentence 'Woman is created to be the meet-helper of man', which is quoted in the entry *meet-helper*, a fitting and suitable helper.

The most famous anti-suffragist of the period was Queen Victoria who had complained in a letter to Sir Theodore Martin in 1870 about 'this mad, wicked folly of "Women's Rights", with all its attendant horrors on which her poor feeble sex is bent, forgetting every sense of womanly feeling and propriety . . . Woman would become the most hateful, heathen, and disgusting of human beings were she allowed to unsex herself; and where would be the protection which man was intended to give the weaker sex.' Expressions such as *the feeble sex*, and *the weaker sex*, along with the verb *unsex*, to deprive a person of the characteristics, attributes, or qualities traditionally associated with their sex, which had been around since Shakespeare, were suddenly being used to disparage the suffragists.

T

for TRAMPS, THE SUNDAY

I expected more famous names in the address books. Instead, the Dictionary was largely a project of the crowd, the auto-didacts, the unknowns. There were pockets of professionals – academics, intellectuals, and writers – but they were in the minority. Of those who were present, I was surprised by the people missing. As advisers on scientific words, there was no Charles Darwin, Luther Burbank, or Thomas Edison. And where were the famous lovers-of-language and literary fig-ures such as Oscar Wilde, Joseph Conrad, Rudyard Kipling, Gerard Manley Hopkins, or Arthur Conan Doyle? There was no William Morris, Beatrix Potter, Margaret Oliphant, or Christina Rossetti. Young members of what became known as the Bloomsbury Set were born too late to get involved – no Lytton Strachey, John Maynard Keynes, E. M. Forster, or Vir-ginia Woolf and her sister Vanessa Bell.

However, Virginia and Vanessa's father *was* one of the Dictionary People. The year Vanessa was born, Leslie Stephen began a correspondence with Murray from his grand house at 13 Hyde Park Gate. Back in the nineteenth century, Hyde Park Gate's residents included the founder of the Boy Scouts, General Robert Baden-Powell, at number 9; the first woman to run for President of the USA, Victoria Claflin Woodhull

Martin, at number 17; and later in the twentieth century the sculptor Jacob Epstein, creator of the *Lazarus* statue in New College chapel, at number 18; along with Winston Churchill, who died at number 28.

Murray wrote under Leslie Stephen's name 'extracts from various sources', alongside symbols including a small Star of David, and codes D and D4 referring to lists of desired words for which Murray lacked quotations and needed skilled Readers to find. Often Murray checked certain words with Stephen, especially if they had been used by Alexander Pope, the seventeenth-century poet and one of Stephen's biographical subjects. One such word was *Brobdingnag*, gigantic, of huge dimensions, which Stephen helped locate in one of Pope's poems; he explained to Murray that the unusual word had in fact been originally coined by Swift in *Gulliver's Travels* to name an imaginary country where everything was on a gigantic scale.

While Stephen was busy answering Murray's queries in Kensington, 30 miles away in the less salubrious location of Surrey County Asylum, Stephen's book on Pope was being read by Dr Thomas Brushfield, who pioneered humane treatment for the mentally ill (see L for Lunatics). The quotations Dr Brushfield chose are particularly striking despite, or perhaps because of, his setting. Most of them pertained to happiness. Brushfield sent Murray slips for *laugh, congeniality, conviviality, courtesy, dazzle* ('Pope seems to have been dazzled by the amazing vivacity of the man'), *playfulness, brilliance,* and *banter,* all of which made it into the Dictionary. The optimistic asylum superintendent sent in 600 slips from several of Stephen's books, some of which seemed especially characteristic of the father of two future members of the Bloomsbury Set: *buck,* a gay dashing fellow; *blandishment,* gently flattering speech; *boozing,* addicted to drinking; and *scribbler,* a writer.

Murray's address book noted when the Dictionary People moved house. The strange thing about Leslie Stephen's entry is that he moved house several times *in the same street.* He spent his entire life in Hyde Park Gate. He was born at number 42, then moved to number 11 where he fell in love with the next-door neighbour, Julia Duckworth. They married and had their two daughters and a son, Thoby. The family moved to number 13, followed by number 22. Once they were old enough, Virginia, her siblings, and friends deliberately moved away from the stuffy atmosphere of upper-class Hyde Park Gate to the then more risqué Bloomsbury.

Virginia Woolf described her childhood at 22 Hyde Park Gate: 'Our duties were very plain and our pleasures absolutely appropriate.' Life was divided into two spaces – indoors, in a nursery and a book-lined drawing room, and outdoors, in Kensington Gardens. 'There were smells and flowers and dead leaves and chestnuts, by which you distinguished the seasons, and each had innumerable associations, and power to flood the brain in a second.' She remembered her father talking with his friend and fellow Dictionary Friend Frederick Pollock 'round the oval tea table with its pink china full of spice buns'. She wrote of Stephen, 'My father was deaf, eccentric, absorbed in his work, and entirely shut off from the world.'

He can't have been too shut off from the world because, during the years that Leslie Stephen contributed to the OED, he started his own crowdsourced project, the *Dictionary of National Biography* (DNB). Just as Murray's Dictionary traced the lives of thousands of words, Stephen's dictionary traced the lives of thousands of people who made a notable impact on British history. Stephen invited 653 people to write 29,120 articles. Sixty-three volumes comprising 29,108 pages were published, the first volume in 1885 and the last in 1900. The DNB is still going today, under the aegis of Oxford University

Press, and it now covers the lives of 55,000 people. Despite his huge workload for his own project, Stephen kept sending slips to Murray for twelve years, until 1891 when, although only in his fifties, but having suffered from a bout of influenza and pneumonia, he decided to give up not just the OED but also his editorship of the DNB (though he continued to contribute articles and engage in other literary work).

There were two types of networks of Dictionary People. Those who were connected by formal membership to certain clubs and societies, and those brought together by more informal and personal communications. One such lively and informal hub was the Sunday Tramps, a group of intellectual men brought together by Leslie Stephen every fortnight, regardless of the weather, to hike together in the countryside on the outskirts of London. The word *tramp* was a popular colloquial term at the time for 'a walking excursion'.

The motto of the Sunday Tramps was *Solvitur Ambulando,* 'It is solved by walking.' Stephen kept a membership book and assigned each member a number to use as shorthand in their records of the walks. There were some sixty in all, with the Russian historian and fellow contributor to the OED, Paul Gavrilovitch Vinogradoff, then living in Moscow, listed as a 'corresponding member'. But only about ten joined Stephen for the tramp on any given Sunday. Walks took place in winter and spring (summers were reserved for climbing in the Swiss Alps), and they were usually 20 to 25 miles in length. Stephen would send out a postcard notifying everyone of the location of the next tramp, along with the railway-station meeting spot.

Stephen was 'Captain of Tramps', choosing the route, striding ahead with his characteristic impatient snort and alpenstock in hand, and setting the topics for conversation. Generally, he encouraged the Tramps to be abstemious – only allowing them to take bread and cheese at local ale houses, or to carry sandwiches in their pockets. But on occasion when the tramping trails passed by the houses of friends of the Tramps, they called in, and they were entertained in this way by Charles Darwin, the jurist Frederic Harrison, and the novelist George Meredith who lived in Box Hill, Surrey, and would relish the opportunity of serving cups of refreshing Russian tea to the 'Learned Tramps' or 'Cranium Tramps', as he often called them.

The Sunday Tramps existed at exactly the same time that its members were most active on the Dictionary, from 1879 to 1895. Most of the Tramps who contributed to the Dictionary did so as Specialists and advisers. Murray consulted Sir Frederick Pollock on law terms and Alexander Kennedy on engineering words. The Cambridge jurist and legal historian (and advocate for women's education) Frederic Maitland helped Murray on current legal terms such as *bail, defend, culprit,* and *deliverance,* and also many obsolete ones such as *couthutlaughe,* a person knowingly harbouring or concealing an outlaw; *abishering,* a misreading of mishersing, freedom from amercements imposed by any court; *compurgator,* a character witness who swore along with the person accused, in order to the acquittal of the latter; *pennyland,* land having the rental value of one penny; and *contenement,* holding, freehold. Maitland co-wrote *History of English Law* with Frederick Pollock. Pollock may have been drinking tea out of pink cups when Virginia Woolf saw him, but the rest of the time this historian and Icelandic scholar was Regius Professor of Modern History at Oxford. He helped appoint William Craigie to the Dictionary and advised Murray on hundreds of words pertaining to law and legal history: *arrest, arrestment, cognizant, cognomen, derogatory, outhouse, parry, affiant, affreight, approve, arraign, arerisement, arson, assign, advalorem,* and *outfangthief,* a tricky entry that took Murray three people and six letters before he nailed its definition as 'the right of a lord of a private jurisdiction to claim for trial a thief captured outside the jurisdiction, and to keep any forfeited chattels on conviction'.

Law was a theme among those of the Tramps who were Dictionary People. The judge Thomas Edward Scrutton advised on the legal sense of *at arm's length* which he defined as 'without fiduciary relations, as those of trustee or solicitor to a client'. Scrutton's entry in the address book is not easy to decode. It has nearly every possible code and symbol: a blue cross, a red O, a Star of David, D, D4, D5, a triangle with a line through it, and a note 'Sent in all he can'. He sent in 736 slips from Swinburne and John Stuart Mill. But it was in the defining of nautical terms that Scrutton made the greatest contribution, which is not surprising given that he became known as England's greatest shipping lawyer, no doubt influenced by his father who was a prosperous shipowner. Murray knew the young Scrutton who had been a pupil at Mill Hill School when he had taught there. Scrutton wrote the definitions of *bottomry*, the action of pledging a ship and its cargo as security for money lent; *dill*, the space underneath the cabin floor in a wooden fishing vessel into which bilge-water drains; and *pink*, a small sailing vessel with a narrow stern.

Leslie Stephen once described a Sunday Tramp as 'precisely the kind of person who writes articles for newspapers'. He could easily have substituted 'dictionaries' for newspapers. Other Tramps who were Dictionary People included the poet and close friend of Henry Bradley, Robert Bridges; the museum curator Arthur Hamilton Smith; the Italianist Arthur John Butler; and the physician Sir Clifford Allbutt who advised on the terms *punctate*, marked or studded with points or dots; and *tellurism*, animal magnetism.

The OED was not their only uniting collaboration. They contributed to the DNB and many of them had been friends since their school and university days. They were a part of exclusive social networks that continued throughout their lives and extended to membership of London clubs and societies such as the Athenæum, the British Academy, the London Library, the Royal Institution, and the Reform Club. The Tramps were particularly in the ascendancy when the Liberals were elected in December 1905.

The Sunday Tramps formed a clique – or 'beloved fraternity' as George Meredith described them – that excluded Murray. Murray was a hiker himself who regularly climbed mountains and, when he hiked, walked an average of 25 miles per day. On the surface it is a little surprising that he did not join the learned group of men who shared a love for walking, nature, and the life of the mind. That's Murray in three. However, Murray differed from these men in many ways, not least education and class. Most of the Sunday Tramps had been educated at Eton and Cambridge, where many had been elected as members of the Apostles, a society of male undergraduates who met each Saturday night for discussion. These men formed strong lifelong bonds. The philosopher Henry Sidgwick summed up his experience of being an Apostle by saying, 'The tie of attachment to this society is much the strongest corporate bond which I have known in my life.' This bond could only have been strengthened by the Sunday Tramps, and would have been intimidating for an outsider, let alone one like Murray who left school at fourteen and never attended university.

It was not only class and education that separated Murray from the Sunday Tramps; it was also religion. Murray was a believer and staunch Nonconformist. He attended church every Sunday, and every morning before going into the Scriptorium he said prayers with his family. The Tramps were professed Agnostics. They believed that nothing is known or can be known of immaterial things, especially the existence of God. The 'Sunday' in the Sunday Tramps was deliberate and was a defiant attempt to 'escape from the dreary London Sabbath', as one of them put it. 'Our very appearance seemed like a challenge of defiance to the orderly church-going world.'

The Sunday Tramps, and Leslie Stephen in particular, were advocates for Agnosticism which emerged and gained popularity in this period. Stephen published a collection of seven essays in 1893 entitled *An Agnostic's Apology*. The word *Agnostic*, which Murray defined as 'one who holds that the existence of anything beyond and behind material phenomena is unknown and (so far as can be judged) unknowable', had been coined by Thomas Henry Huxley in 1869 and first written in an article in the *Spectator* magazine: 'In theory he [Prof. Huxley] is a great and even severe Agnostic, who goes about exhorting all men to know how little they know.'

The entry had caused Murray a lot of bother, and he had written to Richard Holt Hutton for assistance. Hutton was editor of the *Spectator* and he had already been helping Murray spread the word about the Dictionary project by placing announcements in his magazine. Over a series of five letters in 1881, they teased out the word's origin. In the final entry for *Agnostic*, Murray did something very rare. He quoted directly from Hutton's letter: 'Suggested by Prof. Huxley at a party held previous to the formation of the now defunct Metaphysical Society, at Mr James Knowles's house on Clapham Common, one evening in 1869, in my hearing. He took it from St Paul's mention of the altar to "the Unknown God". R. H. Hutton in letter 13 Mar. 1881.'

Murray's Christian conviction would never have allowed him to join the Sunday Tramps in their sabbath-defying hikes. Walking in nature was for him a religious experience, an act of devotion, which went back to a mystical experience when he was thirty-eight years old. Murray was on his annual holiday with Ada and their young family at Easedale in the Lake District. Early one evening, he went out walking alone in the mountains, in anticipation of the rising of the full moon. As night began to fall, he got lost. The moon had not yet risen, he fell in the darkness and badly injured his foot but kept on going. Scrambling down a steep incline, he reached an expanse of deep black in front of him. He stopped and suddenly realized that he was in great danger, and clung to a heather tussock on a precipice overhanging the lake far below.

Writing in his diary afterwards, he explained, 'I could myself do nothing but one thing. I dropped to my knees on the heather tussock on which I stood and earnestly besought God to guide me in this, one of the most dangerous emergencies of my life.' He got up and went to walk in one direction, but a strong feeling told him to turn around and go the opposite way. This decision, he believed, saved his life. 'I have absolutely no explanation save that it was God's answer to my prayer, and such I have ever felt it. One does not proclaim these things from the housetops; they are too sacred. But they are among the most profound convictions of one's soul; and, many a time since then, my faith in the Invisible has been restored by remembering my experience at Easedale Tarn.'

Murray's belief in God sustained him throughout his work on the Dictionary. On his seventieth birthday, he gave a speech which reflected on his lifelong devotion: 'The Dictionary is to me . . . the work that God has found for me and for which I now see that my sharpening of intellectual tools was done and it becomes to me a high and sacred devotion.'

Murray's religious beliefs, his lack of formal education, and his different social class are some of the reasons why he was not a member of the Sunday Tramps. In 1891, at the same time that Leslie Stephen stopped contributing to the OED and resigned as editor of the DNB, he also handed over leadership of the Sunday Tramps to Frederick Pollock. But interest in the group waned and by 1895 it was over. As Maitland put it, 'The deceitfulness of golf and the vanity of bicycles distracted some of those who had been consistent walkers.' The final walk – the two-hundred-and-fifty-second to be precise (these things were noted) – took place in March 1895. Several years later, the sons of the Tramps tried to revive the group, but, without Leslie Stephen's enthusiasm and leadership, it did not endure.

U

for USA

American English was a part of the Dictionary from the very start. Everyone thinks of the OED as quintessentially British, but it also covers thousands of words from other varieties of English spoken around the world. This was intentional. Furnivall always emphasized the democratic nature of the Dictionary – 'Fling our doors wide! All, all, not one, but all must enter', he proclaimed. The founding documents of the Dictionary, grandly called the *Canones Lexicographici*, declare that Americanisms must be admitted 'on the same terms as our own words'.

You can't go a page or two in Murray's address book before seeing a name underlined in thick red pencil. These are the Americans. It is impossible to know exactly how many Dictionary Friends were American – most did not send their slips directly to Murray so they are not always listed in his address books. Because postage across the Atlantic was expensive, American Readers sent their slips via a specially designated 'Secretary in America', first George Marsh in Vermont and subsequently Francis March in Pennsylvania. The Secretaries gathered everyone's slips and sent them to England in large boxes. And because of the hazards of the mail, Murray did not entrust subediting to Americans – 'the risks of the double sea-voyage across the Atlantic deterred me', he told one volunteer.

Some Americans did write directly to Murray, and these – 196 of them – are the ones underlined in the address books. They represent 10 per cent of all the Dictionary People with addresses and produced a total of 238,080 slips that crossed the ocean before coming to rest on Murray's desk in the Scriptorium.

The Americans were a mixed bunch, from the great and the good such as the linguist William Dwight Whitney who wrote his own dictionary (the *Century Dictionary*) and Noah Thomas Porter, who edited *Webster's Dictionary* and became President of Yale University, to relative unknowns such as twenty-one-year-old Miss Carille Winthrop Atwood who loved poetry and Ancient Greece and lived in a large house with several other young women on Clay Street in a fashionable area of San Francisco. The Americans included university professors, politicians, soldiers, publishers, activists,

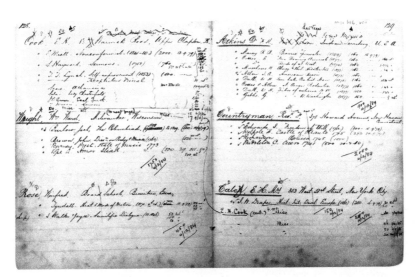

American contributors were underlined in red in Murray's address books.

librarians, booksellers, mothers, lawyers, coin collectors, journalists, pharmacists, and surgeons.

Americans were involved in the OED project right from the beginning. In 1858, the year after the idea of the Dictionary had been mooted by the London Philological Society, the *New York Times* informed American readers of a 'fresh appeal to scholars, and lovers of learning and philological inquiry, for additions to their vocabulary'. The newspaper article argued that a better English dictionary was needed. It highlighted the deficiencies of existing and past English and American dictionaries – Johnson's, Richardson's and Webster's. The article was especially damning of the latter, an American dictionary which, of course, has been improved and revised many times since it was first published in 1828. 'Of Webster it is hardly necessary to speak. His capricious trifling with the rules of orthography, added to the facts that his citations are seldom from original authorities, and his definitions still less accurate than Richardson's, must exclude his labors from serving even as a basis of the complete dictionary of our language.'

The *New York Times* argued that 'any fresh undertaking' needed 'to hold itself independent of all these endeavors, using them wherever they may be advantageously employed, but relying upon their own more catholic plan.' The article proposed that the new English Dictionary's remit should be as wide as possible – admitting slang, taboo words, archaisms, and scientific and provincial words. The following year, the Dictionary stated publicly that it would be following a wide remit.

It is notable that the first public appeal for help creating the OED went out in America – not Britain. When the London Philological Society appointed Herbert Coleridge as the first Chief Editor of the Dictionary in 1859, a request soon appeared in the pages of American newspapers, journals, and magazines. It was George Marsh, a Vermonter lecturing in English Literature at Columbia College in New York and one of the few American members of the London Philological Society, who published this call to his fellow Americans.

Marsh was seeking Readers to gather words for the radical new Dictionary project that was going to rival American dictionaries in its method and reliability. He offered his compatriots the opportunity to co-create the most authoritative dictionary ever produced of the entire English language, and listed rules for extracting quotations for 'every word occurring in the literature of the language'. Then he added, 'The selection is left to the taste of the collaborators.'

When Marsh sent out his appeal for American Readers, what was known as the 'Dictionary War' had been waging for some time between two leading lexicographers, Noah Webster and Joseph Worcester. Worcester had been Webster's assistant on his *American Dictionary of the English Language* (1828) but, a superior philologist to Webster, he went off and wrote his own dictionary which was published two years later as the *Comprehensive Pronouncing and Explanatory English Dictionary*. Webster accused Worcester of plagiarism. A public slanging match ensued, which continued beyond Webster's death in 1843 and only ended a little after the OED project began.

Worcester applied the scientific method to his etymologies (which Webster did not), and wrote a revised and expanded version of his original dictionary entitled *Dictionary of the English Language* (1860). However, four years later, in 1864, *Webster's Unabridged* was published and it marked an important moment in modern lexicography: no longer the idiosyncratic work of one man, this dictionary was the product of a collaborative team with Noah Porter as Chief Editor and the German scholar Carl A. F. Mahn as etymologist. Mahn's etymologies adopted Worcester's scientific approach, thereby producing a dictionary that displayed the best virtues of both. The Dictionary War was over, confirmed by the death of Worcester the following year (1865).

In this context, Marsh invited members of the American public to help create a radical new dictionary of all English which applied the scientific method, was collaborative in its making, and was based on written evidence. They were asked to collect current words and especially to read books from the eighteenth century – because literature from earlier centuries was harder to get in America at the time. Marsh ended his appeal with the warning that Americans would be paid nothing for their help.

Despite that caution, twenty enthusiastic scholars, writers, and publishers immediately responded to the call. American academics, unlike their British counterparts, were keen to be a part of the Dictionary project. Marsh was well connected, from New England aristocracy, which helped. He was also a man of many skills and talents: he spoke twenty languages and wrote popular lectures on the origins of English. He was an early ecological activist, warning against human-induced climate change before anyone else, and publishing in 1864 *Man and Nature: or, Physical Geography as Modified by Human Action.* Marsh was also a politician and a diplomat. In 1861, two years after he assumed his OED responsibilities, he was sent to Turin by President Abraham Lincoln to be the first US Ambassador to the newly united Kingdom of Italy, a post he held until his death in 1882 (he is buried in Rome).

The American Civil War naturally affected contributions between 1861 and 1865. If the first respondents were mainly educated men from universities known to Marsh, very soon all sorts of American amateurs were offering to help document their language. Marsh continued to coordinate the American volunteers from his diplomatic postings in Turin, Florence, and Rome, but the number of American helpers did not increase dramatically until 1879 when Francis March took over as the American coordinator under the new Editorship of James Murray.

Francis March was a Professor of English Language and Comparative Philology at Lafayette College in Easton, Pennsylvania. The study of English in higher education was a development of the nineteenth century, and it took a long time for English studies to gain recognition. March's appointment as a Professor of English in 1857 had been the first in the world that had the prestige of a full professorship – Rutgers appointed its first English professor in 1860, Harvard in 1876, and Oxford in 1885. In addition to contributing to the creation of the OED, Francis March also helped with the etymologies in William Dwight Whitney's *Century Dictionary* (1889–91) and Isaac Funk's *Standard Dictionary of the English Language* (first volume published in 1893).

March was so helpful that Murray considered making him a co-Editor when it was thought that they might need such a person in the USA to secure an American copyright. In the end, that wasn't necessary and March simply remained the contact person for American Readers, informing them of which books to read, keeping a list of books undertaken, and doing everything that could be done to save the time lost by a letter crossing and recrossing the Atlantic.

When Francis March took over, he dedicated so much time to the project that in his first year alone he received and answered around 1,000 letters. 'The truly generous help of Prof March has been so great, that I feel under profound obligations to him, and I shall be glad to see both the Philological Society and the Delegates give some expression to their appreciation of his exertions', Murray reported to the Delegates of Oxford University Press in 1880. Keenly aware that the kinds of professors he could not attract to the Dictionary project in England were becoming Dictionary volunteers

George Marsh (left) and Francis March (right), the
two American coordinators of the Dictionary.

in the USA, Murray was grateful to March: 'Under his influence great and important assistance in the reading has
been rendered by a large number of the Professors in the
American Colleges and Universities, a class of men who in
this country, with the solitary exception of Prof Dowden,
have been too busy even to express interest in the work. In
several instances an American Professor has, with the aid of
his students, undertaken and read whole series of books.'

March's coordinator duties ended in 1882 but he continued reading and advising for the Dictionary for another
twenty-nine years, until his death in 1911.

Academics from many institutions and disciplines, all
over America, gladly volunteered. The chemist Professor
Henry Carrington Bolton from Trinity College, Hartford,
Connecticut, held the world's largest private collection of
early chemistry books and used his library to provide citations for the Dictionary. He sent in hundreds of slips from
Richard Russell's 1678 translation of Jabir ibn Haiyan's *Works*

of Geber. Most of the words Bolton sent in were pertaining to chemical states and were rare or obsolete by the time he found them, but they were all put in the Dictionary regardless, many with his citation as the only proof of the word's existence: *aluminosity*, the quality of alum; *foetant*, fruitful; *fusory*, tending to melt; *ignoble*, capable of ignition; *insignize*, to distinguish; *liquorous*, of the nature of liquid; *lunific*, capable of transmuting other substances into silver; *spissative*, serving to thicken.

Hamilton College in upstate New York was a hub for volunteers and included the chemist Professor Albert Huntington Chester who helped Murray with ornithological and mineral terms. Meanwhile, Miss Elizabeth Gilman Brown grew up at the college where her father was President. She ensured that James Fenimore Cooper was read for the Dictionary. She sent in 150 slips from *The Pioneers* and 75 slips from *The Last of the Mohicans.* Her reading provided the first proof for American words such as *dicker*, the practice of bartering, and *war-paint*, paint applied to the face and body before going into battle. Margaret Catlin Brandt jointly read with her husband Professor Hermann Carl George Brandt, who taught French and German at Hamilton, and they sent in 750 slips from the works of the American Romantic poet, James Russell Lowell, who himself was a contributor to the Dictionary. Lowell joined the ranks of Dr Minor and Fitzedward Hall as Americans living in England who helped the Dictionary. He was American Ambassador to the United Kingdom from 1880 to 1885, during which time (for work) he checked on Minor's health in Broadmoor, and (for pleasure) he visited Murray at the Scriptorium and advised him of the expressions *axe-grinding* and *pegging away.* Murray thanked him in the preface of Volume I for 'various help'. When he returned to America, he helped found the American Dialect Society.

The educator and scientist Dr George Morris Philips sent

in 12,080 slips from books on American history and astronomy. A few years after he started reading for the Dictionary, Philips began sending books to their authors (along with return packages and postage) asking them to sign their book and return it to him. His library eventually grew to be one of the world's largest collections of signed editions. He once sent his copy of John Ruskin's *Ethics of the Dust* to the author for an autograph. Ruskin refused and sent it back by steamer; the ship *Oregon* was wrecked on 14 March 1886 but the book was rescued. Philips sent it back again with a note about its adventure. This time Ruskin signed and added in a note that the book 'was better worth fishing up than most of the things that went down with it'.

The etymologist and Anglo-Saxonist Charles Payson Gurley Scott volunteered as a Reader for the OED in 1883, a year before he started work as etymologist for the *Century Dictionary*. In that one year, he specifically read Chaucer, sending in 300 slips from *The Squire's Tale* and 500 slips from *The Franklin's Tale*. The OED editors also sent him desiderata (D4 and D5). Scott was at one time employed by Andrew Carnegie to support the cause of simplified spelling. He had been a student of March at Lafayette, graduating with a bachelor's degree in 1878 and a doctorate from Columbia in 1881.

Coverage of words from Native American cultures and languages was important, and came from Professor William Stokes Wyman at the University of Alabama, Tuskaloosa, and the linguist Henry Phillips Jnr in Philadelphia. Slips were also sent from the unexpected location of a military base in New Mexico where Dr Francis Atkins was a medical doctor. Atkins read George Gibbs's *Tribes of Western Washington and Northwestern Oregon* and sent in *sweat-house*, a hut in which hot air or vapour baths are taken; *squaw*, defined as 'a North American Indian woman or wife. Now generally considered offensive'; *scalp-lock*, defined as 'a long lock of hair left on the head (the rest being shaved) by North American Indians as a challenge to their enemies'; *to scalp*, defined as 'to cut off the scalp of (a person): chiefly said of the North American Indians'; and *gig*, a fishing handline with barbless hooks.

Atkins also sent in slips from Washington Matthews's *Ethnography and Philology of the Hidatsa Indians* for *pad-saddle*, a soft unstructured horse saddle used by someone learning to ride, 'They make neat pad-saddles of tanned elk-skin, stuffed with antelope hair'; *frontiersmen*, someone who lives on the frontier of a country, 'The whites they had seen were mostly rude Canadian frontiersmen'; *rodent*, 'The rodent teeth of the beaver are regarded as potent charms'; and the *squash* vegetable, a word borrowed from Narragansett *asquutasquash*.

Tribes of the Extreme Northwest by the American naturalist William Dall was another important book on the indigenous peoples and languages of Alaska, western Washington, and north-western Oregon. This was also read by Atkins and provided the words *sphagnum*, a mossy plant, 'A saucer or dish of stone or clay, with a wick, usually of sphagnum'; *rejectamenta*, things rejected as useless, 'Bones, shells, and all varieties of rejectamenta having been deposited here for centuries'; and *to tattoo*, 'The practice of tattooing perpendicular lines on the chin of women'. Atkins's reading of Joel Allen's *History of the American Bison* (1877) put lots of American ranching words into the Dictionary: *rutting season*, mating season; *pronghorn*, a North American antelope; *pound*, an enclosure for cattle; *bison*, a wild ox; *barrens*, tracts of barren land.

There was a high number of librarians among the Americans, such as Charles Ammi Cutter of Harvard and the Boston Athenæum (who produced America's first public library card catalogue). But not all American contributors were scholars or associated with academic institutions – the majority were general members of the public or amateur scholars.

The contributions of American women were many and

often noteworthy. Mrs Anna Thorpe Wetherill was an anti-slavery activist and Quaker who hid escaped slaves in her houses at 901 Clinton Street, Philadelphia, and at Chalkey Hall, a manor house outside the city from where she sent slips to Oxford. She worked with her husband Edward to help them travel to the North safely along the Underground Railroad. She read the plantation diary of Fanny Kemble, and sent Murray 1,000 words which, in the letter A alone, included *abhorrent, abolition, accursed, apoplectic, annex,* and *attack.* Besides collecting words for the Dictionary, Anna kept scrapbooks (preserved today in the Pennsylvania Historical Society). She gathered newspaper articles relating to slavery and its abolition: the death of Harriet Tubman in 1913, who had escaped slavery and then worked on the Underground Railroad; slave auctions in the South; and escaped slaves whom their masters wanted returned – and whom she and her fellow abolitionists sought to help and shelter on their journey North. Her circle included novelist and abolitionist Harriet Beecher Stowe and Quaker abolitionist Thomas Wilmington who described Anna Wetherill as a 'friend and fellow laborer'. Like many abolitionists, she was also a suffragist.

Miss Mary K. A. Stone sent in slips from an asylum in Massachusetts. A poet, she was the daughter of the Revd Dr John Seely Stone, Dean of the (then newly founded) Episcopal Theological School in Cambridge, Massachusetts. She contributed 2,000 slips from books relating to religion and mountaineering. There is a note in the address book that as of January 1881 she resided at the Adams-Nervine Asylum, near Boston's Arnold Arboretum, which implies that she continued to read for the Dictionary while a patient. The asylum was a sprawling three-storey Queen Anne house with a corner tower, a conical roof, and many balconies of different shapes and sizes. It was for women with nervous disorders, rather than serious mental illness, and famously gave refuge to Alice James, sister of William and Henry James, and Clover Hooper Adams, a photographer and socialite who was the inspiration for Henry James's protagonist Isabel Archer in *The Portrait of a Lady* (1881). The asylum is known to have been based on the 'moral treatment' theories of Thomas Kirkbride, a contemporary Philadelphia psychiatrist who believed that asylums should be based on a village plan with a home-style atmosphere that respected the dignity of its patients. Miss Stone's room had a rich rug covering a polished hardwood floor, graceful draperies, and good-quality etchings and books. Patients were frequently restored to full health by living in a community setting within the asylum.

While there, Miss Stone sent Murray 100 slips from the sermons of local Boston Episcopal priest Philip Brooks (who was Rector of Trinity Church, and later Bishop of Massachusetts) – *endearment, escape, mysterious, struggle* – and 500 more slips from books on Greece and the Middle East. After her stint at Adams-Nervine, there are no more titles listed for her in the address book, but she kept up a correspondence with Murray for another two years, perhaps relating to the desiderata he had asked her to find (though alas none of their letters survives).

The Dictionary's coverage of the leading transcendentalist, Henry David Thoreau, is largely due to the monumental efforts of a single woman, Miss Alice Byington of Stockbridge, Massachusetts, who sent in 5,000 slips from books that included several by Thoreau: *Walden, Letters to Various Persons, A Yankee in Canada, A Week on the Concord and Merrimack Rivers*, and *The Maine Woods*. Another of her favourite authors was the female novelist, A. D. T. Whitney, eight of whose books for girls she read for the Dictionary, bringing in the words *dimple-cleft*, 'Her dimple-cleft and placid chin'; *dipperful*, as much as fills a ladle; *gloryhole*, a drawer in which things are heaped together without any attempt at order or tidiness; *brewis*, beef broth; *mitchella*, a trailing plant of North America; and *to scrinch*, to squeeze one's body into a crouched or huddled position.

Byington began reading for Murray when she was thirty-eight years old. She was an activist and schoolteacher at Hillside Home for Young Ladies aged four to fourteen, which operated out of the home of her friend Miss Adele Brewer and her two sisters, with whom Miss Byington lived. In 1904, she and the Brewer sisters staged the first successful sit-down strike in the USA. The New England Telephone Company had planned to put a pole in their front yard and workers from the company began digging the hole. But the Brewer sisters and Byington came out and sat in the hole, blocking their efforts by sleeping there in a tent overnight. The telephone company installed the pole across the road instead, making this a successful result for nineteenth-century Nimby activism.

Byington's father was Judge Horatio Byington who represented the town of Stockbridge in the State Legislature. But it was her uncle, the Revd Cyrus Byington, who had the greatest influence on her life and interests. He had been a missionary with the Brewer sisters' father to the Choctaw Native American Communities at the old mission station in Stockbridge; he had translated the Bible into Choctaw, and wrote a grammar and dictionary of the language.

Byington shared her uncle's interest in and support for indigenous culture and language, serving as President of the Stockbridge branch of the Indian Rights Association, and on the Education Committee for the Women's National Indian Association. But when it came to her reading for the Dictionary, she did not send in words from indigenous culture or language. Nor did George Everett Foster, a Reader who, although he wrote books on the Cherokee, chose instead to read theological books for the Dictionary.

The American who sent in the most slips was a clergy-man in Ionia, Michigan, Job Pierson. A Presbyterian minister, book collector, and librarian, Pierson had the largest private library in Michigan (which included a book published in the earliest days of printing, from Vienna in 1476). Over eleven years, from 1879 to 1890, Pierson, who had studied at Williams College and attended Auburn Theological Seminary, sent in 43,055 slips from poetry, drama, and religion. His correspondence with Murray shows the breadth of his reading, from Chaucer (10,000 slips) to books on anatomy (5,000 slips), and lumbering (1,000 slips). A letter to Murray on 9 March 1882 conveys Pierson's earnestness and the diversity of his reading for the Dictionary: 'My dear Sir, I send you a small package containing the A words from the part of Chaucer you lately sent me. Also some lumber and railroad slips. I enclose a list of compounds of "saw" which I have lately collected. Also a cutting from one of our newspapers containing terms and phrases among the Brokers.'

In addition, he wrote, 'I also send you by mail a catalogue of "lumbering tools" which will pictorially give you an idea of some of the "lumber terms" in use. I send the earliest instance of the use of *cattle guard* which I have been able to find.' I can just imagine the staff of the Scriptorium perusing the American lumber tools catalogue together during their morning tea break.

Pierson's son, Bowen Whiting Pierson, who worked for a hydraulic manufacturing firm in New York, also read for the Dictionary but his interests were less varied and diverse than his father's. He stuck to eighteenth-century novels, sending in 2,000 slips from Samuel Richardson's weighty *Clarissa* and *Pamela* which provided first quotations for *dilly-dally*, to act with trifling vacillation or indecision; *eloper*, one who elopes; *encore*, to call applaudingly for the repetition of something; *girlhood*, the state of being a girl; *hand-to-mouth*, satisfying only

The Revd Job Pierson of Ionia, Michigan, sent in more
slips than any other American.

one's immediate needs, especially because of lack of money;
kill-time, an occupation or amusement intended to 'kill time';
shaming, that shames or puts to shame; and *unlook*, to reverse
a previous act of looking at a person or thing.

Another minister, the Revd Benjamin Talbot, a Congregationalist, sent in 26,725 slips. He was a minister in Colum-
bus, Ohio, and later Council Bluffs in Iowa, where he taught
at the Iowa Institute for the Deaf and Dumb, as it was then
called. Located on 80 acres of land, the Institute was a grand
complex comprising a school, hospital, power plant, and
farm for students and their families. Students were taught
traditional subjects as well as baking, furniture making and
shoe repair.

Talbot's reading for the Dictionary covered geography,
exploration, history, philosophy, and religion. He sent in thousands of words from American newspapers and magazines

in addition to books on Arctic exploration and American geography. His reading of Elisha Kent Kane's *Arctic Explorations* (2,200 slips) and *The U. S. Grinnell Expedition in Search of Sir John Franklin* (1,500 slips), the story of the journey led by fellow Dictionary contributor, Sir John Richardson, gave many new words to the Dictionary: *bergy*, abounding in ice bergs; *coastward*, in the direction of the coast; *flavoursome*, full of flavour; *kayaker*, a person who uses a kayak; *scurvied*, affected with scurvy; and *upstander*, one of two upright posts on a sledge.

It is extraordinary that Talbot found time for the Dictionary given his exhausting schedule at the Institute. Writing about his work, he observed that the teacher of those who cannot speak or hear 'is subject to a constant exhaustion. The very form in which he communicates even the simplest instruction is laborious; and he must, besides this, hold himself in readiness to meet the varied wants of the twenty minds committed to his charge.'

In an article by Talbot in 1856 about his experience of teaching students with hearing and speaking difficulties, we get an insight not only into his reason for teaching but also his view of language and perhaps even the motivation that inspired his later contribution to the world's largest English Dictionary: 'It is to make the mute acquainted with the use of language', he wrote. 'And not merely that, but of the English language, with all its inconsistencies and anomalies; a language as different in its structure and arrangement from the vernacular of the deaf and dumb as could well be conceived; a language, whose irregularities have tried and puzzled scholars of other nations in their efforts to acquire it.'

Perhaps because Francis March had been based in Pennsylvania, the state was quite a hub for contributors to the Dictionary – the antiquarian Henry Phillips Jnr, Helen Kate Rogers, the Honourable James Mitchell, H. S. Brichby,

Mrs S. Clements, George Morris Philips, Mrs E. V. Baker, Miss A. Carter, Professor Thomas Messinger Drown, C. E. Edmunds, J. R. Johns, the Revd E. McMinn, Professor R. B. Youngman, Professor Samuel Stehman Haldeman, and Anna Thorpe Wetherill, of course.

New York City was another hub of activity, with twenty-seven contributors including the literary scholar Richard Grant White who read seventeenth-century English poetry; the philanthropist and mother of four children, Mrs C. F. Richardson, who read the works of the American novelist Nathaniel Hawthorne; and Miss Anna Wyckoff Olcott of 11 West 13th Street, who was responsible for reading Louisa May Alcott.

There were eight Dictionary People living in Boston, one of whom, Nathan Matthews, advised Murray for six years before becoming Boston's youngest mayor and the person who spearheaded Boston's subway system, the first in the United States. But it was his brother, the historian and etymologist Albert Matthews, who was the second-highest ranking American contributor, sending in a whopping 30,480 slips from his reading of American historical sources including the letters of Benjamin Franklin and George Washington, and the works and diary of John Adams. He also read the works of Henry Wadsworth Longfellow and Washington Irving.

Despite the inspiring efforts of the Dictionary People in America to read their local books and send in their local words, when considered in the context of the entire Dictionary, American authors are not cited enough in the Dictionary to be ranked in the top ten quoted sources. It is only a newspaper that makes it into that top ten, the *New York Times* coming in fifth behind *The Times* (London), Shakespeare, Walter Scott, and the *Philosophical Transactions of the Royal Society.*

Surprisingly, the American author who is quoted most in the OED is not Mark Twain or Emily Dickinson or Edgar Allan Poe, but rather Edward H. Knight, a patent lawyer and expert in mechanics who wrote the *American Mechanical Dictionary* and *The Practical Dictionary of Mechanics*. Knight is the seventy-fourth-most cited author in the Dictionary, quoted more frequently than Percy Bysshe Shelley, George Eliot or Ralph Waldo Emerson (who comes in at 116, the next-most quoted American).

American literature was not always read by Americans. Abraham Shackleton, a fifty-one-year-old secretary of a tram company (and, before that, a gasworks), living in Birkenhead, north-west England, sent in a total of 10,092 slips, most of which were from the works of Ralph Waldo Emerson and Edward H. Knight. The works of Edgar Allan Poe were read by an Irishman living in Madras, India. Walt Whitman was read by an English vicar living in Leeds, the Revd John Cross. Mark Twain was read by Georg Herzfeld in Berlin and Thomas Austin in London.

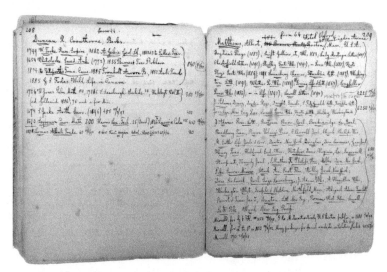

The (somewhat crowded) entry for Albert Matthews
of Boston, the second-highest ranking
American contributor.

A Professor of English at Mason College (later Birmingham University), Edward Arber, kept Murray informed of new American books which might provide Americanisms. He wrote to Murray on Christmas Eve 1884, 'Another book, quite a new one which I would also bring to your attention is Bourke's *The Snake Dance of the Moquis of Arizona*. It is full of the latest Americanisms, such as the verb "to noon" for taking the noontide rest, while a male lover is said to "whittle", what that is, I have no idea. Is it an Americanism for connoodle? It is a most interesting book in itself and would refresh you, if you read it yourself.'

Arber also suggests to Murray in this letter that he should use a typewriter. 'I am quite certain', he wrote, 'that the only way to keep down the cost of corrections is to type-write the copy', suggesting a model called the Ideal Caligraph, no. 2 price £18. Murray did read *The Snake Dance of the Moquis of Arizona* but he did not buy a typewriter.

One of Murray's most helpful advisers on American words was a German living in Boston, Carl Wilhelm Ernst. Ernst was a journalist, the editor of the *Beacon* newspaper, and a former Lutheran minister who had moved to America when he was eighteen years old. Murray wrote to the journalist in a panic when completing the entry for *public school*. 'In working at this, I overlooked the fact that we had nothing for the US use, and find myself now almost stranded, and unable to complete the article.' He wrote to Ernst asking for illustrative quotations and for clarification on the American sense of the word: 'It is said to be synonymous with Common School. I do not know which of these is the official appellation, and which the popular, or whether they are both so used. We should like to know this. The designation in England has a long and rather complicated history coming down from the L. publican schola, which is already used by Jerome of Quintilian.'

Murray started the entry by defining the use of *public school* in England as 'originally a grammar-school founded or endowed for the use or benefit of the public' but more recently, in the nineteenth century, as 'the old endowed grammar-schools as have developed into large boarding-schools, drawing from the well-to-do classes of all parts of the country or of the empire'. He noted that 'the ancient endowed grammar-schools or colleges of Eton, Winchester, Westminster, Harrow, Rugby, Charterhouse, Shrewsbury' are sometimes referred to as 'the Seven Public Schools'. He contrasted this sense of *public school* with that in Scotland, the British colonies and the United States of America, as a school provided at the public expense, usually free. Above six American quotations spanning from 1644 to 1903, Murray added a lengthy note, thanks to Ernst's advice, 'The term has been used in New England and Pennsylvania from the 17th c., and has been adopted in all States of the American Union. An early synonym was "free school", and a later one in some States, "common school" which is now however generally confined to a school of the lowest grade or "public elementary school".'

Murray was uncharacteristically effusive in his reply to Ernst: 'In my Preface to Vol VII which you may have now seen, I have mentioned your help and am only sorry that amid such a "cloud" of helpers, so little could be said about the predominantly worthy.' He signed off, 'with thanks beyond expression, I am Yours, J. A. H. Murray'. In fact, in his preface Murray had called out three people who had helped with American words. In addition to Ernst whom he said 'supplied many early instances of medieval Latin words', Murray thanked Albert Matthews of Boston and the late Mr Wendell Phillips Garrison of New Jersey. On 19 February 1907, Garrison had written a heart-wrenching letter to Murray from his deathbed in a hospital in Orange, New Jersey. The letter exemplifies the devotion of so many of the Dictionary People: 'From my dying bed, dear Dr Murray, I send you a last and long farewell. I can do no more in the Nation for the cause, the work, the bible of the human race over which you preside. May you live to see the end of it as I shall not, and accept any gratitude for the privilege of cooperation with you.' Garrison died a week later.

The *Nation* magazine of which Garrison had been Literary Editor, had in fact been extremely helpful to Murray throughout the Dictionary project. An article on the Scriptorium by the classical scholar Basil Lanneau Gildersleeve, who was a Specialist and had visited Murray in 1880, probably helped recruit American volunteers. 'Everyone who comes within the Scriptorium feels the spirit resting on him', he wrote, 'and under this fresh impulse I desire to call the attention of American Readers once more to this undertaking, for which many eyes and many hands are yet needed.' His description of Murray captures his spirit perfectly: 'It was very interesting to see the machinery in operation, and a high pleasure to talk with the director of the whole undertaking, sunshiny and confident and energetic, with all the keenness and the perseverance of his race. You do not pray that he may complete his work; you count on his doing it, and you feel the strong desire to help which is always inspired by the sight of successful activity.'

A quarter of the Americans in the address books were like Gildersleeve and Ernst, Specialists. The rest were Readers. Proportionally, there were half as many Specialists in America than in Britain, which makes sense because a dictionary editor usually wrote to a Specialist for a quick response, while working on a particular word, and the delay of the post to America would have proved too slow for Murray and his tight schedule. Even so, ten Readers doubled up as

Specialists too, such as Samuel Douglas Luckett of Bedford, Indiana, who advised Murray on American law and sent in 150 slips from Chief Justice John Marshall's *Writings upon the Federal Constitution,* and Jotham Sewall, who was a Specialist in Ancient Greek and the first headmaster of Thayer Academy, a newly established (in 1877) private high school outside Boston. A prize for excellence is still given in Sewall's name at Thayer and students remembered him as 'the white-haired angel' who was an inspiring orator. Sewall sent in slips from an eclectic range of books covering religion, anatomy, Ancient Greek, and satire.

Murray had a healthy respect for contemporary American dictionaries. He praised Noah Webster as 'a great man, a born definer of words'. Dwight Whitney's *Century Dictionary* always sat beside him on his desk in the Scriptorium and the OED drew quite heavily from it, citing it over 2,000 times. It was a serious commercial competitor because it was good quality and came out (in full) when only the letters A and B of the OED had been published. All Murray's team often compared the quality of their work with those of American dictionaries. One of the OED Chief Editors, William Craigie, even moved to Chicago in 1925 to write an American equivalent of the OED, the *Dictionary of American English* (1936–44).

Throughout the making of the Dictionary, Murray and his team were under pressure from the Delegates of Oxford University Press not to include too many American authors or American sources. There was also constant pressure to exclude slang, loanwords (words borrowed into English from foreign languages), and quotations from newspapers (as opposed to books), but Murray ignored them on all counts. This was to be a Dictionary of all English spoken in all parts of the world. On 2 April 1896, the Secretary to the Delegates wrote to him, 'Americanisms should not be inserted unless found in American or English authors of note.' But Murray kept putting them in. His view of English was – like Furnivall's – all-encompassing and all-embracing.

V

for VICARS (AND VEGETARIANS)

One by one the members of the congregation shuffled across the snowy graveyard and through the simple doorway, and found their places on the wooden pews of Cragg Chapel in the Yorkshire village of Rawdon. There was neither the spiced smell of incense nor grand organ music, just a piano. Usually the serious-minded Baptist minister, the Revd Thomas Burditt, stood at the door, but strangely no one was there to greet them on this cold Sunday in late February 1881.

Some members sat in quiet prayer. Others were busy getting the chapel ready for the service. A woman opened a cupboard door at the rear of the chapel. Looking down she saw what she thought was a man's coat. She stooped to pick it up, only to realize that the coat was not just a coat, but their minister – and he was dead.

The Revd Burditt's funeral was held on the following Wednesday and was attended by a large number of the faithful. There were mixed reports on his death. Some newspapers said he had died from paralysis of the brain. But others, perversely, reported that the minister who had been found dead in the cupboard of his chapel had been 'suffering from depression of spirits'. Had it been suicide? Apparently there had been trouble in the Rawdon Baptist community, where

Burditt had been minister for six years. Earlier that month he 'had tendered his resignation in consequence of an adverse vote of the members of his church, and it is said that this circumstance preyed on his mind'.

Whatever the truth of Burditt's death, the last two years of his life had been spent volunteering for Murray. He read twenty-three books for the Dictionary, and sent in 8,000 slips. His contribution was wide and varied – from the book on station life in New Zealand to seventeenth-century English history and poetry.

It was not easy to decide between vegetarians and vicars for this chapter. Vegetarians were an appealing category because vegetarianism was a distinctly nineteenth-century phenomenon – the word *vegetarian* did not exist before 1842 (until then, those who abstained from meat were called 'Pythagoreans' or 'Grahamites') – and many of the Dictionary People joined the movement. But in the end, vicars won out through sheer numbers – ministers from the Nonconformist chapels, like Thomas Burditt, along with numerous Church of England vicars and a handful of Roman Catholic priests, were major contributors to the Dictionary, and made up over 10 per cent of all Dictionary People. Happily, at least one of the vicars was also a vegetarian.

One chilly evening in January 1905, a group of academics gathered at St John's College, Cambridge, in the Senior Combination Room, a club-like room where the dons went to exchange gossip, read the newspapers, and smoke their pipes. They were there to toast a Fellow of the college and retired Professor of Latin on his eightieth birthday: John Eyton Bickersteth Mayor. We do not know if Mayor's friend Frederick Furnivall or his acquaintance James Murray were present, it being a Cambridge event, but the University Vice Chancellor and other academic luminaries attended. The Regius Professor of Greek and adviser to the OED, Sir Richard

Jebb, was the Master of Ceremonies and presented to Mayor a congratulatory address in Latin signed by 170 colleagues. Mayor gave a 'rather racy' reply to this in both Latin and English, though the raciness seems only to have extended to an anecdote about his being caught by the scruff of the neck when he tried, as a boy, to slink into the University Library to read. Mayor got his own back when, in his forties, he became the Cambridge University Librarian.

Mayor seems conventional enough at first glance in his role as an Anglican clergyman and bachelor don. A prolific scholar, he wrote on everything from the Roman poet Juvenal and the history of his college to the seventeenth-century divine Nicholas Ferrar of nearby Little Gidding. He had an easy facility with languages, knew Greek, Latin, Dutch, French, Italian, and German, and was an engaged member of the Cambridge Philological Society. Some regarded him as a fine preacher and an entrancing reader of Latin and Greek, while others found his sermons (packed with the finer details of church history and doctrine) inaudible, his speeches rambling and his lectures boring: there would often be only one student in his lectures by the end of a term. He had the eccentricities of a don: he took on more projects than he could complete, found it hard to organize the amount of material he collected, and was always keen to amass as many illustrations as he could to make a point. His colleagues sometimes laughed at him when he began to trot out facts (at length) in conversation, but his earnestness, kindness, and sincerity meant that he was held in affection. He was a voracious collector of books and when he ran out of space for them in his college rooms (where he lived) he acquired a little house nearby for the overflow. He was generous, often giving books away, and yet he still left 18,000 volumes when he died, bequeathed to the library he had overseen.

So far, so donnish. But Mayor also took up causes that

were perhaps more surprising. He was a suffragist, a supporter of women's admission into higher education, and believed that there should be no barriers of either religion, gender, or class to higher education. When he was eighty-two years old he took up a new challenge – mastering Esperanto – and gave a speech against Esperanto reformists at the World Congress of Esperanto, which would have been attended by quite a few of the Esperantists among the Dictionary People when it was hosted in Cambridge (reminding us of how small worlds can generate fierce battles about keenly held views).

And, of course, he was a vegetarian, a cause he embraced in middle age. Or we might say he thought he was a vegetarian; the college chef was so worried that Mayor was abstemious and getting too thin that he added meat stock to the soups that Mayor preferred to eat. Mayor was also a teetotaller. Although he didn't foist his diet or abstention onto others, he did spread the word in his books: *Modicus Cibi Medicus Sibi, or, Nature her Own Physician* in 1880, *What is Vegetarianism?* in 1886, and *Plain Living and High Thinking* in 1897. He contributed articles to *Dietetic Reformer* and *Vegetarian Messenger*, publications of the Vegetarian Society. He became President of the Society in 1884, a position he held until his death in 1910 when he was eighty-five – and he attributed his healthiness in later life to his diet and ascetic mode of living. Over this period, Mayor had witnessed new words for types of vegetarians: *veg* (1884), *fruitarian* (1893), and *nutarian* (1909). (The word *vegan* would not appear until later, in 1944.)

The rise of vegetarianism in the nineteenth century was part of the reforming spirit that also produced the temperance (against alcohol) and the anti-vivisection (against animal experiments) movements. The Vegetarian Society had been formed in the 1840s, initially prompted by the gathering of several religious groups who had embraced meatless eating.

Still regarded as somewhat crank-ish to many, vegetarianism was nevertheless embraced by some prominent figures, such as Emily Lutyens, wife of the famous architect. If you went for dinner *chez* Lutyens you might be served a rather grim *nut cutlet* (a savoury cake of chopped nuts and vegetables invented in 1908 around the same time as *nut food* and *nut steak*, followed later by *nut roast* and *nut loaf*).

It was Mayor's vegetarian friend Frederick Furnivall who brought him into the Dictionary work. We do not know the exact books which Mayor read or the words which he advised on for the Dictionary because Furnivall made no notes on the work done by contributors in his address book, unlike Murray. We do know that Mayor remained involved in Dictionary work – if on and off – for at least forty years, from 1858 to 1898, and we can glean from his scholarship the ways in which he might have contributed. He was the sort of scholar who could write a 150-line note on the meaning of the word *hortus* in Juvenal's Satire 1, was an enthusiast for Latin lexicography, and wrote a scholarly article on the derivation of the word *akimbo*, meaning 'with hands on hips and elbows turned outwards'. Several of the books he wrote were read for the Dictionary resulting in him being quoted eighteen times for linguistic prosody terms such as *acatalectic*, not short of a syllable in the last foot; *disyllabize*, to make disyllabic; *hypercatalectic*, having an extra syllable after the last complete dipody; and *pyrrhic*, a metrical foot consisting of two short syllables.

But it was not just the clergy at the universities who had expertise to bring to the Dictionary. Clergy in rural, suburban, and city churches all led more leisured lives than they do now, and they had the time to pursue their scholarly interests. The figure of Prebendary Vesey Stanhope, in Anthony Trollope's Barchester novels, absent from his cathedral and parish positions for twelve years while he pursued his hobby of butterfly collecting in Italy, was a caricature – but he was a caricature based in reality.

For the Revd Kirby Trimmer it was not butterflies but plants – with a sideline in fungi – that occupied his days as a Norfolk parson. Trimmer was not only a collector of words, though he was that, with a grand total of 4,690 slips for the Dictionary; he was also a collector of plants for another crowd-sourced project, run by the Botanical Society of London, to catalogue and map the indigenous wild flowers of Britain. The Botanical Society had been founded in 1836 and from its beginnings 'welcomed professionals and amateurs'. Like the Dictionary, the Society had a system of cards or slips for its crowdsourced project. The botanist noted on the card the name of the plant, its location, their own name and the date of the plant sighting. Over the course of his life, Trimmer filled out 84 of these cards: his first when he was thirty-two years old, and his last when he was seventy-nine. He amassed enough knowledge about Norfolk's plants that in 1866 he published a book on the subject: *Flora of Norfolk: A Catalogue of Plants in the County of Norfolk*, and followed up with a supplement to it in 1885. Ever eagle-eyed, while looking for plants he often noticed the fungi growing nearby (at least in East Norfolk) and began to collect them too, compiling 'A list of Fungi met with in East Norfolk, 1842–1872'. This remains unpublished but you can read it in the Norfolk Record Office.

The Revd Kirby Trimmer was Perpetual Curate (in effect, Vicar) of St George's, Tombland, in Norwich, from the age of thirty-eight to his death, aged eighty-three, in 1887. It was a pleasant spot to spend forty-five years: a beautiful medieval flint church just outside the walls of the cathedral close, with a pretty garden. He lived there with two of his sisters (both unmarried, as was Trimmer) and one domestic servant. Trimmer was a dedicated preacher and pastor, but his longevity in the parish and his love of Norfolk meant that he was free to head out to the countryside on fine sunny days to do a bit of plant spotting.

Trimmer brought his expertise in plants to the Dictionary, reading such books as *The English Vineyard Vindicated* (1666) by John Rose, gardener to King Charles II, from which he produced 60 slips, and John Evelyn's 1669 translation of *The French Gardiner* (200 slips). His interests extended to rural life and the pastoral in general and he read William Marshall's *The Rural Economy of Norfolk* (1787) – 40 slips; he probably discussed agriculture with his brother Joshua, a geologist with an interest in farming, who had mapped the drift deposits in Norfolk. Kirby Trimmer also read pastoral poetry such as William Browne's *Shepherd's Pipe* (1614) – 50 slips – and *The Fleece* (1757) by the Welsh poet and painter John Dyer. He read religious books too: John Pearson's *An Exposition of the Creed*, an influential text in Anglican circles by a seventeenth-century Bishop of Chester – 100 slips. Trimmer's own publications on religion included his book *Motes upon Crystal: or, Obsolete words of the authorized version of the holy Bible, critically and chronologically considered* (1864) – perhaps not the most exciting of reads, but it displayed an expertise in rare and disused words which he brought to his Dictionary work.

If you go into the church of St George's, Tombland, today, you will see a stained-glass window on the south wall that commemorates Kirby Trimmer and his sisters. And when you look around, you realize that he never neglected the church for his botany or mycology. In the 1880s when he was growing old, major renovation work began in the church – including the addition of carved angels to the chancel roof. If you go on St George's website, you can read tips for cultivating an eco-life, and learn that the church, dedicated to treading more lightly on the planet, has already received its Bronze Eco Church award and is now striving for Silver. I have a feeling that Kirby Trimmer, the dedicated Norfolk parson who so loved the natural world, would be pleased.

Vicars and ministers were extraordinarily dedicated contributors to the Dictionary; they formed a reliable backbone to the body of Dictionary volunteers. Some provided Specialist expertise, such as the Very Revd Robert Payne Smith, Dean of Canterbury Cathedral, who was an Old Testament scholar and advised on biblical words such as *Boanerges*, the name given by Christ to the two sons of Zebedee. But most were neither newsworthy nor distinctive, quietly and steadily making their contributions over many years. Take the Revd William Lowenberg, curate and then vicar of St Peter's, Bury, in Lancashire: he volunteered for twenty years, from the age of thirty-nine to his death at fifty-nine, and sent in 7,900 slips, was Subeditor for the letters O and P, and a Specialist who tracked down desiderata. Or the Baptist missionary, William Holman Bentley, who advised Murray from the Congo, helping him with Bantu loanwords such as *macute*, a monetary unit in the Guinea Coast and Angola. Or there's the Cambridge-educated Revd William Lees who, by the time he started contributing in 1879, had been vicar of Emmanuel Church at Sidlow Bridge, near Reigate, for nearly twenty years – the church had been recently established for employees of the local farms and estates. Over a period of thirteen years, Lees sent in a total of 18,500 slips. He also introduced one of his daughters to Dictionary work; she began contributing alongside her father, in 1879, and continued for three years. She was listed simply as Miss Lees in Murray's address book, so we do not know which of William Lees's three daughters she might have been, but it was quite likely Beatrice who was then in her early twenties. She would go up to Lady Margaret Hall, Oxford, where she was a Scholar and read History. She became the tutor in History at another of the Oxford women's colleges, Somerville, until 1914 when she went to work for the Admiralty Intelligence Department during the war, and she later held teaching posts at Manchester and again at Oxford. A medievalist, her books included *Alfred the Great* (1915), and *Records of the Templars* (1935). She was just one of the many extraordinary women who contributed to the Dictionary. I wanted to bring them into the light.

W

for WOMEN

From the moment I first held James Murray's address book in that dusty basement in Oxford, I had a burning question: how many women had helped create the Dictionary?

We have known *one* answer from the names of the women listed in Murray's Presidential Address to the Philological Society and in the various prefaces to the Dictionary. But could the address books reveal more? The answer was a resounding yes. There were 234 more women in the address books, bringing to 487 the total number of women who contributed to the Dictionary.

We have already met some of these women – suffragists and an anti-suffragist, lesbians, poets, novelists, activists, a factory inspector, an archaeologist, and a rain collector. There are many more, too many even for this chapter – philanthropists, scholars, translators, teachers, a surgeon, a mummy collector, and an astronomer. And the female Dictionary Friends came from many parts of the world: not just Britain, but also the USA, Canada, Ireland, Austria, India, France, and New Zealand.

Murray's granddaughter, Elisabeth, noted that 'the response from women was particularly warm'. She understood that many intelligent single women, looking after elderly parents or sharing a house with a sibling, found fulfilment in the work. The domestic context of dictionary-making made it easy for these mostly middle-class women to contribute. The volunteer work of reading could easily be done in the corner of a drawing room or by a sick parent's bed, with books borrowed from libraries or pulled from the shelves to hand.

Some of the female Dictionary People were amongst the first university-educated women, and they had scholarly expertise which was vital to James Murray; the majority, however, were women who had never gone to university but overcame their indifferent home schooling to become self-taught or had been fortunate enough to have fathers who had taught them from their private libraries. With enough income to live independently, if not extravagantly, they had the time to do the work without needing to be paid, and they wanted something fulfilling to do.

A core group of women came to be extraordinarily dedicated and important contributors. They were Dictionary People who brought not only time, devotion, and energy to the task but also expertise and, often, personal support to Murray. He couldn't have done it without them.

The Brown sisters, both unmarried and living together in Cirencester in the Cotswolds, began contributing in 1880 while they were looking after their elderly father, Thomas, a successful wine merchant. They had been educated by governesses, and had not gone to school or university, but their father had instilled in them a love of learning and the ethos of service to national projects – he was a rain collector. Jemima (or Miss J. E. A. Brown, as she was always known in the Scriptorium – this was the era of formalities) was a poet and author of spiritual writings. Elizabeth was a distinguished, self-educated astronomer who, as a child, had been taught to use a telescope and observe the weather by her father. They were highly productive Readers and together they produced 16,000 slips; Jemima contributing the lion's share.

For Jemima the Dictionary work was a lifeline out of melancholia. Elizabeth, her protective older sister, knew this and was compelled to write to Murray in August 1882, two years into their volunteering, to ask if he might offer some feedback to Jemima to lift her morale. She wrote that her sister had been hoping 'day after day' to hear that he had been able to examine even a small portion of her work but had refrained from writing to him because she knew how busy he was. Elizabeth had no such compunction in writing with the full story. Jemima had in the past been 'out of health and suffering from low spirits'. The absorbing interest she had taken in the 'Pa's – she was working on incorporating the recently gathered slips for words that began with Pa – had been her only alleviation and amusement. Elizabeth ended by saying that she would be very sorry if Jemima's interest and lift in spirits flagged 'for want of a little encouragement'.

Ironically, earlier that year, Jemima had written to Murray with enormous compassion and understanding when he was facing financial difficulties and battling debates about pronunciation, urging him to take a holiday far away from the mailbox, where 'As cannot pursue you', and assuring him of her prayers. Even though Murray – or someone in the Scriptorium – had written at the top of Elizabeth's August letter 'Ansd', in January 1893 Jemima herself wrote to Mrs Murray, her first letter of the new year, still longing for some gesture of approval and, even, gratitude. Just as the patient tells the therapist the real problem as they have their hand on the doorknob ready to leave the session, it is only in the last sentence of the letter, after four pages of chit-chat, that the plea comes. 'If Dr Murray does not tell me what he thinks of it [her recent work] in its final guise I shall be tormenting myself with the idea that something has slipped in – either incorrect or that he does not like – in which sort of self-torment I am rather clever!'

Jemima brought not only devotion to the Dictionary work but also fluency in German, stamina and skill in subediting – working on the letters B, C, D, I, and P – and speed in reading and producing slips. By 1884, four years into her volunteering, she had already sent in 4,500 slips. Murray's initial neglect of one of his best contributors was soon long forgotten and they became firm friends; Dr and Mrs Murray even visited Jemima in Cirencester. Not only was she an industrious contributor right up to her death in 1907, she was also a generous friend, leaving Murray a legacy of £1,000 which was more than his annual wage and went a long way to alleviating his constant financial woes. Public acknowledgement of her work was given when she was described in various prefaces as 'indefatigable', 'an accomplished lady', and 'one of the most devoted friends of the Dictionary'. After her death, Murray made a special mention in the preface to the letters O and P: 'The large section PIM- to PROF- was laboriously subedited by Miss J. E. A. Brown, one of the most devoted and enthusiastic of our volunteer helpers, between 1900 and her sudden death on 19 February 1907.' In the preface to the smaller section of P, Murray wrote that Jemima's 'lamented death on 19th February last deprived the Dictionary of one of its most indefatigable workers, and the Editor of an honoured personal friend'.

The summer of 1887 was notably wet, good for subediting parts of the letter B, which is what Jemima was doing at home in Cirencester; but not so good if you were trying to observe a solar eclipse, which is what Elizabeth Brown was doing in Russia. The solar eclipse was scheduled for 19 August at Kineshma, just by the Volga. Elizabeth and a female companion had travelled the 2,000 miles by train and boat across northern Europe, visiting the Observatory and Meteorological Institute in Uppsala along the way, to the summer home of Russian astronomer Professor Fedor Bredichin.

Dusty and tired on arrival, the two women were relieved to find that no one changed for dinner as they only had their travelling clothes, and they quickly became a part of the jolly group of family and astronomers, with spirited conversation attempted across English, French, German, and Russian. Soon the serious business of preparation began, as three large telescopes were set up on the lawns outside, along with cameras and clocks, and Elizabeth carefully unpacked her little travel telescope. As the instruments were set up, the villagers looked on, curious and suspicious, even though the government had posted notices explaining the purpose of the astronomers' visit.

For days, the 'hopes and fears' of the weather were the constant topic of conversation amongst the party of astronomers, Elizabeth standing at the window and watching as 'the soft fleecy clouds were constantly passing over a sky of rainy blue'. The weather all week was 'really distressing', she wrote. 'An exasperating fine drizzle would come down for hours, which would clear off for a while, only to come back again.' On the morning of the 19th, Elizabeth was up at 4.30 a.m. to observe the weather, and by 5.30 everyone had gathered outside. As they went to their various stations at telescopes, cameras, and clocks, the gloom descended. At the moment of the eclipse, for two and a half minutes no one could see anything and then, suddenly, everyone voluntarily exclaimed. 'For a second or so we had a view of the coronal light, making it look almost like an annular eclipse, and a glimpse of the rose-coloured prominences, as they are called, on about one-fifth of the circumference, but it was over almost before we had realized it, and I never knew *how* I saw it, whether through a glass or with my naked eye.' A second later a voice rose up, 'The eclipse is over!' It had been a disappointing near-see. As the group got up from their seats, they were silent and could barely look at each other. Elizabeth, the dutiful scholar, immediately went to write her promised report for the Liverpool Astronomical Society, though she did so with 'flagging pen'.

By 1887, when she went to Russia, Elizabeth had stopped volunteering for the Dictionary – which had become her younger sister's great passion – and was devoted to astronomy. But prior to that, from 1880 to 1883, she brought her up-to-date scientific expertise to the Dictionary. She read the evolutionist Alfred Russel Wallace's *Island Life* (1880). Russel's exploration of the astronomical effects on the geology and climate of islands must have fascinated her along with the details of island flora and fauna, and she sent in 150 slips from the book. From James Clerk Maxwell's 1873 *Treatise on Electricity and Magnetism* (cited 158 times in the Dictionary) she produced 250 slips. Tapping her expertise in astronomy she read John F. W. Herschel's 1833 *Astronomy*, from which she produced 200 slips in 1881 (with 146 quotations from it appearing in the Dictionary).

In 1883, Thomas Brown died. The sisters no longer had the duty of parental care and were left comfortably off by their father. Elizabeth was now free to pursue her life as an astronomer. Her reading for Murray largely ground to a halt (apart from a brief stint in 1893, which produced 275 slips from *The Times*), but she did continue to keep up her father's rain record. She even expanded the task to recording temperature, deep-well measurements and thunderstorm activity. As a result, she was elected a Fellow of the Royal Meteorological Society, one of the very few female fellows.

Elizabeth wrote about her journey to Russia in a book published in 1888, *In Pursuit of a Shadow*. A letter in January of that year from her sister Jemima to Murray suggests that the sisters worked on the book together. Jemima was writing to Murray to apologize for not having done much Dictionary work recently because she had taken a fall from her horse while out riding, and the ill health that followed 'had stopped the wheels of labour' for a good many weeks. She had managed one bit of literary work, though, writing a sketch of her sister's trip to Russia. 'We call it "In Pursuit of a Shadow" for that alas it was but it is a story of compensations too.'

Elizabeth had a more successful trip to see the solar eclipse in Trinidad, about which she wrote in *Caught in the Tropics* (1890). She loved the sunshine, the bright plant life, the exuberant birds, and the kindness of the people, as she travelled by Royal Mail steamer, with the same friend who had accompanied her to Russia, via the Azores, Barbados and Granada. On the day of the eclipse, with her telescope set up in a large-windowed tower, clouds threatened to spoil the moment once again but then they cleared, and she saw for the first time 'the silvery light of the corona encircling the death-like blackness of the moon's orb'.

On her return to England, Elizabeth worked with others to establish the British Astronomical Association, which admitted women (unlike the Royal Astronomical Society), and she became the founding director of its solar section and encouraged other women to get involved in the work of observing the sun. 'For ladies, many of whom have ample time at their disposal, and who are often skilful in the use of the pencil, this branch of observational Astronomy ought to have a special attraction. The Sun is always at hand. No exposure to the night air is involved, nor is there any need for a costly array of instruments.' Women could observe the skies, just as they read for the Dictionary.

Elizabeth took her research in astronomy to much deeper levels, having two observatories at her home and making significant contributions to learned journals. In

1892, she was proposed for membership of the Royal Astronomical Society along with two Cambridge-educated women, but none of them was elected. She continued to travel (to Norway, Canada, the USA, Scotland, Ireland, and Spain), always sketching and painting wherever she went – especially landscapes and flowers – and writing vivid accounts to her sister of everything she was seeing. But she preferred the country to the city, and loved her quiet, self-fashioned scholarly life in Cirencester, with regular attendance at her local Quaker meeting house. She was planning a trip to see the solar eclipse in Portugal in 1900, accompanied by Jemima this time, but she died in March 1899, aged sixty-eight, after a bout of bronchitis. She left £1,000 (of a total estate of £37,000 – it was her wealth that enabled her to pursue her astronomy) and her observatories to the female-friendly British Astronomical Association.

The Thompson sisters, Edith and Elizabeth, spinsters who lived together, were also at the heart of this group of female Dictionary Friends, so vital to Murray's work. Like the Brown sisters they began contributing to the Dictionary in 1880 (a jackpot year for Murray) and both continued to do so for the rest of their lives. Edith was the more prolific of the sisters, not only producing slips but (from 1891) also subediting the letter C, and then for many years proofreading the Dictionary from the letter D onwards. She brought to the work a knowledge of Old English, local dialects and historical terms. By 1888, Edith and Elizabeth had produced 15,000 slips between them. That same year, Murray acknowledged 'the ready good will and helpful co-operation of many scholars and specialists, most of them men whose time is much occupied, but whose interest in this undertaking has led them willing to place some of it at the Editor's service'. Edith Thompson was the only woman in the list.

Elizabeth Brown with her telescope.

Reading through the many letters between Edith Thompson and James Murray that are preserved in the OED archives, I was immediately struck not only by Edith's quick intelligence and wit but also by her masterful grasp of semantics and lexicography. She could easily have held her own in the Scriptorium amongst Murray's assistants and co-Editors. This is evident in one of the very first letters she sent to Murray in June 1880 in which she engaged in just the kind of detailed discussion of the finely grained differences of meanings in words that he enjoyed. 'I think I sent you a quotation for the word bridoon [a type of bit in a double bridle for a horse], and that I wrote snaffle [a simple form of bridle bit] against it by way of explanation. I apologize: being instructed that a bridoon has rings at the side, while a snaffle has bars – in short, the bridoon is the less severe part of an ordinary double bridle.'

She doesn't stop there. 'It seems however that it is a purely military word and that civilians, knowing the thing, but not the name, do commonly err by calling it a snaffle. However, the quotation was from a military author, so that will be all right. I suppose bridoon was one of the many technical terms brought in from France in the days when the French were the best horsemen and the best soldiers in Europe.'

As their friendship developed, she and Murray wrote not only about the nuances of dictionary-making, so beloved of word nerds, but also of their lives and families. We know from Edith's letters to Murray that she attended archaeological meetings at Glastonbury, that she holidayed on the Isle of Wight and Exmoor in the summer from August to October, and that when she did so she took a break from Dictionary work.

Edith's interests were not confined to the Dictionary. She was also a historian, and by the time she started volunteering for James Murray, she had already published a popular *History of England* (1872) for schools, which she revised many times. She had been educated at home in Blackheath, London, where her father was a lawyer, and she was launched into a life of writing through her long friendship with Edward Augustus Freeman. In 1869, when she was just twenty-one, Freeman had asked her to write a review for the *Saturday Review,* and she continued to write for both this and other magazines for many years, usually anonymously, sometimes under the pseudonym Evelyn Todd, but only occasionally under her own name. Her sister Elizabeth was also a writer and published a novel, *A Dragoon's Wife* (described as a romance of the seventeenth century). Together they researched the life of their radical politician and abolitionist grandfather, Thomas Perronet Thompson, and Elizabeth wrote up his biography. It was never published, but you can read the manuscript in the archives of Hull University Library along with the intellectually engaged and playful correspondence between Edith and Edward Freeman over many years. Both sisters always lived with their family, moving to Liverpool (when their father became a judge) and Bath (when he retired) with their parents. They have found fame in recent years as the fictional characters Ditte and Beth in Pip Williams's charming novel *The Dictionary of Lost Words* (2020).

This inner group of women had both affection and respect for James Murray and these feelings formed a strong motivation for their commitment to the Dictionary. Miss Jennett Humphreys of Cricklewood in London, one of the Readers of Bulwer's *Anthropometamorphosis* (see P for Pornographer), wrote, 'Volunteer Readers supported the new editor admirably, feeling it an honour and a pleasure to be working with him.' This was in 1882, three years after Murray had taken over the Editorship, and she had visited him at Mill Hill. Afterwards, she wrote an article for *Fraser Magazine* inspired by her trip to the Scriptorium, which she described as an 'Iron Library'. This was the necessary study, workshop, or atelier which was needed now that 'the Master had come'. After the chaos of the Furnivall years, summed up in the two large sacks of papers (full of mice, alive and dead) transported from Furnivall's house to Murray's, what was needed was an 'assembling-place' where 'a group of fellow labourers could be under his direction'. A part of his home, it was a place he could go to at any time 'in all moods and manners, for solitary research and composition, for ever-recurring references by others, and consultation'. In short, it was 'a word factory' where 'the philological raw material, spread abundantly and heterogeneously, could be ground out by division and sub-division, mechanically and afterwards with reason'. Humphreys was enormously admiring of Murray's 'bold grasp of his philological work life' combined with 'his powerful ability to identify himself with the century' (more usual in men of science than men of letters, she thought) and his capacity to select the best 'aides-de-camp' for the task ahead. Once Murray the new Master took over, the Dictionary never looked back.

Besides admiration, Jennett Humphreys also brought enormous energy to the work. She was the number-one female contributor of slips, contributing 18,700 by 1888. During her years of working for the Dictionary, she was also doing historical research on cookery. Her promised book on the subject never appeared, but the Dictionary benefited from her expertise when she sent in 500 slips from Mrs Hannah Glasse's

The Scriptorium in Murray's back garden, described
by Jennett Humphreys as the 'Iron Library'.

Art of Cookery, Made Plain and Easy (1747), which gave the world *mint sauce,* a sauce made of mint and served with roast lamb; *piccalilli,* Indian pickle; *short crust,* pastry made with butter or fat; *gloat,* a species of eel; and *madling cake,* a small cake with currants.

Murray could also be supportive of these self-educated, scholarly female contributors. To Lucy Toulmin Smith, in 1882, he gave crucial assistance as she sought a contract from Oxford University Press for her critical edition of the *York Mystery Plays.* Toulmin Smith had been educated at home by her father; she helped him with his scholarship and was able to complete his unfinished work on English Guilds when he died in 1869. Her expertise was in English and French medieval literature, and she edited a number of manuscripts, some for the Early English Text Society through which she came to know Furnivall. By the early 1880s, when Murray helped her to get her book published, she was volunteering for the Dictionary as a consultant, reviewing the early fascicles and, as a London-based volunteer, verifying quotations in the British Library. In 1894, she moved to Oxford and her days as a Dictionary contributor came to an end as she took up the post of Librarian of Manchester College, the Unitarian college that had opened its new buildings in Oxford the year before. The Unitarians and the college had always been radical – already co-educational before any other college – so the appointment of a female librarian was in keeping with its spirit. Lucy Toulmin Smith, with her extensive scholarship and networks, and from an old Unitarian family, was the perfect candidate.

Toulmin Smith had been recommended to Murray in the 1880s, for the post of paid assistant on the Dictionary. His friend Edward Alber had urged him to employ women because they were 'more conscientious and cheaper'. Toulmin Smith had turned Murray down, but other women were employed in the Scriptorium. Within the first year of taking over the Dictionary, Murray began to employ women: Miss Skipper and Miss Scott were editorial assistants given the huge task of sorting out the sacks of materials sent by Furnivall. Murray described them as 'two young women of fair education belonging to the village'.

Alongside this core group of women who did so much of the subediting and proofreading, and whose support and expertise were so important to Murray, were the 400-odd other women whose reading of books and other volunteer activities were also essential.

These included Dame Elizabeth Cadbury, who went on to be one of the most significant philanthropists of the early twentieth century, creating with her husband George the ideal Bournville village for workers at the Cadbury chocolate factory in Birmingham. Well educated at the formidable Miss Buss's North London Collegiate School, she had passed the exams to go to Cambridge but did not take up her place, choosing the path of philanthropy and service instead, working with the London dock workers, refugees of the Franco-Prussian war, and women in the London slums. As the twenty-one-year-old Elsie Taylor, before she was married, she managed to squeeze in reading John Almon's *Anecdotes of the Life of William Pitt* (1792), and produced 600 slips, alongside her social work, in 1879. When she sat down to read for the Dictionary after a long day on her feet at the London docks, was this simply another aspect of her devotion to service for the public good, or for the pleasure of reading itself?

Many of the other female contributors were active in doing good works, a typical pastime for middle-class women. Miss Eliza Felicia Burton was the founder of the St Mary's Home for Penitents, also known as the Home for Destitute Girls, or 'Fallen Women' as the language of the day put it, in Carlisle in 1872. This was based at the old Caldewgate Workhouse in Carlisle and was run through the (Anglican) Diocese of Carlisle, of which Miss Burton's father was the Chancellor. She was also a campaigner for the rights of female sanitary workers. In the midst of doing these good works, she was a huge contributor to the Dictionary, sending in 12,747 slips over a period of eighteen years from 1880 to 1898. Her reading ranged widely, covering natural history, geology, poetry, insects, drama and hymns, much of it from the sixteenth, seventeenth or eighteenth centuries. An able and trustworthy volunteer, she was also asked to look up a good deal of desiderata.

Lady Louisa Anne Magenis (daughter of the 3rd Earl of Belmore) who sent in 2,000 slips from the works of Edmund Burke and from Herbert Spencer's *The Study of Sociology*, was the driving force behind the founding of the Rehearsal Club in 1892, along with the actress Maud Beerbohm Tree (Lady Tree, wife of the theatre manager and actor, Sir Herbert Beerbohm Tree). This was a place in London where actresses and music-hall chorus girls could go for respite and rest between performances, most not being able to afford a central London home.

Miss Payne of Cuckfield, West Sussex, was likely Edith Payne (rather than her sister), a keen Reader, who founded the Free Library in Cuckfield in 1920, and became its Honorary Librarian. By then she was also a suffragist, taking a lively role in the Cuckfield Suffragists Society, which had its inaugural meeting in 1909. When she died aged seventy-five in 1933, she was described as having had a life of service, taking a prominent part in every good work in the town, from the Women's Institute (of which she was President) to the local nursing institution. Like many of the Dictionary women, it was her Christian faith that motivated her public service, and she was a keen member of her Congregationalist church where she was choir director, organist, and Sunday School teacher. She may sometimes have taken on more than she could manage. In one instance, she was sent 1,000 ready-printed slips by the Scriptorium staff, who ended up having to chase her to return them. She eventually sent in just half of the slips, 500, after reading David Hume's *History of England.*

Agatha Porter was a pioneer, passing her medical examinations as a physician and surgeon in Glasgow in 1891. By then she no longer had time to volunteer for the Dictionary, but in 1879 and 1880 she had read the seventeenth-century philosopher John Locke and poet Phineas Fletcher and sent in 700 slips. After qualifying as a doctor, she chose to serve the neediest. She was the first female doctor appointed under the auspices of the Poor Law, attending to patients in workhouses, via her post at the Chorlton Union Hospital in Manchester. She then moved to the Royal Free Hospital and New Hospital for women in London. In 1912, she was an honorary medical consultant for a committee looking at the Mental Deficiency Bill, a pernicious piece of legislation (which passed in Parliament in 1913) based in eugenics, which sought to take the 'feeble minded' out of Poor Law institutions and prisons and send them to the colonies. There is no record of what Dr Porter thought of this bill, but her experience as a doctor in Poor Law institutions made her an expert to be consulted. Dr Porter's older sister Lela was also a Dictionary Friend, sending in 1,400 slips, some on Locke (like her sister). She contributed over a longer period than Agatha, beginning in 1880. In 1888, she was obviously still in touch with the Dictionary, as James Murray noted in the address book 'now Mrs MacLehose'. Indeed, we can track the changing marital status of several of the female contributors because Murray often made a note of when they married and changed their names. Miss Frankland of Lancaster Gate, London, became Mrs Colense in 1880; Miss Elizabeth Price of Addlestone, Surrey, became Mrs Moore in 1881; and Miss Elise MacFarland of Jackson Street, San Francisco, became Mrs Rickeecker of Santa Rosa, California, in 1881.

For sheer quirkiness Edith (sometimes spelled Edythe) Phibbs probably wins out. She was a mummy collector, along with her brother Owen, who was an avid archaeologist and a member of the Royal Society of Antiquaries of Ireland. Unlike Margaret Murray's mentor, the Egyptologist Flinders Petrie, who kept his collection of mummies under the bed, Edith and Owen Phibbs chose to put theirs on display. They turned a long room on the first floor of their house, Seafield in County Sligo, Ireland, into a museum, where they presented their collection of mummies along with other artefacts from Owen's tours in Egypt and Syria. The presence of the mummies led to reports that the house was haunted. The house's change of name from Seafield to Lisheen in the early twentieth century is sometimes attributed to the family's wish to try and evade its rumoured association with the paranormal. In 1880, Edith contributed 640 slips from a book on geology: Sir Roderick Murchison's *Siluria: the history of the oldest known rocks containing organic remains, with a brief sketch of the distribution of gold over the Earth* (1854). Her reading provided the first quotations for a number of geologically related terms, such as *trappoid*, igneous rock; *siluroid*, fish with no scales; *hydrothermal*, relating to heated water; and *fucoidal*, relating to seaweed. As well as sending in words to the Dictionary, Edith also contributed to the *History of Maunsell, or Mansel* (1903), a book about the history of her mother's family. By 1901 she had moved to London – whether this was because of the presence of the mummies and suspected supernatural happenings, we will never know.

*

Fast-forward to a Wednesday in June 1928, an unsettled, cool, and wet evening. Hundreds of Dictionary People stayed at home and tuned in to a live broadcast on BBC Radio for the Prime Minister's speech from the grand OED dinner in London celebrating the completion of the mammoth work which they, and hundreds who had predeceased them including its former Editors Frederick Furnivall and James Murray, had helped create. 'I am expected in a few words to do justice to the merits of Professor Craigie and his co-editor and the staff, of 15,000 pages of literature, of 400,000 words, of 2,000,000 quotations, and 178 miles of type.'

The Prime Minister stood in the imposing Goldsmiths' Hall in front of four long tables seating 150 men in black tie, sipping Château Margaux. James Murray's son, Sir Oswyn Murray, sat opposite OED Co-Editor Charles Onions and beside the President of Trinity College, Oxford. The Vice Chancellor of Oxford sat between the Earl of Birkenhead and Sir William Jackson Pope.

You could count on one hand (or not at all) the Dictionary People at the dinner – many had died, and others who were still alive were not invited. Instead, the seats were given to journalists from *The Times*, the *Manchester Guardian*, the *Morning Post* and the *Daily Telegraph*. There were heads of Oxford colleges, directors of publishing companies, and notable professors – the anthropologist Franz Boas, and the literary scholars Sir Israel Gollancz and J. R. R. Tolkien.

The event was a marketing opportunity for Oxford University Press. But for those Dictionary People listening from home, they may have felt a slight tinge of recognition when they heard the Prime Minister say, 'We remember perhaps above all others, Dr Murray, Henry Bradley, Professor Craigie, and Dr Onions. We remember with them the subeditors, the voluntary Readers, the assistants, the pressmen, and the compositors, and under and above and around and behind all, the ancient and beneficent University of Oxford.

'Perhaps before I begin, I may make a confession about

the Dictionary,' said the Prime Minister. 'I have not read it. But if ever a work was destined for eternity this is it.'

Laughter echoed through the Hall and reached the minstrels' gallery high above. Three lone women sat in silence, peering down on proceedings. Reader Edith Thompson and editorial assistants Rosfrith Murray and Eleanor Bradley had been denied places beside the men because of the segregation rules at the Hall but were allowed to sit on the balcony and watch from afar. Agnes Carswell Fries, who was invited because her husband Charles was editor of the *Early Modern English Dictionary*, was having none of it. 'I was told that the women would be "skied" if they wished to come. It was explained to me that being "skied" meant that women could sit in the balcony above the hall and watch the men eat. I felt insulted and refused to go under those circumstances.' Funnily enough the word 'skied' is not in the OED.

The sexist cultural biases of the formal dinner did not match the radical and open process of the Dictionary's making, a process which included hundreds of women and gave them roles from editorial assistants and Subeditors to Readers and Specialists. We can imagine the women who were still alive poised by their wirelesses – Margaret Murray, Lady Cadbury, Ada Murray and her daughters, Miss Florence Elworthy, Clara Dorothea Rackham, Miss Blomfield, Mrs Effie Laura Browne, Miss Beatrice Lees, Edith Phibbs, Agatha Porter, Amy Rivington, Edith Payne, and Elizabeth Thompson. But, given the strange guest list at the dinner, there were many male Dictionary Friends listening from home too. The dinner was not only a slight against the women – though it was that! – it was also a slight against the Dictionary People in general, the extraordinary volunteers who had done so much to get the entire massive project to the finishing line over so many decades.

X

for XENOMANIACS (AND ESPERANTISTS)

1879 was a year of three happenings, all of which would strangely relate to the Dictionary People in some way. It was the year when the word *xenomaniac,* someone with an insane fancy for foreigners, was coined; the year when a German priest called Johann Martin Schleyer had a dream that he should invent a new international language called Volapük in order to unite the world; and, of course, the year when James Murray started editing the OED.

Our Dictionary word nerd who pioneered the study of sound and wore the coat with twenty-eight pockets, Alexander John Ellis, could have been described as a xenomaniac. He was not a natural linguist himself, but he was naturally attracted to speakers of other languages. Unlike other Dictionary People who could speak Icelandic – OED Editor William Craigie, Oxford historian Frederick York Powell, and phonetician Henry Sweet – Ellis once lamented that he had just missed meeting an Icelander. He was insatiably curious about new people, new languages, and new cultures. Forever wanting to make comparisons across languages and dialects, Ellis's letters to Murray are full of (mistaken) linguistic theories. On one occasion he wrote with great animation about a supposed connection between Yorkshire words for counting sheep and those found in an Algonquian language in Maine studied by his friend James Hammond Trumbull. He was on firmer ground developing his new spelling systems. He assiduously attended meetings of the Philological Society, regardless of how dry and tedious they might be. In this sense he was quite unlike the Orientalist and fellow Dictionary Friend Robert Needham Cust who is said to have spoken sixteen languages and found Philological Society meetings insufferable. 'We have still half the world to conquer, and I have really no leisure to listen to the way in which a Dorsetshire peasant addresses his cow', he said of the parochial obscurity of the lectures at these meetings. There is an apocryphal story that it was to one of those lectures that the thirty-one-year-old Herbert Coleridge, the first Editor of the Dictionary, was rushing when he was caught in the rain. Sitting through the meeting in wet clothes made him sick, and a few days later, when a doctor told him that he had caught more than a chill and was dying of tuberculosis, he uttered, 'I must begin Sanskrit tomorrow.'

The Dictionary project attracted language lovers and polyglots. At the same time that Ellis was inventing his new spelling systems for English, others were inventing and communicating with each other in entirely new languages with new words, new sounds, new structures and new forms. From Philadelphia to Tokyo to Manchester, there were artificial-language enthusiasts among the Dictionary People.

Most of these enthusiasts were idealists who wanted to create a universal language which would help international relations and unite the world. This noble hope stood in contrast with – and probably in reaction to – the rise of nationalisms in the late nineteenth century. Over 150 new languages were created in this period, the best-known being Volapük (1879), Pasilingua (1885), Esperanto (originally called

Lingvo Internacia) (1887), Spelin (1888), Spokil (1889), Mundolingue (1889), and Ido (1907).

One such idealist and xenomaniac was the linguist and numismatist (coin expert) Henry Phillips Jnr of Philadelphia who started reading for Murray in 1879 and, within six years, had sent in 10,024 slips from books on numismatics and North American Indians from reading his own well-stocked, private library. Small and thin, with round spectacles and a flourishing moustache, Phillips was one of Murray's most valued American contributors. Born and bred into a large, wealthy, and well-known Jewish family, he attended the University of Pennsylvania and was trained as a lawyer. He wrote numerous books including *Additional Notes Upon the Collection of Coins and Medals Now Upon Exhibition at the Pennsylvania Museum* (1879).

Phillips had the resources to collect valuable books and coins, and a natural aptitude for languages, teaching himself Hebrew, Arabic, French, Spanish, Italian, German, Latin, Greek, Hungarian, Turkish, Persian, Sanskrit, Dutch, Russian – along with the artificial languages Volapük and Esperanto. He was Secretary and Librarian of the American Philosophical Society and a member of more clubs and societies than any other American contributor to the Dictionary.

At the same time that Henry Phillips began reading for the OED, a Roman Catholic priest in southern Germany, Johann Martin Schleyer, was 'inspired by God' to create a new international language called Volapük. We do not know how Phillips first discovered Schleyer's work, but it may have been on one of his tours of Europe in the early 1880s. He may have visited Father Schleyer in Baden, Germany, and learned directly from the inventor, or he may have taught himself and attended one of the Volapük conferences held in Munich or Paris. What we do know is that Phillips became one of the first speakers of the language in America, and he set up a Volapük club in Philadelphia. He played an important part in the language gaining a total of 1 million speakers globally within a decade of its invention.

The activities of Volapükists such as Phillips was intense – but short-lived because in the late 1880s most of them turned to Esperanto instead. It was not the complexity of Volapük's structure that eventually killed its global spread, but rather unrest amongst its followers and speakers. History is littered with artificial languages that begin as idealist endeavours, with the aim of uniting all peoples, but turn into political movements that ultimately implode in acrimonious disputes.

One notable exception is Esperanto, which has not only survived but also, Phillips would be delighted to know, continues to thrive today with approximately 2 million speakers, thousands of whom speak Esperanto as their mother tongue. In 1887, the Polish-born ophthalmologist Ludovic Lazar Zamenhof created Esperanto in the hope that it would unify humanity. Both Hitler and Stalin saw the idealist and internationalist objectives of Esperanto as a threat, and persecuted its speakers.

The word Esperanto, which literally means 'one who hopes', was a bit too new to make it into the Dictionary when the letter E was edited by Bradley in 1891, but it did not stop many contributors to the OED being advocates for the new language. Henry Phillips Jnr directed the same passion to Esperanto as he had to Volapük. In 1889 he translated an important early paper by Zamenhof into English, which was read by thousands and helped spread the language. Murray's assistant Arthur Maling translated five sermons into Esperanto under the title *Kvin Paraladoj* (and wore an Esperanto 'verda stelo' green star badge on his jacket each day in the Scriptorium); the vegetarian Cambridge don, the Revd John Bickersteth Mayor, took it up on his eighty-second birthday; and after the English scholar James Main Dixon left Japan (he spoke Japanese, Ainu, Scots, English, and Esperanto), he moved to America and wrote a weekly column on Esperanto for the *LA Times*.

Within the Esperanto community, however, it was Phillips who became most famous. When he died at the age of fifty-seven in 1895, there was no comment from the OED but Esperantists hailed him as 'la unua Amerika Esperantisto', the first American Esperantist. One of his admirers wrote, 'Kiam Henry Phillips, la pioniro de la lingvo en Ameriko, mortis, la movado por Esperanto en la lando recevis forton baton' (When Henry Phillips, the pioneer of the language in America, died, the movement for Esperanto in the country received a heavy blow). Sometimes Murray recorded the deaths of the contributors beside their names in the address book (W. C. H. Glazier of the US Marine Hospital in Key West, Florida; Professor George Stephens of Denmark; and the Very Revd Robert Payne Smith, Dean of Canterbury), but there is nothing beside Henry Phillips's name.

Readers who look closely, however, will see it is within the Dictionary itself that Phillips's legacy sits. Phillips was another rare instance of someone who read his own books for the Dictionary, sending in 500 slips from his own works, contributing words such as *alated*, having wings; *alto-relievo*, carving or stamping in which the sculptured shape projects from the surface; *to chase*, to engrave; *didrachm*, an Ancient Greek silver coin; *die*, an engraved stamp; *dollar*, a Spanish peso used in the British North American colonies; *festoon*, a carved ornament representing a hanging garland; *fiscal*, pertaining to financial matters; and *hub*, a cylindrical piece of steel on which the design of a coin is engraved in relief.

Y

for YONGE, CHARLOTTE, AND OTHER NOVELISTS

Charlotte Yonge and her elderly mother hurried along the platform just as the train pulled out of Corby station with a loud rush and a puff of steam. There was a three-hour wait for the next train. It was the start of the hot weather in July 1864, and they took shelter from the sun in the small railway refreshment room. Mrs Yonge took out *Sylvia's Lovers*, a sad novel by Elizabeth Gaskell that she was reading for the Dictionary. Her novelist daughter took out her quill and ink. On this occasion, it was to write not one of the five novels she published that year, but a letter to Frederick Furnivall, a friend of the Yonge family and Editor of the Dictionary at the time.

Before going on summer holiday, Charlotte had been subediting the letter N. She sat beside her mother and wrote to Furnivall, 'Just at present we are wanderers, very decided wanderers at this moment for I am writing at a little station on the Great Northern having missed our train by two minutes.'

She had been pressured by Furnivall's printer to take the letter N slips, or 'extracts' as she called them, with her on her travels. 'I was obliged to write to him that it must wait till my return, for I can only settle doubtful words by reference to the extracts', she explained to Furnivall, 'whereupon he wrote to me again to ask if I could not get my papers sent after me! Fancy carrying about all the extracts from NI onwards to NY! But I am afraid I must remain guilty of the delay, for my correcting would be of no real use without the extracts.' In addition to subediting, Charlotte also read for Furnivall, sending in slips from a dozen books including Samuel Johnson's periodical *The Rambler* and Richardson's epistolary novel, *The History of Sir Charles Grandison*.

Ten years later, Charlotte was no longer working for Furnivall. 'I am afraid I cannot now read the books mentioned as they have drifted out of my reach and I have much less time than I had in the old times when it was undertaken.' She was in her fifties, her mother had died, and she had greater responsibilities – financially bailing out her brother Julian and caring for her sister-in-law who had come to live with her – as well as the demands of her growing success as a writer.

We can imagine her irritation when the chaotic Furnivall wrote to her in 1877 to ask for the work she had done on N. Her one-sentence reply was tart. 'You must have my Ns somewhere, for I put them all into their sack and sent them back to you I should think four or five years back, I know it was just as a friend came to live with me, and I had to make room for her possessions.'

Twenty years later, James Murray wrote to Charlotte asking her for clarification on the plant *cliders* (or *clithers*), which had appeared in two of her books, *The Heir of Redclyffe* and *The Herb of the Field*. Murray hinted to her that she might want to contribute to the Dictionary again: 'We know your hand well in the earlier Dictionary material, though it has not been my fortune to see it often in later times.' She politely told Murray, however, that her Dictionary days were behind her: 'I was sorry to drop the dictionary work

This photograph of Charlotte Yonge was taken four
years before she wrote to Furnivall from Corby
station about her subediting of the letter N.

but occupations thickened on me so that I could not keep
it up.'

Yonge's books and essays are quoted over 1,300 times
in the OED with most quotations coming from *Cameos from
English History, The Daisy Chain,* and *Womankind.* They were
predominantly read for the Dictionary by women: Miss Gertrude Ewan in Cheshire, Miss Catherine Gunning of Eccleston Square, London, and Miss Elizabeth Thompson of

Reigate. Yonge was later read again by the twentieth-century writer Marghanita Laski (who founded the Charlotte Yonge Society and co-edited a book of essays on her) and as a result hundreds more quotations were added to the Second OED Supplement in the 1970s and 1980s.

When Yonge died, Murray noted her death in his meticulous handwriting in his letter catalogue. Beside the entry for 'Yonge, C. M. Miss', he wrote, 'Died 25 Mch. 1901.' Unusual for Murray, he got the date slightly wrong – Charlotte Yonge died of pleurisy at the age of seventy-eight on 24 March.

Although little-known now, Charlotte Yonge was one of the most successful of all Victorian novelists. 'Prolific' is a word often overused when describing a writer, but it is an accurate description of Yonge's facility for producing novels and all kinds of other books, including many for children. She was widely read in the nineteenth century, but today her didactic messages about the duties of a Christian and the subordinate place of women (as ordained by God) strike an old-fashioned note. She lived in the same village her whole life, Otterbourne in Hampshire, where she taught at the village school for sixty years, was a devout worshipper in the parish church, and – paradoxically, given her view of women's place – exercised her influence as an educational reformer to international effect.

Charlotte was a cousin of one of Murray's best Subeditors and proofreaders, Henry Hucks Gibbs, 1st Baron Aldenham, who was Director of the Bank of England from 1853 to 1901. Gibbs was a mentor to Murray, frequently helping him negotiate with the tricky Delegates of Oxford University Press. He had often come to Murray's rescue with personal financial loans, as he did during the Eleanor Marx fiasco. Letters from Gibbs stand out in the archive because until 1864 his writing slanted to the right, but afterwards it slanted to the left. He had been out hunting and accidentally shot off his right hand. But this neither slowed his contributions to the Dictionary nor dampened his opinions.

Much of Gibbs's advice on Dictionary matters bordered on the prescriptive. He often disagreed with the words Murray was letting into the Dictionary, considering some of them, such as 'accommodated', to be 'mere vagrants knocking at the door'. 'If you must honour such words as "accommodated"', he wrote to Murray, 'you should have a separate limbo to which to relegate them – a hot one, I should suggest.' Charlotte's second cousins (Henry's sons), Vicary, Alban, and Kenneth, were also volunteers.

Should women writers be read for the Dictionary? They were, of course, though not in the quantity that male authors were read, but Gibbs was the Dictionary contributor who raised the question with the editors, taking a more conservative position than they did. He wrote to Murray in May 1883: 'Furnivall has a fancy that it is good to quote women, because the writings of women are a characteristic of the Age. But the Dicty is not meant to be a record of the progress of the Emancipation of Women but of the birth, life, and death of words; and that a word has or has not been written by a woman doesn't touch the matter.'

Gibbs's generalizing views on female novelists reveal his bias. He believed that they 'did not give themselves time to think' or, if they did, they could not write well. In a letter to Murray, citing his own cousin, he declared, 'Many who do think have not the faculty of writing clear intelligible English, witness my cousin Miss Yonge – popular as she is.'

In the hastiness of his prejudice, Gibbs could forget his own declared belief in the Dictionary's purpose to record the birth, life, and death of words. Of another female novelist, Mary Elizabeth Braddon, whose work was quoted in the Dictionary even more frequently than Yonge's, he wrote that, 'Miss Braddon sometimes, often, indeed, writes good strong English. My objection to her as an authority, where better can be had, is that she is a hasty writer – grinds out novels by the yard and does not give herself time to think whether she is writing good English or not. I say of her, in a much less degree, what I have said before of newspaper writers, gener-aliter, and the D. J. in particular – not that the writers are not sometimes masters of English but though they have good horses in their stable, they bring out very sorry hacks sometimes.'

What Gibbs could not see, because he was too busy making judgements about the quality of her writing, was that Braddon used language in innovative ways and was therefore important to the Dictionary's record of the birth of words. She was the first person to coin or write many words – *twilit*, lit by twilight; *tight-lipped*, suppressing emotion; *past-mistress*, a woman adept or expert in a specified subject or activity – as well as having a penchant for turning nouns into adjectives – *splotchy*, covered in splotches; *port-winey*, resembling port; *curranty*, full of currants.

Charlotte Yonge was in her time probably the best-known of the novelists who contributed to the Dictionary, unless we count Murray's questions to Robert Louis Stevenson, Lewis Carroll, and George Eliot, and Thomas Hardy's request to Murray asking him to include some words in the Diction-ary. In 1887, Murray asked Stevenson about the word *brean* in one of his short stories. The Scottish novelist wrote back to Murray explaining that it was a misprint for *ocean*, and ended his letter, 'I live and long for your dictionary. Ah, why was I not born later!' In 1879, Murray had questioned George Eliot (a novelist whom Gibbs deigned to describe as 'good') about her use of the word *adust* in place of *dusty* in her novel *Romola* (1862). In Eliot's courteous response, she said she could not remember why she had chosen the word seventeen years earlier, but she believed that it had been determined by 'the feeling of rhythm' which accompanied her prose writing, and 'the (perhaps fallacious) impression that by "adust" the imagination was less restricted and would be led to include other conditions of which dustiness is one sign'. She did not intend to represent the Latin *adustus*, but rather 'dared to form my word analogically'. Finally, she noted, 'I wish always to be quoted as George Eliot', though she signed the letter M. G. Lewes. Murray wrote straight back the next day, even allowing a little fandom to enter into his letter: 'I am happy to have had, so to say, a peep at such a genius.' He added his own gloss on *adust* and her use of it. 'Your instinct – shall I call it? – was quite correct as to adust, which, in strictest analogy, means in a dusty state, i.e. not merely dusty but "affected by dust" in every way that it could affect clothes, skin, eyes, or throat.' He continued with a comment on how language is made, keen perhaps to display his own knowledge and expertise to this famous novelist whom he admired. 'It is of course by such extension of analogy – instinctive most of it – that language is made; not by conscious synthesis of roots and particles which have independent existence only on paper, but exist in living speech – in the concrete, and by analogy.'

Thomas Hardy, unprompted by Murray, wrote in June 1891 to suggest three 'well-known English words' which he could not find in any dictionary. These were *eweleaze*, defined by him as 'an upland pasture where sheep feed, differing from a meadow in never being laid up for mowing'; *hogleaze*, 'ditto pigs'; and *cowleaze*, 'ditto cows'. Hardy wrote that he had 'been recommended to send these words to you, and you will perhaps excuse my doing so'. He also noted that it was in the West of England that these terms were most generally used, in speech amongst all classes, and in print. *Lease*, with the variant spelling *leaze*, meaning meadow, made it into the Dictionary in 1902, with the cow-, ewe- and horse- (but not hog-) variations. An illustrative quotation was taken from Thomas Hardy's 1898 poem 'In a Eweleaze Near Wetherbury' in *Wessex Poems*: 'The years have gathered grayly / Since I danced upon this leaze.'

A few years after Murray's death a budding novelist and talented scholar came to work on the Dictionary for a year. The twenty-seven-year-old J. R. R. Tolkien was not yet famous for his novels when he worked as an editorial assistant with Charles Onions. The two men worked on the letter W together and became firm friends. After Onions's death, Tolkien described him as 'my dear protector, backer, and friend' who 'was the last of the people who *were* "English" at Oxford and at large when I entered the profession'. On one of my visits to Giles Onions, he had told me a funny story about a family lunch with his parents and all his ten brothers and sisters. 'Jirt', as the children called Tolkien (short for J.R.R.T.), 'was over for Sunday lunch and my brother John was hitting golf balls in the back garden', recalled Giles. 'A ball came through the window, bounced around the dishes on the table, and nobody took any notice. Jirt always remarked how funny it was, but for us it was normal.'

Life in Murray's hallowed Scriptorium was far more ordered than life in Onions's house. Beatrice Harraden was a friend of Furnivall, or 'Ferney' as she called him, and he helped arrange her visit to Murray's back garden so she could do some research for a novel she was planning. Ferney sent a postcard to Murray, stating Miss Harraden's wants and, with characteristic enthusiasm and indiscretion, setting out the plot of her proposed novel 'with unguarded truthfulness'. Despite or because of this, she had a good visit in which 'some of the secrets and complications of dictionary-making were unfolded to me with a willing generosity which I shall never forget', as she wrote in a reminiscence of the time, and she left 'armed with fresh knowledge and with new friends'.

Harraden's novel, *The Scholar's Daughter* (1906), transplants the Dictionary and its Scriptorium to the countryside, to Yew House, where Professor Grant (based on Murray) has presided for years over a dictionary 'which was to be the abiding pride of the Anglo-Saxon race'. There his three secretaries live and assist him. In the midst of this entirely male household (even the house parlourmaid is male, a former coastguard) is just one woman, Geraldine, daughter of Professor Grant who, at the opening of the novel, has just returned from college. She is a breath of fresh air – literally, as the first thing she does on arriving is open all the windows. The secretaries, or 'the bookworms' as she has called them since she was a child, speculate on what she will do now, wishing that she would work for the Dictionary for 'she has a wonderful grasp of etymology' and, if only she were to work with them, they might stand a chance of reaching the middle of the letter E in five years' time – but in their hearts they know she won't. The novel puts Geraldine, the scholar's daughter, at its centre, but the plot of reunion with the mother she never knew, now a famous actress, also leads to the softening of the scholar's heart. Professor Grant is portrayed as a man 'who doesn't care for women or for anything, indeed, except dictionaries', but the final melodramatic scenes see him confessing his hardness of heart to his daughter which leads to his touching reunion with her mother.

Like the Geraldine of her novel, Harraden had been well educated, at Cheltenham Ladies' College, followed by Queen's and Bedford College in the University of London, where she received a First-class degree in Latin, Greek, and English in 1884. She entered London literary life in the 1890s and her first novel, *Ships that Pass in the Night*, was a success, subsequent novels less so. Given her acute observation of the 'maleness' of the Scriptorium, as reflected in her novel, it isn't a surprise that she was also a suffragist. She went on to join the more militant Women's Social and Political Union (WSPU), formed by the Pankhursts, frequently speaking on its platforms and contributing to its magazine, *Votes for Women.*

As far as we know, Harraden never became a Dictionary Friend, her only contribution being her fictional recreation of its inner workings. She is memorialized in the Dictionary through her novels which are quoted fifty times and which exemplify words from *tea,* a meal at which tea is served, 'A rattling good tea – hot rolls, fried potatoes, and quail'; to *unsaintly,* 'A most unsaintly pair of shoes'.

While Harraden wrote in *The Scholar's Daughter* about that which was deeply familiar to the Dictionary, other contributors imaginatively explored other universes. The rise of science also saw the rise of science fiction as the reading public became increasingly fascinated with other worlds and what the future might bring. The Revd George Theodosius Boughton Kyngdon, who ministered in both England and New Zealand, had a dry spell in the 1870s with no church ministry, and used the time to write a science-fiction novel, *Skyward and Earthward* (1875) under the pen name Arthur Penrice, which imagined life in other parts of the universe. The central character travels in an advanced balloon to the Moon, discovers a race of telepaths there, travels on to Mars and returns to Earth. Kyngdon's reading for the Dictionary, four years after the publication of his novel, was entirely earth-bound and religious, and he produced just 250 slips from the seventeenth-century Isaac Barrow's sermons.

Another science-fiction writer and vicar among the Dictionary People was the Revd Edwin Abbott Abbott, who came by his repeated last name because his parents were first cousins. He was celebrated in his day as a liberal theologian and innovative educationalist, and Murray thanked him in the prefaces for 'various help' in the first part and volume of the Dictionary.

Abbott Abbott became headmaster of City of London School at the young age of twenty-six, where he introduced a new curriculum that incorporated chemistry, brought new life to the Classics – even enabling some pupils to study Sanskrit – and encouraged the performance of Shakespeare. He is now best-known for a strange science-fiction novella, *Flatland: A Romance of Many Dimensions*, which he published under the pseudonym 'A Square'. The protagonist, a square from Flatland, visits Pointland, Lineland and Spaceland to explore the possibility of other dimensions; but it is a sphere – the other-universe or divine character – that has a fuller knowledge of those dimensions, beyond that of the square's understanding. Abbott Abbott was speaking into the Victorian attempt to negotiate the impact of science on Christianity while also introducing readers to non-Euclidian geometry as it was being developed in the nineteenth century. But the book is also a plea for openness to dimensions which are beyond our initial understanding, and a satirical commentary about the hierarchical nature of Victorian society. Eighteen words from *Flatland* eventually made their way into the Dictionary. Two, added by Murray in 1896, were used for the first (and only!) time by Abbott Abbott: *dimensionable*, capable of being measured; and *nondimensional*, lacking dimension. Abbott Abbott wrote three other novels, less successful, on Christian themes, in an attempt to encourage people to read the Bible and embrace a broad and open faith, as well as other books on language and theology. The latter are quoted over fifty times in the Dictionary, including another word which he invented but which was never picked up by anyone else: *crinanthropy*, judgement or criticism of other people.

Other Dictionary Friend novelists may have been minor writers but they were dedicated contributors. On 3 June 1912 Edward Peacock wrote in shaky handwriting to James Murray from his deathbed: 'I have been so long ill – more than a year and a half, and do not expect ever to recover, that I have made up my mind to discontinue The Oxford English Dictionary for the future.' He added in a postscript, 'I am upwards of eighty years of age.' By then Peacock had been a volunteer for the Dictionary for fifty-four years, making him one of the longest-serving contributors. He had submitted 24,806 slips and had given great service to Murray not only as a Reader but as a Subeditor and Specialist too.

Peacock was a gentleman farmer and writer in Lincolnshire, though towards the end of his life the farming failed and he had to rely on grants from the Royal Literary Fund to sustain him. The extensive library in his home of Bottesford Manor enabled him to pursue his life of letters, which included antiquarian interests (he was a Fellow of the Antiquarian Society), history and archaeology, journalism and reviewing, Dictionary work, and his contributions as a founder member of the English Dialect Society.

Peacock was also the author of four novels: *Ralf Skirlaugh: the Lincolnshire Squire* (1870); *Mabel Heron* (1872), *John Markenfield* (1874) and *Narcissa Brendon* (1891). If a twenty-first-century reader does not recognize these titles, it's hardly surprising – very few of Peacock's contemporaries would have known them either. While none of his novels had much success in their reception and sales, strangely they did find success in the Dictionary. Peacock is quoted 993 times in the OED, a huge number for any author let alone a not very popular one. His novels were read for the Dictionary by Miss Emma Fowler in Essex and her younger brother the Revd Joseph Thomas Fowler in Durham.

Peacock used words that were new at the time, especially regional terms from Lincolnshire, such as *blob*, a bait used in fishing for eels; *clat*, noisy talk; *eighteener*, a cask holding 18 gallons; *nattering*, chattering; and *slated*, scolded – none of which had ever appeared in writing before. Despite Peacock's novels being flops, they are quoted more times in the OED than the works of either E. M. Forster, Joseph Conrad, or Arthur Conan Doyle.

Edward Peacock's son, Edward Adrian, known as Adrian, was also a Dictionary Friend and novelist. He was an Anglican priest and, like Kirby Trimmer, a collector and cataloguer of plants. Despite a weak constitution, he would walk several miles a day in the countryside of his native Lincolnshire, spotting plants and making copious notes in his diary, which he carried, along with a pen and inkpot, in one of the many special inner pockets that he had sewn into his jacket. He published extensively on the plants of Lincolnshire, pioneered the ecological approach to the recording of natural history, and helped found a museum for Lincolnshire. His father had got the whole Peacock family interested in local dialects and Adrian edited *The Lincolnshire Place-Name and Dialect Dictionary* which the family members had compiled together. Like his father, he was an unsuccessful novelist who was successful in getting quoted in the OED. His book *Only a Sister*, which he wrote under the pseudonym Walter Adam Wallace, is quoted in the Dictionary over forty times for entries including *popinjayess*, a beautiful woman; *squinny*, to direct the eyes obliquely; *swilly*, a whirlpool; *flim-flam*, nonsense; *fairly and squarely*, in a just or honest manner; and *wizened*, shrunken and dried up. Unlike his father, Adrian's time volunteering for the Dictionary was brief: in 1891, he sent in just 75 slips. His heart was more in the recording of plants than the recording of words.

Z

for ZEALOTS

By the time the word *zealot*, someone who is fervently or passionately devoted to a cause, was published in the OED (in May 1921), the Dictionary's greatest zealot had already died.

It was in the summer of 1915 when James Murray's strength began to fail. He had always put the success of the Dictionary ahead of the well-being and health of himself and the Dictionary People, and his final months were no exception. Earlier in the year, he had undergone X-ray treatment for prostate troubles, but still he worked relentlessly on the letter T. The words contained in it presented some incredibly tricky problems which he handled with his characteristic brilliance, but it was a huge effort and he had time for little else except every now and then tending to his stamp albums.

The last Dictionary entry bearing his handwriting was the word *twilight*, or at least that's what biographers say, but when the archivist and I went back to the boxes, we discovered the slip was missing. So in the absence of that final slip, I can only imagine that Murray sat alone in a quiet Scriptorium that Saturday evening in July. He took out a clean slip, and with a slight tremor in his fingers wrote, 'The light diffused by the reflection of the sun's rays from the atmosphere before sunrise, and after sunset.' He paused, and wondered how to distinguish between the soft glowing light of twilight and the period or state of twilight. He heard the familiar bells of St Margaret's church, and was suddenly inspired; he dipped the nib in ink, and marked the definition with a semicolon followed by 'the period during which this prevails between daylight and darkness'.

Murray wearing his scholar's cap in The Scriptorium
not long before he died in July, 1915.

It had been thirty-six years since he had started on the letter A. He remembered the first day as though it were yesterday. It was the end of one of the coldest winters on record, and the family had watched from the main French window of the sitting room at Mill Hill, under the portraits of William Gladstone and John Bright, as a horse-drawn carriage had delivered 2 tons of slips from Furnivall's house. As the horses had made their approach the children had run outside, and James and Ada had followed. The air had been crisp and Murray had never felt so alive in his forty-two years. It had been the beginning of the family's 'Dictionary Days', and now – two years shy of his eightieth birthday – he put the finishing touches on the entry for *twilight*, sat in the gloaming, and knew those days had come to an end.

He had been relentless in his pursuit of perfection and rigour. Nothing had been able to thwart his resolve and dedication – not hopeless contributors or kleptomaniacs or bad reviews or competition from America or mercurial Furnivall or the miserly Oxford University Press or utterly numb-skull staff. From the moment when, as a teenager, he had published the article on wild flowers in the *Hawick Monthly Advertiser*, he had been resolved to see his name in print. The ambitious eighteen-year-old had invented his middle names 'Augustus Henry' in order to add gravitas to that of James Murray, common on the Borders of Scotland. He had vowed then to rise beyond his village and to lead a bright future worthy of another Denholm native whom he admired greatly, the poet John Leyden. He had seized every opportunity that had come his way. Despite having left school at fourteen, Murray had used his prodigious memory to teach himself twenty-five languages. He had attended a holiday course on phonetics in Edinburgh with Alexander Melville Bell and that had taught him to speak with a standard southern English accent.

He had worked harder and longer than anyone he knew, from labouring on a dairy farm at the age of twelve to being a schoolteacher and even spending a stint as a bank clerk. Taking on the Dictionary project had been an opportunity to better himself and his family, to enter a more prestigious world which was usually denied to men like him. A lesser person might have felt intimidated in Oxford because of his outsider status – he was Scottish not English, a Nonconformist not an Anglican, liberal not Tory, and a non-smoker and teetotaller within an indulgent academic setting – but Murray had been confident of his ability, describing himself thus: 'I am not a man of letters like [Samuel] Johnson . . . but I am a Philologist, and I enter on the task of editing or writing the Dictionary with advantages due to my own especial training and my own studies, and therefore I consider myself ten times better fitted to make the Dictionary than Mr Ruskin, or Mr Carlyle or Matthew Arnold or Professor Jowett, and so a hundred times better than Dr Johnson, no Philologist, only a man of letters.'

No amount of self-confidence could disguise the reality that Murray was continually excluded from Oxford academic circles and never made Fellow of a college. His insecurities can be detected by the fact that as soon as he received an honorary degree of LLD by the University of Edinburgh in 1874, he wore his scholar's cap every day. Perhaps to compensate for being snubbed by Oxford's collegiate university, he busied himself with civic activities in the city of Oxford, engaging with the 'town' rather than the 'gown', attending public meetings for church, Liberal Party politics, the YMCA, stamp collecting, natural history, and temperance. He was knighted in 1908 but his outsider status in the university was painful for him. Writing to his sons Oswyn and Harold about the various honours that finally flooded in towards the end of his life, Murray stated a little too vehemently, 'To tell the truth, my work . . . was so long so little appreciated, that I learned . . . not to care a scrap for either blame or praise.' He even expressed a reluctance to accept any accolades that came his way: 'I should prefer that my biographer should have to say, "Oxford never made him a Fellow or a D. C. L., and his country never recognized his work, but he worked on all the same, believing in his work and his duty." ' Finally, in the year before he died, he was given an honorary doctorate by the University of Oxford.

Murray had been sustained and supported by three main things throughout the Dictionary Days: his God, his family, and the Dictionary People. 'God give me help to do my work', was a prayer he often repeated. 'Inspire me with fresh effort when I am tired, and use me as an instrument to do your will.' In his seventieth-birthday speech he had said, 'I never could have stood the work I have done at the Dictionary, and the special difficulties which threatened at times to overwhelm me, without earnest prayer every morning. There are many articles in the Dictionary which could never have been done by me without this earnest and sometimes agonized appeal to higher wisdom.'

Although he had hoped to finish the Dictionary by the end of 1916, in time for his eightieth birthday and Golden Wedding anniversary, it was not to be. He was suffering from chest pain and he was finding it painful to breathe. On the day that he defined *twilight*, despite not knowing whether the Dictionary would ever be finished, he did know he had done his best. He put down his pen, placed his scholar's cap beside his inkpot, and shuffled out of the Scriptorium, across the garden, and into the house, calling out, 'Where's my lovey?' for the last time.

Murray went to bed with pleurisy and died two weeks later on 26 July 1915, surrounded by Ada and all his children, except for Wilfrid who was still abroad. He was buried at Wolvercote Cemetery beside his friend the sinologist and fellow Nonconformist, James Legge. The Scriptorium was disbanded and all the slips and pigeonholes taken to Bradley, Onions, Craigie, and the team working at the Old Ashmolean. Ada continued living at 78 Banbury Road until 1929 (she died in 1936 and was buried with James), at which time the house was bought by an American historian, Robert McNutt McElroy. McElroy demolished the Scriptorium in 1930.

I had always wanted to see the site of the Scriptorium

and my chance came on the hundredth anniversary of Murray's death, 26 July 2015, when I joined a small group of his relatives for a gathering at Wolvercote Cemetery. It rained incessantly and we huddled together under umbrellas around Murray's tombstone. Next we had planned to visit the sacred spot where the Scriptorium used to stand behind the house at number 78, by then owned by the zoologist and surrealist painter Desmond Morris. It began to thunder and lightning, and we were soaked to the skin when we arrived on Morris's doorstep. He showed us through to the back garden along a side path. I had remembered reading in *Caught in the Web of Words* that Murray had enjoyed growing ferns along this draughty pathway and had nicknamed it 'windy lene'. The ferns were long gone, but it sure lived up to its name on that blustery morning. Morris vaguely pointed to a landscaped area that looked the same as any garden in north Oxford. I wish I could tell you that we had a mystical experience and were able to conjure the ghosts of the Dictionary People but, to be honest, it was so wet, and uncomfortably cold, and, as much as I like to get romantic, it was pretty difficult to imagine the iron house of Murray's glory days. Those times are better captured in the ten volumes, 414,825 entries, and 1,827,306 quotations that were finally published in 1928.

*

My own journey with the Dictionary People is almost at an end. It began eight years ago in the dark basement of Oxford University Press, and it is ending in the bright sunshine of Australia where I was called to the bedside of my dying mother a month before the book was due. Looking back, I must admit that from the moment I lifted the lid on that dusty box, a little of Murray's zealous and determined energy entered me. I became obsessed with unearthing the lives of the people in his address book and reclaiming their place in the story of the creation of the OED. I feel as though this quest has been led by something beyond me. I could not have anticipated the generous support of Stanford University in funding the early days of the research. Nor did I expect the joyous enthusiasm of my student researchers, or the generosity of archivists and librarians around the world, or the camaraderie of Casper Grathwohl and the team of lexicographers at the Oxford English Dictionary.

It made sense to finish the book in Australia. This is where, thirty years ago, I first met one of the Dictionary People. You may not know this, but people still send in slips to the OED today. And one of the most zealous contributors of the twenty-first century, in fact of all time, lived in my home town of Brisbane, Australia.

Mr Chris Collier collected two things: words and movie posters. He was so successful at collecting words that he sent in a total of 100,000 slips to the OED over thirty-five years from 1975 to 2010. He lived in Paddington, a suburb close to where I grew up, but I had no idea of his fame at the time. No one did. More people knew of him in Oxford than in Brisbane, even though he rarely left his neighbourhood, let alone Australia. As far as his neighbours were concerned, 'Chris' was the local eccentric who lived alone, and was known to walk through the quiet, hilly streets at midnight. He lived on French Street in a humble Queenslander, a house raised on stilts in the local style, with a front verandah, and a corrugated-iron roof, surrounded by leafy rubber trees and frangipanis. Piles of newspapers and movie posters blocked the windows and made it difficult to get past the front door.

Mr Collier was a night owl. Every evening, after the fruit bats flew overhead in dark clouds at sunset, he sat barefoot at a wooden table in his kitchen by the light of a fluorescent tube. The local newspaper was spread in front of him, with a pair of scissors, a pot of glue, and hundreds of freshly cut slips alongside. Regardless of the heat and humidity, Mr Collier spent hours focused on his Dictionary work. I don't know if he knew the lineage behind him, the other Dictionary People in equally hot corners of the world – Margaret Murray in Calcutta, Donald Ferguson in Ceylon, John Bruce Moffat in the Kalahari, Dr Atkins in New Mexico – faithfully copying out slips in the hope that they might get one word into the Dictionary.

Mr Collier had a special technique. He cut out the quotations and, dipping a brush in sweet-smelling Perkins Paste glue, he stuck the quotation onto the slip. It was quick, and some nights he could get through 100 slips. Just him and the sound of his scissors, the incessant croak of cicadas, and the greasy smell of the neighbour's lamb chops hanging in the close air. Around midnight, he would stop work, gather up the scraps of paper, clear the table, turn off the light, and take off his shirt, his shorts, and his underwear. Standing naked in his kitchen, he was ready to go out.

Mr Collier was a naturist. There was no word for someone who practises or advocates a natural way of life, especially nudity, until 1926. Nothing on earth was more splendid than freeing his body of restrictions and communing with nature. Even after all these years he still got a thrill from leaving the house naked. But nothing quite matched the exhilaration of that first time. It was November. He walked down the front steps from his verandah onto the quiet tree-lined cul-de-sac. The sudden rush of night air hit parts of his body which were usually covered. He turned right out of his gate and up the hill towards the main street. The shock of no one stopping him. Paddington lay in silence before him and he revelled in his freedom. Nature was at its most splendid in Brisbane in November. The weather was warm and the jacaranda trees were in full bloom, a profusion of pale purple blossoms which looked white in the moonlight. A faint talcum-powder scent and a soft carpet of cool petals underfoot. This was Mr Collier's happy place – wandering the streets of Paddington, and collecting newspapers from the neighbours' bins for the next day of Dictionary work, while everyone slept.

None of his neighbours knew that Mr Collier volunteered for the OED nor that words from their local newspapers would eventually find their way onto its authoritative pages. Thanks to his work, there is a weird bias in the OED towards quotations from the Brisbane *Courier-Mail.* It is now the three-hundred-and-ninetieth-most frequently quoted source in the Dictionary, with more quotations from it than from either Virginia Woolf, T. S. Eliot, or the Book of Common Prayer.

I first discovered Mr Collier and his prodigious work for the Dictionary, not when I lived in Brisbane but in 1990 when I was a twenty-one-year-old grad student, employed in my first job for Oxford Dictionary in Canberra, Australia (I wasn't to move to the mother ship in Oxford until later). It was my job to open the mail each day, which included unwrapping the parcels of slips sent in by volunteers. Mr Collier's bundles stood out from the others because they were eccentrically wrapped in old cornflake packets with pieces of cereal and dog hair (or at least I hoped it was!) stuck to them. I filed the slips into the large word-collection drawers so the editors could access them when it came to drafting entries and putting new words into the dictionary.

A few years later, when I left Australia to work at the OED in Oxford, one of the first questions I was asked was, 'Do you know Mr Collier?' Little did we know at the Oxford Dictionary offices in Canberra that he also sent thousands of slips to Oxford each month. Open any of the drawers in the

OED Quotations Room and you will find slips from Mr Collier. All the quotations have one thing in common – they hail from the Brisbane *Courier-Mail*. There are thousands of Australian words – *kit off*, nude; *sickie*, a day's sick leave; *Mad Max*, denoting situations and objects similar to those portrayed in the Mad Max films (set in a futuristic world characterized by violence); *paceway*, a racecourse for trotting; *rawk*, roll music; *sea changer*, someone who undergoes a significant change of lifestyle; *snaky*, angry; *gurgler*, a drain; *petrolhead*, a car enthusiast. Many of his words did not get into the Dictionary, such as one for *Brizvegas*, the local nickname for Brisbane, but thousands of others did.

Brizvegas (see prior)

2003 *Courier-Mail* (CBne) 4 Jan 3/1 (heading)

Brizvegas boy had affair with Britney

THE mystery man named yesterday as the cause of the break-up between pop stars Britney Spears and Justin Timberlake has been revealed as a former Brisbane boy.

One of Mr Collier's 100,000 slips. This word for
Brizvegas, a jocular name for the city of Brisbane
where he lived, never got into the Dictionary but
thousands of others did.

To me and my fellow lexicographers at the Dictionary, Mr Collier was a mysterious and private figure. The parcels he sent only gave a return PO box address. We therefore knew that he lived in Brisbane but not exactly where. Until 2006. That year, I was on secondment from Oxford, at the Dictionary Centre in Canberra, and I asked the staff if they ever heard from Mr Collier. 'We still get slips and occasionally he calls,' a colleague said. Spookily, the very next day, as we were drinking our morning coffee, he rang and I spoke to him. I said I would like to meet him. He told me to meet him at his 'office'. And where is that? I asked. 'A park behind the Paddo Tavern,' he replied.

I flew to Brisbane and got a taxi to the park. An elderly man sat at a bench reading a newspaper. His blond hair shone in the sunshine. He looked about seventy years old, skin weathered by the sun, dressed in a simple blue T-shirt and very short shorts with a matching backpack beside him. I walked over and introduced myself. Mr Collier smiled and with a broad Australian accent said, 'G'day.' I could see the newspaper was the Brisbane *Courier-Mail*. Of course it was, I thought to myself.

We sat and chatted for a couple of hours. I could have been talking with one of Murray's zealous volunteers from a hundred years before. His life story was not dissimilar from them. An autodidact, he had left school at fourteen and eventually ended up working in the Queensland Patents Office. In 1975, he had read an article in the Brisbane *Courier-Mail* about the then Chief Editor of the OED, Robert Burchfield, who was calling for public contributions to the Dictionary. 'I thought to myself, imagine if I could help get one word in the dictionary,' Mr Collier said.

I suggested to him that, as a token of appreciation for all his work on the Dictionary, the OED might fly him to Oxford to see the work of the editors first-hand. He paused. 'No way', he replied. 'Imagine all the *Courier-Mails* waiting for me on my return!'

Mr Chris Collier reading the Brisbane *Courier-Mail* in
2006 in his 'office', a park behind the Paddo Tavern
in Brisbane, Australia.

Mr Collier said he was going to remain at Paddington for
the rest of his days. It was Friday 18 June 2010 when he watched
the fruit bats fly overhead and sat at his kitchen table one last
time. He was seventy-nine. As usual he scissored quotations
and stuck them onto freshly cut slips, but they never reached
the OED. Two days later he suffered a heart attack and was
rushed into the Royal Brisbane Hospital for surgery. He died
on the operating table. His funeral was attended by a few of
his neighbours, none of whom knew the extent of his contribution to English scholarship. They spoke of their quirky
'salt-of-the-earth' neighbour who mowed his lawn naked and
was 'always there to help us and others when needed'.

After meeting Mr Collier, I had set the ball rolling for
him to receive an Order of Australia, an honour that recog-
nizes Australian citizens for outstanding service. I figured
that his dedicated efforts to get the Australian language

represented in the largest English dictionary in the world was worth some acknowledgement. Sadly he died before the process was completed. I can only hope that in the telling of his story, and the placing of him in the lineage of the thousands of other faithful, skilled, and devoted Dictionary People, his legacy will be remembered and valued.

Looking back, I see that my interaction with Mr Collier over thirty years – from unwrapping the slips he sent to the Dictionary each month to meeting him in person and trying to get him officially honoured – influenced my view of lexicography and the making of the OED. Without knowing it, he set me quietly on the path of wanting to find out more about the unsung heroes of the OED.

This book has gone a small way to give them credit for their devotion. May we always remember the people who fervently and passionately committed themselves to the Dictionary: William Douglas in St George's Square who obsessively recorded words relating to the human body; Michael Field who read the Romantic poets in their William Morris-lined study in Bristol; Henry Spencer Ashbee who ensured that the language of pornography, flagellation, and sex got into the Dictionary. May we never forget John Dormer carrying Murray's letters in his pocket and becoming unhinged from too much Dictionary work. Not to mention the hundreds of others whose lives were untraceable.

This has been a story of ordinary people doing extraordinary things in the name of recording the English language. My hope is that I have done justice to their lives and their efforts for the Dictionary. It is now up to all of us to do our part in honouring James Murray's wish, expressed in 1892, 'that lovers of our language will not willingly let die the names of those who, from unselfish devotion and service to that language, have laboured in the cause of the Dictionary'.

Acknowledgements

My gratitude goes to Jane who is always my first interlocutor and best critic.

To friends and family who generously provided me with encouragement and places to write, especially Dom for her flat in Sydney; Skye for her farmhouse in Bowral; and Sandie and John for their garden studio in Norfolk.

To my student researchers at Stanford – the talented Gabe Previte, May Peterson, Riya Verma, Isi Okojie, Kenny Smith, Tyler Lemon, Mirae Lee, Sandhini Argawal, Vihan Lakshman, and Luz Tur-Sinai Gozal.

To Stanford University for their generous support: Mike Keller and the Stanford Libraries; Margaret Levi and the Center for Advanced Study in the Behavioral Sciences – and the Berggruen Foundation for funding my year-long fellowship there; the Roberta Bowman Denning Fund for Humanities and Technology; the Center for Spatial and Textual Analysis; and John Etchemendy, when he was Provost, for a generous research grant.

To Caroline Michel and Rebecca Carter for their wondrous editing and agent skills.

To Erroll McDonald for believing in the Dictionary People and in me, and to all at Knopf, especially Reagan Arthur, Michael Tizzano, Erinn Hartman, Kelly Shi, and Ellen Whitaker, who helped bring this beautiful object into your hands.

To my colleagues at the University of Oxford: Campion

Hall, Harris Manchester College, the Humanities Division, and the Faculty of Linguistics, Philology, and Phonetics.

This book would not have been possible without the support of many librarians and archivists. To the staff at the Bodleian Libraries at Oxford, especially Elaine Anstee, Oliver House, Neil Iden, and Mike Webb; Bev McCullough and Martin Maw at Oxford University Press Archives; David Luck and Colin Gale at the Bethlem Museum of the Mind; Joy Wheeler at the Royal Geographical Society in London; Diane Shaw at the Skillman Library, Lafayette College. I travelled to many places researching the Dictionary People, and am grateful for the kindness of staff at the Huntington Library in California; the Oxford and Cambridge Club and the Athenaeum in London; University of St Andrews Archives; the National Library of Scotland; University College London Library; Berkshire Record Office in Reading; Mill Hill School; Furnivall Sculling Club; and the British Library.

A few weeks before the book was done, my mother suddenly fell ill and was given two weeks to live. I flew to Sydney with Jane, and the whole family gathered around her bedside. On the Saturday before she died, I was sitting quietly in the corner tapping away on my laptop, oblivious to the fact that the room had fallen silent and my mother had asked, "how are the Dictionary People going?". I passed the laptop to Jane, who kindly read a chapter out loud. I guess it might sound a little strange that the Dictionary People were present at my mother's deathbed. I suspect they will be with me at my own. That's obsession, that's love.

List of Illustrations

Every effort has been made to trace copyright holders and obtain permission for use of copyright material. The author and publishers apologise for any omissions and would be grateful to be notified of any corrections that should be incorporated in future editions of this book.

Page 5: A 4 x 6- inch 'slip' sent in by one of the most prolific female contributors, Edith Thompson of Bath, by permission of Oxford University Press

Page 10: Some pages of Dr Murray's address books, by permission of Oxford University Press

Page 13: Dr Murray and his editorial team working on the OED in the Scriptorium, by permission of Bodleian Libraries, University of Oxford

Page 21: Margaret Alice Murray © Archive PL / Alamy Stock Photo

Page 25: Dr Murray writes to Frederick Furnivall in 1887, 'Austin's *is* a painful case', by permission of The Huntington Library, San Marino, California

Page 32: Photograph and signature of Sir John Richardson as recorded in Frederick Furnivall's photo album, by permission of Bodleian Libraries, University of Oxford

Page 51: An image of Alexander John Ellis in Furnivall's photo album, by permission of Bodleian Libraries, University of Oxford

Page 58: A section of a wall of slips in the Grimmwelt Museum, by permission of the author

Page 68: The Murray family on an annual hiking holiday, by permission of Bodleian Libraries, University of Oxford

List of Illustrations

Page 74: A photograph from a family photo album of James Murray and Ada linking arms with their eleven children, by permission of Bodleian Libraries, University of Oxford

Page 99: Hopeless contributors in one of the address books, by permission of Oxford University Press

Page 103: A page of one of the address books showing the various symbols and codes used to track a volunteer's work, by permission of Oxford University Press

Page 134: John Dormer took pride in his work and stamped each slip with his name, as seen here for hanky-panky, by permission of Oxford University Press

Page 140: Photo of John Dormer taken on admittance to Croydon Mental Hospital in 1907, by permission of Bethlem Museum of the Mind

Page 146: One of the 151,982 slips written out by William Douglas, by permission of Oxford University Press

Page 150: Furnivall pictured with the world's first female rowing team, by permission of Furnivall Sculling Club

Page 167: One of the 62,720 slips sent in by Dr William Chester Minor, by permission of Oxford University Press

Page 186: Herbert-Jones's demonstrative speaking style, by W. Blomfield, from *The New Zealand Observer,* Vol XV. – No. 832. New Series, No. 141, edited by W. J. Geddis (8 December 1894)

Page 197: Edward Ellis Morris, by permission of National Library of Victoria, Melbourne

Page 207: Joseph Wright and Walter Skeat often joined Murray for tea, by permission of Bodleian Libraries, University of Oxford

Page 220: Henry Spencer Ashbee © Volgi archive / Alamy Stock Photo

Page 227: Katharine Bradley and Edith Cooper, photographer unknown

Page 236: A personal card of Whym Chow, by permission of Bodleian Libraries, University of Oxford

List of Illustrations

Further Reading

In writing the Dictionary People, I have uncovered lives that have not necessarily been written about in the history books. For these I went through censuses, marriage certificates, death and burial records, regional newspapers, and private collections, many of which I accessed via The National Archives.

Oxford University Press stores the OED archive and the dictionary slips, along with the address books, internal administrative documents, letters, and papers belonging to James Murray and the other editors. The Bodleian Library holds the Murray Papers which comprise letters, family photographs, and unpublished materials belonging to the Murray family. Some of the letters from this collection are available online at the website Murray Scriptorium.

A useful resource was the prefaces of the facsicles of the OED, where Murray often mentioned consultants, readers, and subeditors. The prefaces were reprinted by Darrell R. Raymond in *Dispatches from the Front* (1987). Murray also mentioned contributors in his Presidential Addresses to the London Philological Society which were published in the *Transactions of the Philological Society.*

Some of the Dictionary People have short entries in the *Oxford Dictionary of National Biography,* the *American National Biography,* and the *Australian Dictionary of Biography,* which you may find helpful.

Longer, published biographies and autobiographies are available for a small number of Dictionary People. The archaeologist, Margaret Murray, published a charming memoir on the occasion of her one hundredth birthday called *My First Hundred Years* (1963). Sir John Richardson wrote an engrossing book called *Arctic Searching Expedition* (1851) about his second journey to recover Franklin's ships. His diary of the first Arctic expedition with Franklin is a compelling read and was republished in *Arctic Ordeal* (1984) by Stuart Houston.

John Dormer's medical records while he was in Croydon Mental Hospital are stored at the Bethlem Museum of the Mind. Dr Minor's papers, letters, and medical records from his time at Broadmoor Asylum are held at the Berkshire Record Office in Reading, England. Many aspects of his story are wonderfully captured by Simon Winchester in *The Professor and the Madman* (1998). For more on mental health and asylums in the nineteenth century, I recommend *Broadmoor Revealed* (2011) by Mark Stevens and *Inside Broadmoor* (2019) by Jonathan Levi and Emma French. For the other murderer, Eadweard Muybridge, see *River of Shadows* (2003) by Rebecca Solnit and *The Scoundrel Harry Larkyns* (2019) by Rebecca Gowers.

There is no biography of Alexander John Ellis, but I found helpful details about his life and personality in the papers of his friend, Alfred Hipkins, which are stored in the British Library. The colourful John Stephen Farmer deserves his own biography but until that is written, there are details about his slang dictionary with William Henley in volume 3 of Julie Coleman's *History of Cant and Slang Dictionaries*.

The outsider, Joseph Wright, is captured with tenderness by his wife Elizabeth Mary Wright in her two-volume *The Life of Joseph Wright* (1932), which also contains their love letters. For others, I highly recommend *Eleanor Marx* (1972, 1976) by Yvonne Kapp; *Doubts and Certainties* (1997) by John Poynter, which discusses the group of Melbourne-based contributors; *Charlotte Mary Yonge* (1903) by Christabel Coleridge; *George Perkins Marsh, a prophet of conservation* (2000) by David Lowenthal; and *Francis A. March* (2005) by Paul Schlueter and June Schlueter.

For more on the pornographer, Henry Spencer Ashbee, you may enjoy *The Erotomaniac* (2002) by Ian Gibson, and for further reading on the general topic of sex, bondage, and pornography in the nineteenth century see *Pleasure Bound* (2011) by Deborah Lutz, *The Other Victorians* (1966) by Steven Marcus, and *The Secret Museum* (1987) by Walter Kendrick. On some of the suffragists, see *Emily Davies and the Liberation of Women 1830–1921* (1990) by Daphne Bennett. William Whyte wrote a great essay on the Sunday Tramps (2007) in the *Oxford Dictionary of National Biography* and Frederic Maitland, one of the tramps and a Dictionary Friend, published *The Life and Letters of Leslie Stephen* (1906).

The Bodleian holds the Michael Field Papers which contains correspondence, photographs, and drafts of their writing. Their diaries have been digitized by Dartmouth College and are available online at The Diaries of Michael Field. I also recommend *We are Michael Field* (1998) by Emma Donohue and *The Fowl & the Pussycat* (2008) by Sharon Bickle.

If you are interested in more general histories of the OED, *Caught in the Web of Words* (1977) is a glorious description of the making of the Dictionary and the life of James Murray, written by his granddaughter K.M. Elisabeth Murray. There was an excellent biography of Murray by his son Wilfred called *Murray the Dictionary Maker*, which was published in South Africa in 1943, but it is difficult to find. There is also a marvellous unpublished biography of Murray by his son, Harold, called *Sir James Murray of the Oxford English Dictionary*, which is held in the Murray Papers in the Bodleian Library. If you prefer something a little more recent and scholarly, then I recommend *Making the OED* (2016) by Peter Gilliver, *The*

Meaning of Everything (2003) by Simon Winchester, *Lexicography and the OED* (2000) and *Lost for Words* (2005) by Lynda Mugglestone, and *Words of the World* (2013) by Sarah Ogilvie.

For more on Frederick Furnivall, there is *Dr F. J. Furnivall* (1983) by William Benzie, and the Furnivall Papers which are housed at the Huntington Library in California. The Furnivall Sculling Club in London has photographs of Furnivall with his female rowers. The papers of William Craigie are held at St Andrew's University Library in Scotland and the National Library of Scotland in Edinburgh. Charles Onions' papers are stored in the unlikely location of Canberra, at the Australian National Library.

If you would like to delve into the weeds of the practice and theory of lexicography, and who doesn't, then I recommend subscribing to *Dictionaries: the Journal of the Dictionary Society of North America* and to the *International Journal of Lexicography*.

For those of you with a penchant for dictionary-themed fiction you might like *The Liar's Dictionary* (2020) by Eley Williams and *Everything Under* (2018) by Daisy Johnson, and two novels that are set in the Scriptorium and are wonderfully evocative of Murray's world: *The Scholar's Daughter* (1906) by Beatrice Harraden and *The Dictionary of Lost Words* (2020) by Pip Williams.

In the end though, nothing beats sitting down with the twelve volumes of the OED itself. However heavy and cumbersome the large leather-bound volumes of the first edition are, reading the prefaces and dedications of each volume and smelling the dusty and spicy pages will transport you directly to Murray's desk. The entries and the quotations sent in by the Dictionary People are often all we need to imagine their interests, inclinations, and predilections. If you are anything like me, you will be left in awe at the scale and precision of their work.

Index

About the Author

Sarah Ogilvie teaches at the University of Oxford, and specializes in language, dictionaries, and technology. As a lexicographer she has been an editor at the Oxford English Dictionary and was Chief Editor of Oxford Dictionaries in Australia. As a technologist she has worked in Silicon Valley at Lab 126, Amazon's innovation lab, where she was part of the team that developed the Kindle. She originally studied computer science and mathematics before taking her doctorate in Linguistics at the University of Oxford, and then taught at Cambridge and Stanford.

A Note on the Type

This book was set in a type called Baskerville. The face itself is a facsimile reproduction of types cast from the molds made for John Baskerville (1706–1775) from his designs. Baskerville's original face was one of the forerunners of the type style known to printers as "modern face"—a "modern" of the period A.D. 1800.

Typeset by Scribe,
Philadelphia, Pennsylvania

Printed and bound by Berryville Graphics,
Fairfield, Pennsylvania